JEANNIE

JEANNIE

---

54 YEARS AND 10 DAYS
NOT LONG ENOUGH

JAMES BROWN

JEB

Contents

Dedication

This book is dedicated to my wonderful daughter Brandy Lea
Starr, and my six grandchildren, Ryan (Starr) Ottavio,
Spencer Haines, Mason Haines, Joseph Starr, Jonathan Starr,
and Cooper Starr.

One

In the Beginning

I met Jeannie in the fall of 1960—October 7, to be exact.

My best friend and Alpha Tau Omega fraternity brother, Rich "Pete" Peterson, came to my room and asked if I wanted to go on a "picnic" with some Delta Gammas who didn't want to attend the fraternity party to which their sorority had been invited. There were seven of them, so he needed seven of us to make the numbers even.

Back then, at least at the University of North Dakota, a picnic did not involve solid food unless someone happened to have a snack tucked in a jacket pocket. Nourishment came in a sixteen-gallon keg and was served in plastic cups.

I told Pete to count me in. Off I went in search of my least used clothes before jumping in the shower. It might have been a good idea to take my clothes in with me if there had been time to get them dry and pressed. But there wasn't, so I didn't.

When our small group walked into the DG House, my eyes fell on a sight that was at once both delightful and terrifying. Delightful because she was so beautiful and terrifying because I knew I had to somehow dredge up the courage to introduce myself to her, a girl obviously way above my pay grade. Seated on the bench in front of a grand piano, her strawberry blonde hair curled up at the collar of a tan jacket that couldn't hide the fact a gorgeous girl was contained inside.

She and I rode in separate cars to a place called the gravel pits, a location outside Grand Forks where our kind of picnic was frequently held. This left me time to think about the seemingly impossible task that lay ahead.

The first order of business at the gravel pits was for someone to tap the keg while others got a good fire going to fight off the North Dakota chill. I helped with the fire, trying to keep the object of my hopes and fears in sight.

After the fire had burned down a bit—and after I was fortified with a cup or two from the keg—I noticed an empty spot beside the girl who made my heart stand still. *Now or never.* I walked over on wobbly knees and introduced myself.

"Hi, I'm Jim Brown," I said with only the slightest quiver in my voice.

She took a sip from her cup and looked up at me with a soft grin. "I'm Jeannie—Jeannie Ratliff." I detected the hint of an Oklahoma accent.

I sat down next to this magnificent girl, fully expecting her to find an excuse to get up and mingle with the others. But to my surprise she didn't.

"Where are you from?" I asked.

"Oklahoma City."

"What brought you here?"

"My dad was transferred to Williston. You?"

"I'm from Bakersfield." A puzzled look crossed her face. "California," I added. "But I was born here . . . in Grand Forks."

I babbled on, telling her that everyone on both sides of my family who had gone to college went to UND, and my brother and two cousins from Denver were here now, and another cousin from Milwaukee had just graduated, and I was a junior, and finally I took a breath and shut up.

Jeannie Ratliff, the *it girl,* got up and walked to the other side of the fire. I had blown it.

But to my delight she filled her cup and came back smiling what I came to learn was her mischievous grin. Jeannie told me she was heartbroken when she learned of her dad being transferred to North Dakota right before her senior year of high school.

She said her parents promised she could go back to Oklahoma for one year of college if she didn't make a fuss over leaving Oklahoma City and all her friends. After that she had to go somewhere with in-state tuition. She took them up on their offer and attended Oklahoma State her freshman year.

"What's your major?" I inquired.

"Nursing."

Within minutes Jeannie's calm, easy manner put me at ease. We spent the whole evening together, laughing and talking about everything we could think of. She was so cool, and I was trying so hard to be.

Too soon, the fire burned to glowing embers and the keg burped. It was time to head back to campus. Jeannie and I rode together in an old Chevy, scrunched in the back seat with another couple. She sat on my lap. Seat belts weren't yet in vogue.

We didn't talk much on the drive back from the gravel pits, probably because others could listen in. When we arrived at the DG house, I walked Jeannie to the door and we stepped inside. I didn't want this night to end. In the bright light of the foyer I saw Jeannie's beautiful green eyes, flecked with gold, looking up at me. I leaned down and we shared our first kiss—wow! Tingles raced all the way to my toes.

Impulse overtook me to the point of asking her to go to a dance the next Friday. It was homecoming weekend and I already had a date for that night. I had to cross that bridge with the other girl later. I did, but not well.

Jeannie & Jim (1960)

Two

Newcastle

Jeannie and I dated often over the remainder of that school year, both of us claiming we didn't want to be tied down to a single relationship. I believe she told the truth. Not me. In any event, by the time the school term ended and Jeannie was about to head off to Newcastle, Wyoming, where her father's job had now taken him, I thought we had a pretty strong relationship. We parted with a passionate kiss. I was staying at UND for summer school—penance for my failed attempt to master thermodynamics without bothering to attend many classes—I only managed to make to three out of 51, actually.

The eight weeks of summer school seemed to crawl by as I eagerly looked forward to my trip home to California which I designed to take me through Newcastle. Anticipation of quality time with Jeannie dominated my thoughts. We had exchanged a couple letters about this. The plan was for me to hitch a ride to Newcastle with another summer school student who lived in Wyoming. He agreed to drop me off at Jeannie's home. After several wonderful hours with her, I'd ride the Greyhound to Bakersfield.

What did Robert Burns say about plans of mice and men? I made the trip to Newcastle as planned, but that was about it.

Jeannie greeted me with a kiss—more of a peck, actually—that fell miles short of our glorious goodbye kiss two months earlier.

There is something I failed to tell you about our conversations when we were dating at UND. It becomes important here. Jeannie told me in no uncertain terms her absolute, unwavering, iron-clad, rule for a future husband was he *must* have a ski boat. She loved to water ski. I did not have a ski boat nor did I have the prospect of acquiring one—and I had never been on water skis.

Back to Newcastle . . .

After the disappointing greeting kiss, Jeannie very casually said, "I'm going water-skiing this afternoon. You can come along."

"Who are you going with?" I asked with my head somewhere between Rome and Peking.

"A man my mother introduced me to."

Before long the *man* pulled up in a shiny new pickup towing a spectacular ski boat. Don Thorson, age 27, handsome, charming, and rich.

I felt like a lump of mold on someone's favorite sandwich. It soon became obvious that Jeannie and Don Thorson were not just acquaintances or water-ski pals. They had chemistry, a team of two, getting the boat launched, the truck and trailer parked, and everything ready for skiing.

Jeannie was first to go into the lake, smiling and waving as Don Thorson set a slalom ski on the water and pushed it toward her. A perfect push. He then tossed her the tow rope. A perfect toss. He handed me an orange flag and told me I was the spotter. Not so perfect.

When Jeannie gave the signal that she was ready to go, Don Thorson eased the boat forward. The loops in the tow rope straightened. A perfect easing.

Then WHOOM, the boat shot forward and Jeannie popped up like a cork. She wore a spectacular, one-piece red swimming suit and cut gracefully back and forth through the wake, swinging out wider with each turn and getting more air with each wake jump. I sat there, transfixed, holding the orange flag. I was the spotter.

At the end of Jeannie's glorious ride, *the man* helped her into the boat. She was grinning her "boy, was that fun!" grin. I had seen that grin before, but this one wasn't for the spotter. She barely looked the spotter's way while drying off and taking a seat behind the steering wheel. Now it was Don Thorson's time to ski and her time to drive the boat. My job remained the same. I was the spotter.

The cycle continued. Each time Jeannie got back on the ski, she looked more beautiful, and my heart felt more like a block of concrete.

Out of abject sympathy for the spotter, I won't relate the details of what happened when he was offered the chance to ski. He survived—just barely. Jeannie and Don Thorson seemed to enjoy his floundering, but the spotter didn't. Not at all.

After the water-skiing misadventure, I have no memory of how I, the erstwhile spotter, got to the bus station. But I clearly recall the indescribably miserable Greyhound ride to Bakersfield. Visions of two beautiful people having a splendid time water skiing, laughing and enjoying each other's company, kept me awake the whole time.

Earlier I failed to mention something—this time on purpose. Don Thorson had a chink in his armor. He was unlucky. And he made a terrible mistake—one he probably never saw coming. At the end of that summer, he asked Jeannie to drop out of school, stay in Newcastle, and become his wife. It should have worked. After all, along with everything else, he had the requisite ski boat. If he had just not included the drop out of school part, he probably might have been okay. The spotter never would have made that mistake because he knew Jeannie had her mind set on getting her degree and no way, no how, and for nobody was she going to drop out of school.

The "unlucky" part for Don Thorson was that Jeannie's dad was again transferred, this time to Farmington, New Mexico, and Jeannie never returned to Newcastle or to Don Thorson's ski boat.

Three

—————

Hope Springs Eternal

My six weeks in Bakersfield that summer of 1961 fighting mountain fires gave me hope that I might win Jeannie back. No real basis existed for such thinking. I had written to her, and she had responded. There was nothing in her response that any rational person would interpret as hopeful, given what happened during my ill-fated trip to Newcastle. But one thing I've never been accused of is being rational. Therefore, I made the trek to Grand Forks and good old UND clinging to the memory of that first night at the gravel pits with Jeannie.

Cool but gracious (on her part) is a good way to describe our first encounter back on campus. She was always gracious and, as I said before, very cool. The kind of cool I'm talking about here, however, is the kind cartoonists depict with icicles. I didn't yet know about Don Thorson's proposal. She told me about that later—much later.

It's not that Jeannie refused to go out with me. It's just that the oomph wasn't there like it had been the year before. Undaunted, I persevered and time worked in my favor over the next two years.

Neither of us had a car and we both were short on spendable funds so most of our time together was spent either on walks through the snow or in the "green room" of the DG house where boys were allowed to watch television, black and white television complete with a grainy, snowy picture. We also spent much time talking on the phone in the wee hours of the morning when the one phone in the DG house was available without someone else clambering to use it. Phones in those days were rotary, the kind where you put your finger in a numbered hole and turned it to the right until encountering a silver metal crescent.

During those two years we found we had much in common. Coincidentally, we read the same books such as Harold Robbins' *The Carpetbaggers* and Ayn Rand's *Fountainhead* and *Atlas Shrugged.* We enjoyed the same music, The Kingston Trio, The Limelighters, Gordon Lightfoot, and even Vince Guaraldi. We both liked playing golf and fishing. We were, in a word, simpatico.

"We're buds, huh?" was Jeannie's favorite thing to say when we discovered things we both liked or liked to do.

* * *

A sprinkle of rain pattered down one nice Saturday morning in the spring of 1962. Nice for Grand Forks, North Dakota, that is. "Let's go for a walk," Jeannie said. She had told me she enjoyed walking in the rain. The winter snow had melted, and grass was sprouting here and there.

"Where should we go, down to the park?" I asked. What we called Theta Park occupied several square blocks east of the Kappa Alpha Theta sorority house, a short jaunt down University Avenue. We paid many a visit there during the winter to play in newly drifted snow.

"I'd like to visit your mother's grave," Jeannie said. I had told her that my mom was buried in Calvary Cemetery about a half mile north of the DG House. She held my hand and gave it a squeeze. "I wish I could have met her."

"So do I." I squeezed back.

I hated talking about my mom's death. It hurt deep inside where a big hollow place lived. She died the summer after my freshman year at UND, ten years to the day before Neil Armstrong took "One small step for man—one giant leap for mankind." Although mom died in California, the family plot was in Grand Forks.

We continued to hold hands while meandering north past my temporary basement living quarters. "How old was she when she died?" Jeannie asked.

"Forty-seven." My mind drifted back to that day.

"So young. Was it cancer?" Jeannie stopped walking and looked up at me with those beautiful green eyes. She wasn't wearing a hat so I couldn't tell if the moisture on her cheeks was rain or tears.

My dam broke. "No. First, Mayo Clinic diagnosed multiple sclerosis. That's why we moved to California. Then a doctor in Pasadena thought she had a brain tumor. He did surgery where he lifted up a big flap of her skull to get to where he thought the tumor was. He said there was no tumor, just evidence of repeat bleeding episodes in her brain. He told my dad she had little chance of surviving the next one. She didn't."

"Were you living in Pasadena then?" Jeannie started walking again and pulled me along.

"Just north of there, in Altadena."

"How'd you get to Bakersfield?"

"My dad asked the FBI for a transfer so he could be closer to home. Mom died two and a half years later."

"Were you home when she died?"

"Sort of . . ."

Jeannie looked at me with knit brows. "What does that mean?"

The big, twisting squeeze hit my stomach again. "I had a summer job working for the Kern County Fire Department at a station in the mountains. My schedule was eight days on, four days off. I didn't have a car so Dad and Mom drove me up to the station for my next eight-day shift. Mom was doing really well." I took a couple deep breaths. "Two days later, a sheriff's car pulled up to the station—red lights flashing."

I held Jeannie close, wrapping my arms around her. "The deputy said my dad asked him to come get me. My mom was in the hospital in a coma. She stayed in the coma about a week before she died. It was the only time I ever saw my dad cry."

Jeannie and I stood in the street, hugging, for a long time before continuing our trek to the cemetery.

The rain stopped before we reached the open gate. Foggy mist hung in the old trees dotting the grounds. No one was there to guide us to the grave where Mom lay next to my grandparents, great aunts and uncles, and other relatives. I had not been there before.

Thirty minutes or so of wandering through the monuments and grave markers led us to the spot. A flat marker read "Margaret Patricia Brown: March 17, 1912 – July 20, 1959". My tears flowed freely. Jeannie's did as well. The twisting in my gut eased and the big hollow spot shrunk a tiny bit.

Four

Trains

Travel by train was common in the early sixties. Two train trips taken by Jeannie in our last year together at UND stand out among my clearest memories, one in the fall of 1962 and the other on New Year's Day 1963. Both occurred because Jeannie's major took her away from campus to study pediatric nursing in St. Paul, Minnesota. I had to get along without her for several weeks before the Christmas break, plus a few weeks after.

When the time came for Jeannie to leave for St. Paul, I borrowed Pete's car and took her to the train station.

I was dreading this period of separation. But a bright side hung on the horizon.

Jeannie planned to spend Christmas vacation with her parents in Farmington, New Mexico, where as far as I knew there was no Don Thorson lurking about. I would be in Denver with relatives for the holidays. Jeannie agreed to take a short flight on New Year's Eve Day from Farmington to Denver—her first time on a plane, a DC3 no less. I promised to buy a train ticket for her return to St. Paul the following afternoon. That way we could ring in 1963 together.

* * *

So, enough of the silver lining for now. Back to the train station in Grand Forks for Jeannie's trip to St. Paul.

We said a tearful goodbye and waved to each other as the train pulled out of the station. I watched until the caboose rolled out of sight. Then I climbed into Pete's car and headed back to campus. On the way, I stopped at a place called Henry's for a fifteen-cent chocolate milkshake to ease my sorrow.

When the clerk handed me the shake and a straw, I removed the plastic lid and stuck in the straw. As I drove away, I raised the cup and got my lips on the straw. I then tipped the cup as if intending to pour the milkshake down the straw. Why I did that, I have no idea. I was majoring in engineering and had taken fluid mechanics. I knew a chocolate milkshake wouldn't pour down a straw when it had the whole open top of the cup from which to make its escape.

The laws of fluid mechanics prevailed, and my entire front and lap became a gooey mess of cold, sticky, chocolate yuck. Somehow, I managed to avoid getting in a wreck.

* * *

Now, back to Denver. The New Year's plan went without a hitch. Jeannie arrived as scheduled. The evening we spent together was divine. And the surprise I conjured up for the next day came off better than I had dreamed.

I had, unbeknownst to Jeannie, purchased *two* train tickets from Denver to St. Paul. The second one was for me, continuing on to Grand Forks. My cousin drove us to the train station in Denver where Jeannie and I again said a tearful goodbye before I deftly slipped into the following passenger car and waited for the train to pull away.

After a few minutes, I approached Jeannie from the rear of the car, thankful another Don Thorson hadn't taken the seat next to her. In my best disguised voice I asked, "Is this seat taken?" Her reaction, with tear-drops still running down her cheeks, warmed the cockles of my heart. A delicious ride to St. Paul began.

* * *

A few weeks later, Jeannie returned to Grand Forks and very soon Don Thorson and his ski boat vanished from the picture forever. I knew this when one night Jeannie looked up at me and said words that burned themselves into my brain, words I once feared she might never speak.

"I love you, Jim Brown." She always called me Jim Brown back then, not just Jim. I never did know why. Maybe it was to separate me from all the other Jims who were pursuing her. I didn't care. She said she loved me and that freed me to tell her how much I loved her.

* * *

About two centuries ago, William Cowper wrote a poem that began with:

> *God moves in a mysterious way,*
> *His wonders to perform.*
> *He plants His footsteps in the sea,*
> *And rides upon the storm.*

I believe the events that happened in rapid succession in the spring of 1963 fit these words.

First, for some reason I still can't explain, I spent $10—which at the time could have purchased forty bottles of beer in a bar—and took the Law School Aptitude Test (LSAT) while Jeannie did her pediatric stint in St. Paul. Even though I took the test, I had never given thought to studying law. My brother Bill followed in our father's footsteps and would be graduating from the UND School of Law that June. I hoped to receive my engineering degree at the same ceremony and intended to pursue that career path.

Second, one of my friends who also took the LSAT and seriously wanted to go to law school, came up to me several days later with a scowl that announced his displeasure. "You son-of-a-sea-cook!" (He didn't really say *sea-cook*.) "They just posted the LSAT results. You don't even want to go to law school, and you got the highest score."

Third, I got mail—from local draft board 78 in Bakersfield—ordering me to report for a pre-induction physical in July. Careful reading of the letter convinced me that I hadn't actually been drafted but that a *pre-induction physical* just cleared the way in case they wanted to draft me on down the road. Direct involvement of the United States in the decades-long conflict in Vietnam didn't come until more than a year later, after *The Gulf of Tonkin Incident.*

And fourth, I received a phone call from Olaf H. Thormodsgard, Dean of the University of North Dakota School of Law, a position he had held since before my father attended. Dean Thormodsgard suggested there might be some scholarship money available if I chose to study law. He obviously hadn't looked at my undergraduate transcript. Unlike my brother Bill—every parent's dream of a model son and student—I had treated college as more of a social experiment than an academic endeavor.

Then I called my dad. "Pop, I'm in a bit of a dilemma." I gave him a shorthand explanation of the situation.

"If you're going to go to law school, you'll go in California. You won't be practicing in North Dakota." Adopting his FBI persona, his tone carried no hint of suggestion or opinion. Just the facts.

I sent off an application to the University of California law school at Berkeley, then known as Boalt Hall. A postcard came by return mail rejecting my application, stating that the deadline for 1963 had passed, but inviting me to apply for admission in 1964.

I called Pete Lewis (not to be confused with Rich "Pete" Peterson), then in his first year of law school at Hasting College of the Law, UC's San Francisco campus. He and I graduated from high school together in Bakersfield but didn't really get to know each other until we became Alpha Tau Omega fraternity brothers at UND.

"You can get in here," he said, "they take anyone still breathing who has three hundred bucks and a college degree—any degree from any college. The school's nickname is *Fear Tech.* Half flunk out before graduation."

"Doesn't sound like the place for me. I'd prefer *Easy sledding Law School.*"

"Any place is going to be hard, Jimbo. Places like Boalt Hall are picky and prestigious. They only take top-flight students and hardly anyone flunks out. Here, they give everyone a chance to get in, but if you can't cut it you're out."

"How are you doing so far?" I dared ask.

"Don't know. There's only a final exam in each class. Your grade is what you get on that." He let out a small chuckle. "It's nervous time, but the faculty is outstanding. Probably one of the best in the country. Most are members of what they call *The Sixty-Five Club*, all retired professors from other law schools. There's even one from UND."

"I'll give it some thought."

Shortly thereafter, Jeannie returned to campus from her pediatric training in St. Paul while the North Dakota winter still raged in the early months of 1963. Calendar spring approached, but Grand Forks spring remained a long way off. Below zero temperatures in March surprised no one. We bundled up and took long walks, talking about what the future may hold. My graduation date lay two months away. She had one more year to go. Would I be going to law school, and if so, where?

* * *

I don't know what ailment laid me low when most of the snow had melted. Perhaps some combination of food poisoning, dysentery, and cholera got me. No common bug was going around that I can recall. Whatever befell me wreaked havoc on my innards to the point of seemingly emptying my body of all its precious fluids and rendered me semi-comatose.

How I got to the hospital—the same one in which I was born—I don't know. I have a vague memory of being placed on a cot, stripped of my stinky clothing, and then being wheeled on this narrow bed to the hallway—wearing nothing more than the day I was born—covered only with a thin sheet and the remnants of what had been expelled from my innards.

My mind couldn't stay focused. All I wanted to do was sleep. I closed my eyes and drifted toward dreamland when soft hands lifted the sheet and gently began cleaning my soiled body. I may have dreamt feeling the warm touch of lips on my cheek and hearing the whispered words, "I love you, Jim Brown."

When I next awoke, comfy flannel pajamas covered my body and limbs. I opened my eyes and found Jeannie standing by my bedside.

"How do you feel?" she asked.

"Like I've been washed too many times on the hot cycle. When did you get here?"

"I was working as a student nurse yesterday when your friends brought you in. I asked if I could stay on and take care of you overnight. The charge nurse said it would be okay since I'm not on their payroll."

"Are you the one that cleaned me up?"

"Un-huh."

I felt the warmth of embarrassment in my face. "Do you still love me?"

She nodded. "Yup."

If I go to law school in California, will she still love me after a year apart?

* * *

In the spring of 1963, I graduated. Jeannie had one more year to go. We were facing a year of separation before we could begin our lives together as husband and wife. I never formally proposed marriage, and Jeannie never had an engagement ring. We just knew.

I headed off to law school in California where Jeannie agreed to join me as soon as she graduated and completed her nursing board examinations. By this time she had told me about Don Thorson's blunder, and I dared not repeat it.

Jeannie & Jim (1963)

Five

Our Year of Separation

Two thousand miles lay between us. Still, I felt as close to Jeannie during our year apart as ever. With none of the forms of instant communication that exist today, letters served as the basic means of conveying what was going on in Jeannie's life and mine. "Via Air Mail" allowed for a weekly exchange.

Her letters were elegant, mine clunky.

In one of her letters Jeannie described President Kennedy's visit to the University of North Dakota. His helicopter landed in an open field directly across the street from the Delta Gamma House. She was able to get up close enough to see the lines in his face. "He looks so old," she wrote.

Long distance phone calls were quite expensive so there were few of those. The first phone call from Jeannie came on November 22, 1963.

"Isn't it awful? I can hardly stand it." I heard her sniffing and trying to fight off tears. The tears won. She mourned the passing of our young president, who looked so old.

For a long time the whole world seemed to be in shock. Lee Harvey Oswald. Jack Ruby. The Zapruder film. John-John's salute. The Warren Commission. The "magic bullet". Conspiracy theories. Would things ever return to near normal?

* * *

Later, she told of her battles with sub-zero temperatures in Fargo, where she had been assigned to receive the Public Health part of her training. During the day she trudged through snow from house to house seeing her patients. Returning to her *home* provided little relief. The furnace that supposedly heated the room she shared with another student-nurse barely kept it above freezing. Her description of the cold could have been the inspiration for the bleak opening scene of the movie *Fargo*, where ice crystals blew in waving ribbons across the highway.

* * *

Following her Public Health stint in Fargo, Jeannie moved to her psychiatric training at the State Mental Hospital in Jamestown, North Dakota. The event this training led to still sends shivers down my spine.

Her first letter from Jamestown read in part:

> *We have each been assigned one patient –*
> *just one. The challenge is to win our pa-*
> *tient's trust. Mine is Richard, a 21-year-old*
> *diagnosed as sociopathic. Just the other day*
> *he set another patient's bed on fire. This*
> *may be tough.*

I don't know what Richard had done to land himself in a state mental hospital, but I know one thing he did after he got out. He went to see Jeannie at the Delta Gamma House. It was after her graduation. Only a few other DGs were still there.

She called me right after Richard's visit. "I was studying for my state boards when Suzy Leifer told me there was someone outside on a motorcycle who wanted to see me. I asked her who it was. She didn't know. I went outside, and there was Richard. He wanted to take me for a ride."

Then she told me that she went for the ride.

I went numb.

"Why in the world did you do that?" I could barely contain my anger.

"I knew it was dangerous. But I spent so much time building up trust. If I hadn't gone, the trust would have."

For an instant—only an instant—I almost changed my mind about marrying someone so . . . I don't know what. All I could picture was her dead body in a ditch and sociopathic Richard riding off whistling a happy tune.

The instant passed, leaving me thankful she was okay, and Richard was gone.

For that and a litany of other reasons, someone once pondered, "How can so wise a woman be such an airhead?"

Six

The Best Wedding Ever

June 19, 1964, was to be our wedding day with Jeannie arriving by train on the 18th in time for us to get our marriage license that afternoon. She planned to spend the night with Pete and Mary Lewis who were to be our Best Man and Matron of Honor. Mary had been Jeannie's roommate at UND. Pastor Erickson would then pronounce us *man and wife* the next morning.

So much for planning.

June 18 came and went with no appearance by Jeannie. It was neither the first nor last time she was late. She was no slave to the clock for most things. This time, however, the tardiness was *not* her fault. Massive flooding occurred in the Pacific Northwest, and Jeannie was stranded at the train station in Portland, along with all her earthly possessions packed in two cardboard boxes.

The train arrived from Portland a day late, and Jeannie stepped off and into my waiting arms. The kiss we shared put all others to shame. I felt about to burst with happiness. She laughed her wondrous, joyful laugh as we hugged and kissed over and over again. Finally, we loaded her two cardboard boxes into Pete Lewis' car, which I had borrowed because I still didn't have one.

On the way to Pete and Mary's I showed Jeannie the one-bedroom apartment that was to be our first home. I had managed to save up enough from a part-time job to acquire $100 worth of used furniture and pay $37.50 for half a month's rent.

The next morning, we were married. A grand total of twelve people attended the ceremony, three of them unborn. Those three all made their appearance in the next couple weeks—Jennifer, born to Pete and Mary Lewis, and twins, Jim and Meg, born to my brother Bill and his wife Ruth. Because of this, only nine saw the holes in the soles of my shoes as I knelt before the altar.

At just the right (or wrong) time during the wedding ceremony, a noisy, horn-honking, procession passed by the church, rattling the windows. This probably distracted my brother. He didn't object to our marriage when Pastor Erickson gave the assembled throng the opportunity to do so. Bill got even for that later. Twice.

My father, one of the few in attendance, with a twinkle in his eye muttered, "Quit your blubbering" to Jeannie as we walked down the aisle at the end of the service. Tears streamed down her face, but she assured him—and me —they were tears of joy. Many times thereafter she shed "tears of joy" at the happiest moments.

Wedding photo taken by brother Bill
(June 20, 1964)

A combination reception and honeymoon took up the rest of our wedding day. First, we went to Jack London Square and a quaint pub called *The First and Last Chance*. Legend has it that Jack London wrote most if not all of *The Call of the Wild* in this converted ship with its slanted floor and clanging bell that rang to announce, "there's a pigeon on the pot."

It seems as though the proprietor delighted in spoofing unsuspecting female users of the "Ladies' Room"—a facility akin to an outhouse

—through the use of a speaker placed in the chamber below where one sat.

"Excuse me, ma'am, I'm painting down here," the barkeep said when he heard the *pigeon* take her seat. "Could you hold off just a bit?". It was funny for all but the one sitting.

From *The First and Last Chance* the assembled group wandered over to another pub at Jack London Square where adult beverages flowed freely and no bell rang. When dinner time arrived, we crossed through the Tube from Oakland to Alameda and gathered at a very nice restaurant called The Odyssey where my father hosted an order-from-the-menu meal.

Unfortunately for Jeannie, she didn't get to eat much. It became the first of the times brother Bill made up for missing the opportunity to object at the church.

Seated next to his new sister-in-law who had ordered a steak—something Jeannie and I had little prospect of providing for ourselves for quite some time—he made his move. Before Jeannie had taken more than a bite or two, Bill speared her steak with his fork, saying something like, "well, if you're not going to eat this." He then devoured her steak before setting off to invent *photo bombing*.

With Jeannie's meal resting comfortably in his belly, along with copious amounts of ethyl alcohol, brother Bill wandered into a room at The Odyssey that had been set aside for another wedding's reception. A huge cake sat on a small table next to a larger table groaning under the weight of wrapped gifts.

As the bride in all her finery opened each wedding present, she held it up and smiled at the photographer. Later, when she or anyone else looked at the pictures, there would be brother Bill, all six foot three of him, standing behind her with his goofy smile. They probably wondered, "Who is that guy?"

From The Odyssey, the journey to our little apartment consisted of a two-minute, 75-cent cab ride. We were alone at last, newlyweds with a year apart to make up for—our honeymoon of sorts.

At three in the morning the phone rang. By that time, we had made up for way less than the full year. Nevertheless, I answered the phone thinking a call at that hour could only portend something bad had happened.

"What are you guys doing?" slurred the voice of the worlds' first photo bomber. I hung up in the middle of his laugh, and Jeannie and I returned to making up for lost time.

Seven

Culinary Queen – Not Exactly

Jeannie looked over the kitchen of our tiny apartment. "My mother never taught me how to cook." On the first full day of married life, I really didn't care.

I had managed to scrape up the funds to assemble a few pots and pans, some Melmac plates, a smattering of old flatware, and paper cups. Food presented a different problem. We had none. We also didn't have a car.

Fortunately, a Safeway grocery store was just four blocks down the street. We took inventory of the combined cash we had available and set out for our first grocery shopping adventure.

On the way, Jeannie ticked off a list of things she knew how to make—food things, that is.

"I can fix breakfast. Eggs, bacon, sausage, that kind of stuff. Fried chicken. Hamburger soup... "

Hamburger soup?

"What's hamburger soup?"

"We had that going at our house all the time. Basically, it's left-overs with some crumbled ground beef tossed in. That big pot will be perfect." She started to skip as the Safeway came into view.

I kept a running total as Jeannie loaded items into the cart. Food was really cheap—inexpensive I should say—back then, especially over-ripe bananas.

"Oh, and I know how to make banana bread." She pointed to bags of bananas at the end of the fruit aisle. Each bag was marked, "19¢." A dozen or more of the mostly brown crescents resided in each one. "These will be perfect."

When our loaded cart arrived at the check-out stand, I prayed that my accounting total matched that of the cash register. If it did, we might not have to put anything back, leaving a few coins to jingle in my pocket on the way home.

We made it.

Now, how to get the grocery sacks to our little *home*. Grocery bags were bigger and stronger in those days, heavy brown paper with carrying handles. But between us, we only had four hands. So Jeannie had an idea.

With her sweet smile she asked the checker, "We don't have a car but we live just down the street. If we promise to bring it right back, can we use the cart to get these groceries home?"

"Of course, dear," the clerk said with a wink. Jeannie had made another new friend. For the next two years, every time we went to Safeway, Jeannie looked for this gal and got in her line, no matter how many others stood there.

We pushed the Safeway cart thumpeldy-bumpeldy down the street and trucked all the bags of goodies up the stairs to the second floor and into the kitchen. Jeannie put everything away while I ran the cart back to the store. She was starting her first batch of hamburger soup when I returned.

"I'll make breakfast in a minute. Just let me get this soup going." She put some canned vegetables in the big pot while hamburger crumbles sizzled in a fry pan.

I came up behind her, turned off the fire under the pan, hugged her around the waist, and whispered in her ear, "Breakfast can wait. Let's take a nap." She knew napping was the last thing on my mind as we went hand-in-hand into the bedroom.

Eight

First Jobs

Our honeymoon lasted over that weekend. On Monday, I started my summer job working as part of a sandblasting crew. Jeannie was still waiting for the results of her State Board Nursing Examination. She had to pass in order to start her job as an RN at Children's Hospital in Oakland. Waiting was the order of the day in 1964. There was no email, no fax, no anything other than wait for the mail.

Jeannie got up early that Monday morning, fixed my lunch and packed it into a lunch pail she brought from North Dakota. She kissed me goodbye and sent me on my way, lunch pail in hand. The walk to work only took about fifteen minutes. I got there ten minutes early. Had I known what my job entailed, I might have been more like a week late.

When I got home that first day, all stinky and sweaty, with sand packed into every place sand could be packed in a person's body, I was greeted with a big hug and the proud announcement, "I passed!"

She didn't just pass; she scored at or near the top of every category of the test—and there were many.

"I called the hospital and told 'em. They said I could start on Thursday. But we need to get a garbage can."

That last part didn't make any sense. What did a garbage can have to do with her work at the hospital?

I hunched my weary shoulders. "That's great. But why do you need a garbage can?"

"For the garbage." She pointed at the grocery bags she had filled up with trash. "They pick up on Thursdays. I don't want plastic. I want metal. Mary says they got theirs in Oakland for three dollars."

"Did she say where?"

"I have the address." She held up the paper it was written on.

I looked at my filthy, sweaty clothes. "I need to take a shower."

After showering and digging a cupful of sand from each ear, I announced that I was ready to head to the bus stop and go garbage can shopping. Off we went.

We found the address in Oakland Mary had given Jeannie. The place might have been named "Garbage Cans Galore." Our choices seemed endless.

"I like this one," Jeannie said, pointing to a large galvanized can with its lid connected to the body by a stout chain. "What do you think?"

A garbage can is a garbage can, right?

"I'm fine with that." Then I looked at the price tag. It wasn't $3. "How much you got?"

Together we scraped up enough nickels, dimes, and pennies to close the deal and leave us with enough for bus fare home.

The three of us waited at the bus stop, hoping we didn't have to pay extra to get our galvanized child aboard. We didn't, but some funny looks came our way as we carted the can down the aisle to a bench seat where we could sit side by side.

It was still light out when we got home, so we took 'Junior' around to the side of the building where a narrow walkway led to the garbage can area.

There in the slot for Apartment "D", our apartment, stood a galvanized can that could have been our guy's big brother. Neither of us had bothered to check.

Jeannie just laughed until her tears began to flow.

How could so wise a woman be married to such an airhead?

Nine

Edgar

I came home from collecting sand in my ears and put my lunch pail on the kitchen counter. "Jeannie," I called out. It was her day off.

"In here," came a weak voice from the living room.

I poked my head in to tell her I was going to take a shower. She sat on the couch with her forehead resting on the upturned palms of her hands, elbows on her knees. A torn shopping bag and a pile of clothes lay on the floor beside her.

Tears ran down her cheeks when she looked up at me. "What have I gotten myself into? This is *not* how I pictured my life."

"What's the matter?" I knelt in front of her and kissed her forehead.

"Look at these clothes. They're filthy." Still sitting, she kicked out at the torn bag. She missed. "I had to use this stupid thing to carry 'em to the laundromat." The back of her hand wiped a tear from her cheek. "On the way home, the bag tore and the clean clothes wound up in the gutter. . . I sat on the curb and bawled. . . People must have thought I was crazy."

I tried to give her a hug, but she pushed me away. She stood and gave the bag a good kick, sending it flying. "Taking the bus from work at night is bad enough. I'm not going to carry laundry in paper bags." With that, she stormed off into the bedroom.

Not knowing what to say without making things worse, it seemed a good time for my shower.

With water splashing on top of my head, and fingers cleaning sand out of my ears, I barely heard the voice from the other side of the door.

"Right! Just go hide in there!"

By the time I dressed, Jeannie had composed herself a bit.

"Maybe we can find a cart of some kind," I said.

An almost smile crossed her face. "The hardware store downtown might have just what I need."

Off we went in search of a solution. On foot, that is.

A mile or so into our walk, Jeannie said, "let's look in here."

I don't remember which store it was, but it wasn't the hardware store. I didn't think they carried what Jeannie wanted—and said so.

Wrong.

She found a two-wheeled wire cart large enough to hold our laundry and then some. It cost $4.

Jeannie wheeled it home—forward down the curbs and backward up to the sidewalks.

Not too many days later, my sandblasting job came to an abrupt end. The union rep showed up. I wasn't in the union. I became unemployed.

That evening, I called Pete Lewis. He had a summer job working on a special project for the East Bay Municipal Utilities District (East Bay MUD). He had joked about it, saying it was like being back in kindergarten. The special project team he worked for put the finishing touches on documentation of the completed construction of a new aqueduct. His assignment was to color-code a long strip-map identifying the type of property interest East Bay MUD held for each parcel the aqueduct passed through.

"Do you need help?" I asked him.

"Not hardly," he chuckled. "I need to slow down or I'll work myself out of a job."

"Could you ask if they need another kindergartner to do something else?"

"Sure."

The next day Pete called. "They could use an extra draftsman to do as-builts. I told the boss you had an engineering degree. He said he'd put you to work."

"You're a magic man, Pete. Do I owe you a finder's fee?"

"Naw . . . well . . . how about two beers?"

"Done."

I could hardly wait for Jeannie to get home so I could tell her the good news. She worked the evening shift from three to eleven, sometimes not getting off the bus at the end of our block until nearly midnight.

The sound of her footsteps on the stairs raised my heavy eyelids and I sat up straight on the couch.

"What are you doing up?" she asked. I was usually in bed asleep by the time she came in.

"Pete found a job for me at East Bay MUD."

"Doing what?" she set her purse on the floor and sat down next to me.

"As-built drawings of an aqueduct."

She furrowed her brow. "What are they . . . as-built drawings?"

"I don't know for sure, but I think it's converting field construction notes to an engineering drawing. Probably to show what was built matched the plans."

"Oh."

"Can you ride with Pete?"

"He said I could. We'll be working in the same building."

*　*　*

In the morning, after some discussion, I said, "You need a car . . . all you have is a $4 cart." We agreed to cash her first nursing paycheck—and my first and last sandblasting paycheck—and go on another search for wheels.

I looked in the paper and found a green 1951 Chevy with an asking price of $200. We got on the bus to go check it out. No radio. No defroster. Crank windows. No anything but a steering wheel, a gear shift, and pedals. We talked the owner down to $175. Jeannie named the thing Edgar.

She no longer had to take the bus to and from the hospital. She drove Edgar and fell madly in love with him. The first road-trip for Edgar was to Sacramento for the baptism of Bill and Ruth's twins Meg and Jim.

Jeannie even took Edgar to the laundromat.

Jeannie, Ruth with Jim, the pastor, Me with Meg
Photo by Bill Brown

Ten

Early Days of Fishing, etc.

Jeannie liked to fish. I learned that before we were married, and she learned the same about me. During our nearly four years of courtship, however, we never wet a line in each other's company. Our first fishing adventure together came in the summer of 1964 when her parents came to Alameda for a visit. They hadn't been at our wedding, waiting about a month before making the trip from Williston, North Dakota, where they again lived.

Jeannie's folks, Bill and Bertha, both avid anglers, made the decision for us to take a weekend camping-and-fishing trip to Clear Lake, an hour or two north of San Francisco. Jeannie and I didn't have camping gear other than two flimsy sleeping bags that zipped together to make one large bag—and no fishing equipment at all.

Bill found an open campsite on the west side of Clear Lake. He parked their camper and started a fire while Bertha pulled out some folding chairs. We sat by the fire and chatted until darkness set in and the campfire had burned down to coals perfect for roasting hot dogs on a stick and heating up some beans.

Each of us held our sticks over the glowing coals, taking part in an unspoken challenge to see who could roast the perfect hot dog. After eating and a little clean-up, Bill and Bertha retired to their bed in the camper.

Jeannie and I struggled to zip our bags together. We put them on the top of a picnic table because Jeannie said, "I don't want to be exposed to whatever critters prowl the ground at night."

An essentially sleepless night on the concrete top of the table in our large, thin, conjoined bag marked the start of our misadventure. The fairly narrow space required us to cuddle together. Nothing bad about that except sometime during the night, when we both had at long last drifted off to sleep, Jeannie rolled left and I rolled right. We wound up each hanging off our respective sides of the table, wrapped like two sausages in flimsy sleeping bag material. How we got out, I don't recall. All I remember is the laughter, and Jeannie saying, "bring on the ground critters."

The following morning, after a cold breakfast, Jeannie and I set out in search of basic fishing tackle. And by *basic* I mean a length of black line wrapped around cardboard, and a hook to tie on the end. Two of each. And a Styrofoam cup of worms, of course. We found this gear at something resembling a miniature general store.

With our newly acquired paraphernalia in hand, we began looking for a likely spot where we could fish from shore. Bill and Bertha had gone off to see if they could find a small boat for rent.

"Look over there." Jeannie pointed to a large pine. "Someone's fishing off that tree."

The pine must have fairly recently toppled over into the lake. Its needles hadn't yet turned brown. A lady had made her way out on the trunk almost to the tip-end and was pulling up a fish.

We hustled down to the base of the tree and watched the gal catch one fish after another until she had a loaded stringer to carry ashore. When the coast was clear, Jeannie crawled out to take her spot. Slipping a worm onto the hook, she let the black line down between branches. It didn't take long before she called out, "I got a bite." She pulled on the line. "Now I'm hung up."

Using a branch for support—or at least that's probably what she thought she was doing—she tried to get her hook free. The branch bent, and bent, and bent with Jeannie doing a slow-motion dive into the water. She came up sputtering and laughing—my only catch of the day.

* * *

A few weeks later, with newly acquired rods and reels in hand—courtesy of Bill and Bertha—we tried our luck in San Francisco Bay. Scrambling out onto a rock jetty at the west end of Alameda Island, next to the Naval Air Station, we cast lures into the murky water. Nary a bite all day. We decided to concentrate on golf for a while.

* * *

During my second year at Hastings, Pete Lewis introduced me to one of his classmates, a fellow named Ralph Temple. We became friends. He was an avid golfer and a native of the Bay Area. Jeannie and I joined him to play many of the public courses with green fees we could afford.

When his graduation date approached, Ralph arranged for me to inherit his job as a law clerk for two brothers, the Sills. They practiced out of a dinky office in Freemont with a staff of one lady, Lillian, who served as receptionist-secretary-bookkeeper and general factotum. She worked with a manual typewriter, making copies with carbon paper. I don't know what the Sill brothers paid her, but it was not enough.

My job consisted mainly of research projects that often took me to the county law library. What the Sill brothers called their library occupied a single shelf no more than five feet long. Being paid $1.75 an hour to do what I was putting out good money for as a law student seemed like a gift from heaven—until Lillian took her one-week summer vacation. I took over her job for that week. That's how I know she wasn't paid nearly enough. Somehow, Ralph Temple forgot to tell me about that part of the job.

After Ralph graduated, I lost contact with him for over a year. The next time I saw him, at a time and place neither of us expected, we only had the chance to talk briefly. That encounter will be described later.

Eleven

The Job Offer

In the summer of 1966—the height of the war in Vietnam—President Kennedy's policy that married men were to be at the end of the draft call-up list—those with children at the very bottom—remained partially in place. President Johnson rescinded the Kennedy policy effective August 26, 1965, but the old rule still applied to those of us who were married before that date.

Jeannie and I had the marriage protection but no children. So, after I graduated from law school, we set about starting a family. Success came easily, too easily it seemed. Home test kits had not yet been invented.

"Still good," Jeannie beamed. "Five days late." She winked as she headed toward the door in her crisp white nurse's uniform, complete with white hose and white shoes, a starched white cap bearing a green stripe, and her pin signifying she was a registered nurse from the University of North Dakota. I smiled and gave her a kiss and a thumbs-up.

Jeannie's period had always been regular as clockwork. Five days late seemed too good to be true. I went back to my studies for the bar exam that hovered less than three weeks away. Visions of a new life forming in her womb captured my imagination.

The next day, I received a letter from Kit Nelson, the District Attorney in Bakersfield, offering me a clerk's position in his office while I waited for the bar results. Pete Lewis, then a Deputy DA had put in a good word for me. If I passed the bar, I would become a deputy, ready to go to court and put criminals where they belonged. I couldn't wait for Jeannie to get home so I could tell her.

When Jeannie opened the door, I ran up and hugged her, lifting her off her feet. "I got the job—six hundred a month! Can you believe it?"

"That's great!"

She wrapped her arms tightly around my neck and gave me a long sweet kiss, her feet still a good six inches from the floor.

"Let's call Pete and Mary," she said as I set her down.

Her little book where she dutifully recorded the address and phone number of everyone she cared about lay next to the black, cradle-style phone in the living room. She opened the book while dialing "O."

"Long distance to Bakersfield, California, person-to-person to Mary Lewis at Fairview 4786 please." She waited as the operator completed the call.

"Mary? Jeannie. Jim got the job." Jeannie laughed. Mary laughed. I laughed. The conversation went on longer than we could afford at long distance rates, but what the heck. Life was good.

When she hung up, Jeannie told me Mary and Pete were hosting a barbecue the following Friday for a bunch of DA people.

"She said we should come down. I'm off next Friday and Saturday, so…" She lifted her eyebrows.

"I don't know," I said, looking at the books and papers strewn on my study desk.

"Come on, you deserve a break. We'll leave as soon as I get off work Thursday and come back Saturday."

"Okay, if you drive so I can read."

* * *

Jeannie drove down to Bakersfield the next Thursday and we stayed the night with Pete and Mary. Friday morning I took the opportunity to pay a visit to Local Draft Board 78 to check on my status.

"Yes, how may I help you?" the nice lady behind the counter asked.

I gave her my draft card. "Have you started drafting married men yet?"

She glanced at my card, gave me a quick once-over and said, "Not yet. But when we do, you'll be the first."

With a small lump in my throat from her apparent familiarity with my situation, I pressed on. "What about those with kids?"

"Oh, that's a long way off."

That welcome bit of news buoyed my spirits as I headed back to Pete and Mary's house to help with preparation for the evening barbecue get-together with the DA crowd. I found Jeannie and Mary in the kitchen talking quietly about baby things. Mary had a two-year-old and a second on the way. As a pediatric nurse, Jeannie knew all about kids from birth on. But pregnancy was a new experience.

I interrupted the maternal discussion to tell Jeannie what I had learned at the draft board. She opened her eyes wide and gave a knowing smile to Mary when I got to the part about kids. We knew that a confirmed pregnancy was considered a child by the draft authorities.

* * *

The evening's festivities brought many laughs, we met some wonderful people, and listened to much shop talk about this trial and that.

After a while, Jeannie excused herself to the ladies powder room as I got an earful about what to expect working as a clerk in the DA's office, all the while being tormented about what the bar results might bring. She returned a few minutes later with an expression that made it totally unnecessary for her to whisper in my ear, "I'm not pregnant." That message was etched all over her face.

Twelve

The Letter

As best my muddled brain can recall, it was a beautiful Thursday afternoon in the East Bay, four days before the start of the Bar Examination. After those three days of torturous testing Jeannie and I intended to pack up and move our meager belongings to Bakersfield with fingers crossed. My 26th birthday was four months away and with it there would be no more worries about the draft.

I decided to get up from my books and take my glazed-over eyes for a short walk. Jeannie hadn't come home from the hospital where her co-workers were throwing a going-away party for her.

Random thoughts flowed aimlessly through my head as I strolled just as aimlessly around the neighborhood. A few blocks west of our apartment the San Francisco skyline came into view beyond the sparkling waters of the bay. The Bar Examination lurked there.

Before long, I found myself approaching the side of our apartment building—actually a converted house carved into four units—where the mailboxes were fastened to the outside wall. The box for our apartment sat on the far right. A brown envelope peeked out the top, the ugliest envelope I have ever seen, with an equally ugly letter inside. A knot twisted in my gut as I read, "Greetings from the President of the United States . . ."

I made a futile attempt to get back to preparing for the bar exam. Visions of the jungles of Vietnam swam through the words on the pages. Viet Cong hid behind every tree.

I was halfway between panic and despair when I heard Jeannie coming up the outside stairs. I went to meet her at the door with the envelope in my hand. My expression must have been dour.

"What's the matter?" she asked, a fading smile on her face and a boatload of goodbye gifts in her arms.

"I've been drafted."

I held up the ugly brown envelope.

In the second or two it took for this news to sink in, Jeannie's smile disappeared and the color left her cheeks. She nearly staggered into the tiny living room of our one-bedroom apartment and plunked down on the faded couch.

"When do you have to report?" Her voice was thin and desperate.

"Not until September."

"What are we going to do?" Tears were forming in the corners of her eyes.

"I don't know." I sat down beside her and took her hand. "Maybe you should move in with your folks."

Jeannie shook her head. I knew what that meant. She would not run back to her mom and dad who then lived in Seminole, Oklahoma. She had her heart set on repaying her parents for her college education, not moving back in with them.

"What about Canada?" she said softly through her growing tears. "Lots of people are doing that."

Silence prevailed. I didn't need to answer. She knew how I felt about those running away. I just hugged her and held her close, feeling her heart thump in her chest, as she must have felt mine.

"We'll get through this somehow," I finally said. I didn't know if I spoke the truth or not, but at the time it seemed like the right thing to say.

The next few weeks are blurred in my memory. The bar exam came and went. I knew I failed miserably and the next opportunity to take it again lay at least two and a half years away—if I survived that long. By then I'd have forgotten too much to ever have a chance of passing.

Jeannie got her job back at Children's Hospital and made an attempt to return her gifts. Everyone declined but they all accepted her with open arms—particularly a certain amorous doctor.

The rest of July, August, and early September flew by. The date for reporting to the Induction Center in Fresno loomed just around the corner when Jeannie announced, "I'm going to stay right here."

"All your family is in Oklahoma. Why don't you go back there?" I protested to a made-up mind.

"This is *our home*. I'm staying."

Thirteen

Induction into the Army

When the dreaded day arrived for me to report to the Army Induction Center in Fresno, Jeannie drove me to the Greyhound bus station in Oakland. She parked at the curb and we hugged for a long time.

"Are they going to send you right to Vietnam?" she asked.

My knowledge of the military came mostly from two years of mandatory ROTC at the University of North Dakota. That wasn't much. Obviously, Jeannie knew even less.

"No. I have to go through basic training first. Maybe more after that." I wiped a small teardrop from her cheek.

"Where will that be?"

"I don't know. I'll write you as soon as I can."

We kissed goodbye. And hugged. And kissed some more. I breathed in her scent to take with me. Our fingertips parted as I trudged backward toward the bus for Fresno.

When the bus pulled out, I waved to Jeannie, still parked at the curb. She waved back. I knew she wouldn't leave until the bus rolled out of sight. She might even follow it a few miles.

I rode to Fresno in silence with an empty seat beside me and a larger emptiness in my heart. *When will I ever see Jeannie again?*

* * *

When my bus arrived at the induction center in Fresno, jammed with draftees from all over the San Joaquin Valley, I was placed with the Bakersfield group, mostly 18- and 19-year-olds. One fellow with hair flowing over his shoulders earned the nickname "Cinderella" from the soldier in charge of our processing.

Our Bakersfield group of inductees rode an army bus to Fort Ord. The greeting when we arrived reminded me of a scene from a movie. A drill sergeant barked commands nonstop from the time the bus door opened until all of us were out and in a straight line.

For the next few days we went from one long line to another waiting to get our heads shaved, waiting for needles to be stuck into our arms and elsewhere, waiting to be fitted with boots and clothing, waiting to have our eyes and teeth checked, and on and on. It was days of "hurry up and wait." The only fun I had was watching Cinderella's long locks hit the floor.

* * *

After those hurry-up-and-wait days, I became separated from my Bakersfield group to receive the Officer Candidate School (OCS) pitch. All draftees with a college degree received the pitch—a good one, well delivered. I fell for it. Fortunately, I washed out of the program for the same reason I suffered suspension from the University of North Dakota. More on that later.

By then, my Bakersfield guys had moved on, so I joined a group from Houston. This band of misfits included the original *Zero* from the *Beatle Baily* comic strip, the soldier who couldn't tell his left hand from his right. Others were similarly challenged. Collectively, we became the Fifth Platoon of Company B, First Battalion, Third Brigade (B-1-3).

Basic training began.

After a few days, we got permission to send out a short letter advising the recipient we were at Fort Ord, California, and that visitors could come the second Sunday of October.

At an age six or seven years older than the rest of the Fifth Platoon, I received the great honor of being named their leader as *trainee sergeant*. My advanced age, coupled with the few remaining hairs that adorned my pate, also earned me the nickname *Grandpa.* Due to our general ineptitude—in spite of my faultless leadership—we became known as *The-raggedy-Ass-Fifth.*

I hoped to take away some of Jeannie's fear with my first letter telling her I was still in California, less than 100 miles south of our Alameda apartment, and about Visitors' Sunday. When the day came, she made the two-hour drive to Fort Ord. The final stretch of road took her along beautiful Monterey Bay to the main entrance gate of Fort Ord. The weather was perfect.

Then things became more difficult.

Jeannie wasn't a good navigator under the best circumstances, but she later told me that when she showed my letter to the guard at the gate and asked for directions to B-1-3, he might as well have been speaking Swahili. Nonetheless, my sweet wife said she eventually made it to the 3rd Brigade area and began asking anyone who would talk to her, "Where is B-1-3?"

I waited impatiently, keeping an eye out for our old car. When I saw her pull up and park I wasn't allowed to go to her. I had to wait for her to run across the small patch of grass and jump into my waiting arms.

"I'm sorry to be late, but the people here are so stupid," she said between sweet kisses.

"What do you mean?"

"I drove right by here half an hour ago and asked that guy for directions to B-1-3." She pointed at the soldier guarding B-1-3, one of *The-Raggedy-Ass-Fifth.* "He said he didn't know." Apparently my fellow platoon member didn't know what building he was guarding. I shook my head thinking someday soon my fate might be in his hands.

In less than an hour the drill sergeant curtly and loudly informed the visitors they must leave.

I gave Jeannie a hug and kiss. "You can come back on Thanksgiving, spend the whole afternoon."

"Can I bring food?" She asked.

"As much as you want." A major mistake on my part.

I watched her walk away and get into Edgar. As she drove off she shook her fist at the dummy who couldn't tell her how to get to the building he was guarding. Good thing he didn't see her, or he might have shot at her with his unloaded rifle.

Fourteen

Basic Training
Thanksgiving

Thanksgiving took forever to arrive. When the day finally came—Jeannie didn't—at least not when every other visitor did. Except for her nursing work, she paid little attention to the clock.

While I watched for Jeannie, I spotted a friend, the aforementioned Ralph Temple, who had been a year ahead of me in law school. Even at a good distance away I saw the silver bar on his lapel.

"Ralph . . . I mean . . . Sir." I snapped up a salute as we walked toward each other.

"Brown, what are you doing here?"

I hunched my shoulders. "I got drafted."

"So did I. Why didn't you get a commission?"

I told him the story about getting washed out of the OCS program. "They said if I put in for Infantry OCS, I could get an automatic transfer to JAG. That sure sounded like a good deal."

"You are *sooooo* lucky. They told me the same thing." He shrugged. "I didn't know they had a license to lie. My request for transfer to JAG came back *denied* and I went to Nam as a 2nd Lieutenant leading search and destroy missions . . . don't know how I got out of there alive."

His head was on a swivel, as if he feared Viet Cong might be sneaking up on him.

He seemed to be in a hurry, so I gave him another quick salute and went back to my vigil watching for Jeannie. While I waited, I shot up a prayer of thanks for having been washed out of the OCS program.

When I caught sight of our little green car pulling up, every parking place was taken—save one. Jeannie drove right into that open space, the one reserved for the Commanding General of Fort Ord. A big sign said so. She hopped out, went around to the back, opened the trunk and waved for me to come over.

"Permission to go to the parking lot, Sergeant?"

"Granted. Double time, soldier."

I ran to the parking lot, grabbed a quick hug and then bent into the trunk to lift out two heavy bags of food and drink. Before I straightened up, a shadow appeared from behind me with flapping wings on each side. Never in the prior seven weeks of basic training had General Charles R. "Monk" Meyer visited B-1-3. That day—of all days—he did.

I stood, trembling, as I attempted to raise my right hand in salute without dropping the load in my arm. The stone-faced General Meyer, sitting in the rear seat of the Command Vehicle, returned my clumsy salute. His driver, a second lieutenant, did the same while glaring daggers.

Jeannie was just Jeannie. She shrugged her shoulders with a wide-eyed *whoops* look on her face. "Oh, I'm sorry, am I in your spot? I'll move."

With flags waving on each front fender, General Meyer let himself out. Rather small for a highly-decorated combat veteran and former West Point football star—runner-up for the first-ever Heisman Trophy —the general more than compensated for his lack of size with his military bearing. He stepped close, eyes flicking back and forth between Jeannie and me.

"That's all right, Miss," he said with a wry smile, "my driver will find another place to park. Soldier, take this lovely young lady to the yard and have a wonderful Thanksgiving."

With that, General Meyer turned, climbed back into the Flag Vehicle, and off he went.

I, Private Brown, with knees ready to buckle and a loaded bag in each arm, led Jeannie to the place on the lawn where my blanket reserved our spot in the sun.

The yummy smelling feast in those two bags calmed my nerves somewhat. One bag held turkey and mashed potatoes—plus gravy—all still steamy hot in insulated containers. In the other I found cranberry sauce, pickles, olives, rolls, soft drinks, salad, and pie. Jeannie may not have packed enough to feed 5000, but it might have come close.

Time sped by and soon the visitors had to leave. I again got permission to go to the parking area in order to carry the two bags—still quite heavy—back to the car.

We hugged for a long time. "Thanks for coming, sweetheart, and for all the goodies. Drive carefully."

"I will."

We parted with a kiss and I said, "I love you." She mouthed the same to me as she climbed into the car and backed out of the spot clearly marked for the Commanding General.

Who else but Jeannie?

Fifteen

Bar Results

Sunday, December 4, 1966, the day after basic training graduation, I had fallen into the dreaded category of *hold-over*. Most of my fellow draftees had received their orders for Advanced Individual Training (AIT) and were gone. Behind my name on the "Orders List" appeared the words: *Science and Engineering – orders to follow.* They didn't.

I was sitting in the Day Room watching a football game with a few other hold-overs when a member of the cadre barged in and barked, "Private Brown, report to the Orderly Room."

My orders must have come.

Making my way down the hallway toward the Orderly Room where the drill sergeants and officers conducted business, the last thought on my mind was the bar exam. I knew I had failed and hadn't thought about it at all during basic training. Nor did I have any idea when the results might come.

When I rounded the corner into the Orderly Room, the Officer of the Day was standing just inside the doorway.

I snapped to attention and saluted. "Private Brown reporting, Sir."

"At ease, Private. There's someone here to see you."

That someone stepped out from behind the lieutenant. Jeannie.

In one hand she held a bottle of champagne; in the other a fat envelope. Her face beamed with a big old smile: *ear-to-ear* as they say. "You passed!"

She threw her arms around my neck and gave me a fine congratulatory kiss.

I looked at the envelope. It was from the State Bar of California, but it hadn't been opened. My heart sank. I remembered talk about fat envelopes and skinny ones—one being good and the other bad—but I couldn't recall which was which.

"How do you know I passed? You didn't open it."

"It came yesterday. I was afraid to open it so I called Lee Archer. He said fat envelopes are good—all the forms you have to fill out and stuff. He passed, too. So did Lance Russom." She was bouncing up and down with excitement. "It was in the paper today. Didn't you see it?"

The Sunday *San Francisco Chronicle* had been on the table next to me in the Day Room and I hadn't even bothered to pick it up.

"You can't open that bottle here, ma'am. In fact, it shouldn't be here at all. But . . . this calls for a celebration, don't you think?" The lieutenant pulled out a form, scratched some words on it and held it out to me, an off-post pass for the night. I didn't have to report for duty until noon the next day.

"I'll arrange a room for you two at the VEQ (Visiting Enlisted Quarters) for tonight. It's not fancy, but it'll do for what you need." He winked at us and picked up the phone to call the VEQ. I gave a quick salute. He returned it, phone in hand.

I couldn't resist tearing open the envelope to make sure there hadn't been a horrible mistake. "Congratulations . . . " That's all I had to read.

"All set. Check in before you leave post. Now get out of here. Your wife says she has some civvies for you in her car."

Another quick salute and we were gone.

When we got to the VEQ, which was surprisingly nice, I changed clothes—allowing sufficient time for some extracurricular activities. I dressed in my civvies as Jeannie put back on the clothes she had been wearing. She hadn't planned on spending the night.

A stunning sunset greeted us as we pulled through the gate to leave post. The broad expanse of the Pacific glowed with merging streaks of orange, pink, and violet that reflected through the largest of the breaking waves. The colors seemed to dance on the horizon, a hard scene to turn away from in order to head up the Coast Highway to a little restaurant we had found long before I was drafted.

If corkage fees were in vogue then, we weren't charged. And if credit cards existed then, we had none. Between us we had enough cash to order anything on the menu. Plus, we always kept a roll of quarters in the car for pay-phone emergencies. Cell phones were decades away—even dumb ones.

We toasted each other with the champagne Jeannie brought—chilled in an ice bucket the restaurant graciously provided—ate heartily, ordered a decadent dessert of ice cream drenched with gooey caramel and chocolate, and made a list of all the people to call from the phone booth outside the front door. Our roll of quarters was sorely tested that night.

Back at the VEQ . . . little sleep. I did manage to make it back to B-1-3 by noon—just barely—and sadly waved goodbye as Jeannie again backed out of the Commanding General's parking place. She pulled in there out of pure orneriness, laughing as she did. "I have my very own lawyer to take care of me if I get in trouble."

I went back to being Private Brown, hold-over, the dark cloud of Vietnam looming over the same horizon that dazzled us the evening before.

Sixteen

The Generals

Hold-over status meant reporting for general duty at 7:00 a.m. Monday through Friday for work assignment along with a group of misfits the Army didn't otherwise know what to do with. Most days, supervision came from soldiers freshly back from combat in Vietnam, proficient in the art of cleaning latrines. Under their tutelage, I obtained similar proficiency.

Every once in a while, I was fortunate enough to be placed with a crew picking up roadside trash. Not a single cigarette butt escaped our squad-leader's eagle eye. But fresh air and no walls for barked orders to echo off made for a welcome break from latrine duty.

* * *

After seven weeks of grunt work, my AIT orders still hadn't come. The low risk of being killed or wounded in a Fort Ord latrine as opposed to the jungles of Vietnam didn't outweigh my reluctance to hover my face over one more toilet or urinal. So, I went AWOL—in a manner of speaking.

Rather than reporting for my 7:00 a.m. assignment, I strapped on my temporary sergeant stripes from basic training and marched down to Headquarters Company intent on finding out what happened to my

AIT orders. As I stepped into the first official-looking building I came to, a civilian lady greeted me with a cheery "May I help you?"

"I've been a hold-over for seven weeks waiting for AIT orders. I'd like to know what the Army intends to do with me." She looked puzzled but directed me to the next building in the row of single-story, white structures.

The same process repeated itself in four more offices before I found myself in the first building facing the same civilian lady I started out with. She glanced at the name tag on my field jacket. "Brown. Are you the lawyer-engineer?"

When I nodded, she pushed away from her desk. "I'll be back in a minute." She then negotiated her way through a maze of desks to reach an office in the back. True to her word, she returned in a minute. "It seems you fell victim to conflicting DOD (Department of Defense) regulations. If you have a degree in engineering or a natural science, the regs require you to be assigned for AIT at Aberdeen Proving Ground in Maryland. With a law degree, you're supposed to get AIT as a legal clerk."

"So?" I asked, lifting my shoulders.

I then heard words no other drafted soldier in the history of the world ever had.

"What do you want to do, and where would you like to do it?"

Am I dreaming?

My mouth stayed still for several seconds. I didn't want to go to the east coast so I said, "AIT as a legal clerk at The Presidio in San Francisco sounds good."

She laughed. "There's no legal clerk training at the Presidio. If you want to stay in the Sixth Army area, your training will be here."

The deal was done, and the next day I moved into barracks at Headquarters Company, donned my class A uniform, and reported to the JAG Office. On weekends—unless I had KP or guard duty—I was able to go home to Alameda and see Jeannie. So much better than cleaning latrines.

* * *

During my AIT at the JAG Office, I worked with two other drafted lawyers, one from Virginia, the other from Texas. They were in training before I arrived and completed their AIT while I was in the midst of mine.

The military operates on a multitude of acronyms, among them is MOS (Military Occupational Specialty), one of which is *Legal Clerk.* The three of us discussed where we might be assigned as legal clerks at the completion of our training. Even in Vietnam, office duty didn't register as being particularly hazardous. What we didn't appreciate at the time took a bite out of the fellow from Virginia first. He came back from his daily check of the order board looking as if he had suddenly been stricken with the disease that laid me low at UND.

He staggered to the chair behind his desk, plopped down and grabbed his head with both hands. "My orders came . . . Nam, light weapons infantry."

Creepy-crawlies slithered up my spine. Ralph Temple's image flashed into my head. "No way," I said. "You're a legal clerk."

"Captain Armstrong just told me legal clerk is a *secondary* MOS. The primary MOS for all of us is *light weapons infantry.*"

How will I break this news to Jeannie?

Virginia left the following day. Texas suffered the same fate two weeks later.

My AIT ended four weeks after Texas departed to Vietnam and my daily check of the order board gave me the jitters. I still hadn't told Jeannie.

Days turned into weeks, and weeks into months, but no orders came for me. Meanwhile, three other lawyers completed their AIT at the Fort Ord JAG Office and followed Virginia and Texas to the combat zone as light weapons infantry soldiers. This time, I felt no need to make waves over the lack of orders coming for me.

* * *

In late 1967 I achieved the desired status of *Short-Timer*, the point at which I was no longer at risk of receiving orders to go to Vietnam. I could then live off post, so I rented a small apartment in Pacific Grove, a fifteen-minute drive south of Fort Ord, and Jeannie and I loaded our meager possessions onto a U-Haul trailer. During the move down from Alameda, the worn cover on our old mattress ripped completely open—beyond repair.

Two nights of sleeping on the box springs inspired Jeannie to embark on a search for a mattress we might be able to afford. She had sent all the money she saved while in Alameda to her parents in thanks for her college education.

"Look at this." She held out a copy of the latest Fort Ord newspaper. "It's a horse-hair mattress for only ten bucks."

I looked at the ad. The Commanding General of Fort Ord, Jeannie's old friend, General "Monk" Meyer, was retiring and having a big moving sale. She called and found out the mattress was still available. We grabbed some rope and jumped into the car. General Meyer and his wife met us at the door. If General Meyer remembered Jeannie from his encounter with her fifteen months earlier, he didn't let on. In fact, he didn't say much at all. Mrs. Meyer was in charge of sales.

"William Westmorland slept on this mattress," she proudly proclaimed.

I was impressed. If this mattress was good enough for the general in overall command of the combat operations in Vietnam, it certainly must be good enough for us.

Neither Jeannie nor I had any prior experience with horse hair beyond occasionally sitting on a horse's back. Sleeping on the back of a trotting horse would have been more comfortable than this mattress turned out to be. Truth in advertising demanded the sales pitch include something like "General Westmorland had the choice of sleeping on this mattress or a pile of sharp rocks. He regretted not choosing the rocks."

After one miserable night, our ten-dollar sack of lumpy horse hair found itself again lashed to the top of our car, this time bound for the sanitary landfill to join our former mattress. We went back to sleeping on the box springs.

Jeannie laughed until she cried.

* * *

At the Fort Ord Bayonet Golf Course, the first and tenth holes run nearly parallel to each other with their tee boxes close together. We were on the first tee and Jeannie went through her usual warm-up routine, preparing to take her opening shot of the day.

A golf cart pulled up to the tenth tee. American flags fluttered on each side of the cart. Two grey-haired gentlemen got out and pulled out their drivers (golf clubs, not cart drivers). They stepped up to their tee, paying us no mind in spite of our close proximity.

When Jeannie finished her pre-shot routine, she stepped to her teed up golf ball. One of the generals on the tenth tee did the same. Then something happened I had never witnessed on a golf course before—or heard of in over a half-century since.

I watched as Jeannie and the general simultaneously took their clubs back and started their down-swings. Suddenly the air was filled with a piercing scream.

"*AIIIEEE!*"

It was Jeannie. Her ball went rocketing straight and true down the fairway, while the startled general barely nicked the top of his ball, sending it hopping to the front of the tee box.

"It worked," Jeannie exclaimed, beaming.

Words of extreme displeasure came from the tenth tee.

I could find no hole to crawl into.

When Jeannie realized what had happened on the tenth tee, she did her wide-eyed shoulder-shrugging *whoops* thing. "I'm so sorry. I read about it in *Psycho Cybernetics.*"

"Sure did work," the non-dribbling general offered. "Your ball went a mile."

"Probably not fit for the golf course," the dribbler grumbled as he picked up his ball and put it back on the tee.

It was an otherwise quiet day on the golf course, and no one was waiting behind either the generals or us, so Jeannie had time to explain.

"Last night I was reading in this book, *Psycho Cybernetics,* about why karate guys scream when they break a stack of bricks or something. It's supposed to concentrate their power."

She never used that scream on a golf course again. But I know she wanted to.

* * *

Yellow-jackets, hornets, wasps, honeybees, or whatever, all were *bees* as far as Jeannie was concerned. She wanted no part of any of them.

One day at the Fort Ord golf course, the starter sent us out with another couple. They appeared to be in their early fifties.

"We are the Browns, Jeannie and Jim," I said, offering the man my hand.

"Jack Morris, and this is my wife, Vivian." No ranks were mentioned.

As the round progressed, they learned that Jeannie was an RN and I was a lawyer with my time in the army growing short.

About a third of the way through the round, the unexpected happened. One of those flying insects Jeannie knew as *bees* landed on the collar of Vivian's golf shirt.

"Oh, my! There's a b-bee on you," Jeannie stammered.

Vivian froze. Her eyes went wide. "Get it off. Get it off." She seemed terrified, apparently having been born with the same *bee* loathing as Jeannie.

Jeannie stepped up to do her duty. But as she swatted at the *bee*, she flinched; and the little, yellow, winged critter escaped.

"Oh, no. It went down inside your shirt!"

Both women started jumping around like crazy. Vivian pulled off her shirt and swung it around before flinging it as far away as she could.

There she stood in her bra and golfing shorts still yipping and yowling, not knowing what had happened to the *bee.*

I couldn't believe what I was seeing. Nor could I imagine what Jack was thinking.

Then I heard Jeannie's infectious laugh.

Vivian quickly joined in, as did Jack while he retrieved the tossed shirt. He shook it out to make sure the potential assailant no longer resided there, and handed it to his wife. Jeannie did her best to provide some sort of shelter for the re-dressing.

As it turned out, Jack and Vivian were as nice as could be. Vivian and Jeannie laughed with each other the entire rest of the round. After the 18th hole, we sat around and visited for a while and learned that Jack was in fact General Morris. I was most grateful he didn't arrange for me to be sent to Viet Nam.

Seventeen

Mustering Out

Our time in Pacific Grove passed quickly. Jeannie worked the evening shift (3:00 to 11:00) at the Ave Maria Convalescent Hospital in Monterey. My day at Fort Ord started at 7:00 a.m. and ended at 4:00 p.m. so we saw little of each other except on weekends. These we filled to the brim. We toured the Monterey-Pacific Grove-Carmel area, and further down the coast looking for local, inexpensive eating spots, not tourist-traps. We rented bicycles when the weather allowed us to ride warm and dry. And, of course, we played a lot of golf.

* * *

When my *short timer* calendar showed about four months left of Army captivity, I became aware of a new regulation issued by the Department of Defense that allowed a soldier to be discharged up to 90 days early. The regulation only applied to those taking a job in law enforcement.

I told Jeannie about my intention to apply for this *early out* if I could get Kit Nelson, the Kern County District Attorney, to renew the job offer from two years earlier. Surely working as a deputy DA qualified as "law enforcement."

Jeannie wasn't so sure.

I called Pete Lewis, who was still working in the DA's Office, and he typed a job offer for Kit Nelson's signature. Then he got Mr. Nelson to sign it, and Pete put it in the mail to me. Meanwhile, I filled out my application—in quintuplicate—for early discharge. I attached Kit Nelson's job offer as soon as it came in the mail and hand-carried the paperwork to the Adjutant General's Office hoping for quick approval.

I was wrong. Again.

Jeannie was right. Again.

Actually, I was right about *quick*. The denial came the next day. The AG's Office was next door to the JAG Office where I worked. A *grunt* from the AG's Office brought the denial over and plopped it on my desk. "Sorry," came from his lips. "Ha-ha!" came from his eyes.

The denial bore a brief explanation. The department of Defense regulation applied to police, sheriff, highway patrol, and correctional officers, and other peace officers who were allowed by virtue of their job to carry firearms. The regulation was intended to alleviate the manpower shortage in police departments due to the Vietnam War.

I hit the books. The California codes bailed me out. A deputy district attorney didn't cut it, but a DA investigator did. With Pete's help, Kit Nelson's offer was amended to hire me as an investigator in his office. I resubmitted the application along with a copy of the California code section.

It worked. I told Captain Armstrong.

"That's great news," he said with a sly grin. "Did you ever wonder why you never got orders to go to Nam?"

"Every day. I still get a knot in my gut thinking about it."

"Actually, you did . . . three times."

My stomach did flip-flops. "I never saw 'em."

"That's because they were pulled by the Old Man."

I had only spoken to the Colonel in charge of the Fort Ord JAG Office twice, both times he asked me to make court appearances in Salinas.

Why did he pull my orders?

Captain Armstrong explained that other than the Old Man, I was the only one licensed in California. "The Old Man said, 'Until we get another California lawyer, Brown stays.' He's not going to be happy you're leaving."

* * *

One of the things a drafted soldier remained ignorant about until the very end of his tour of duty centered on what needed to be done in order to get out. That information came in real time, two weeks prior to the discharge date, a process called *clearing post.*

When the time came, I was given a sheaf of papers along with instructions to obtain signatures from each department listed in those documents clearing me to go. I had no idea that many of those departments even existed, let alone their location. George Sadler bailed me out.

George and his wife, Henry (Henrietta), a couple we met on the Fort Ord golf course, became fast friends. They came from Hollywood, Florida, and George's discharge date was the day after mine. He knew all the locations. I tagged along with him as we both cleared post. It took us all of twenty minutes a day to collect the needed signatures.

Each morning of the post clearing process, we left Jeannie and Henry at the golf course to visit over coffee while George and I picked off signatures. Then, we all teed it up. The four of us played a minimum of 27 holes a day before Jeannie had to leave for her 3 to 11 shift at Ave Maria. On the two weekends when Jeannie didn't have to work, we played 45 holes a day.

Playing golf at Fort Ord remains my one fond memory of army life. Not only because of the two beautiful and challenging courses, but also because of the price. $5 a couple. Not each time. For a whole month. George and I figured the last month cost less than a penny a hole.

* * *

On my discharge date, I reported for pay, turned in my paperwork, and bid Fort Ord and the Army goodbye. From there, I rented a trailer and drove to our apartment to load it. Everything we owned had been packed in boxes. Two hours later, the road to Bakersfield beckoned. Our new civilian life waited at the end of that road. But not a motel room.

Bakersfield at that time enjoyed the reputation of being the roller-skating hub of America. A local girl carried the crown of national champion and hoped to retain it at the championships hosted that weekend at her father's roller rink. Every motel in town sported a "No Vacancy" sign. When we asked if there might be a room somewhere, all we got was a head shake and, "every place is booked solid."

Turning back the way we came, we found something resembling a room in something resembling a motel in Wasco, a town about 25 miles northwest of Bakersfield. "Plan Ahead" never was our motto.

* * *

The next day, Saturday, had to produce an apartment so I could relinquish the trailer without an additional fee. We found one. Actually, Jeannie did. I found several, but she didn't like them. She liked the one she found. It had a pool. We paid the first and last month's rent and moved in. After I returned the trailer, we went for a swim.

That night, George and Henry arrived. They had a long drive ahead of them to get back to Florida, but they wanted to have one more day of fun with us. Sunday morning breakfast followed by golf, lunch, bowling, dinner, and many hands of card games, wore us out by midnight. Jeannie insisted they sleep at least a few hours before getting back on the road. They did.

Early Monday morning, the Sadlers crawled into their hippy-looking Volkswagen van and we waved goodbye to each other as they turned the corner and drove out of sight.

"I'm going to miss them," Jeannie said.

"So will I."

We went inside and I donned my one suit. "Next time you see me, I'll be a DA investigator."

Jeannie laughed.

* * *

The swearing in took place in front of the County Clerk. Pete Lewis and Kit Nelson stood by my side. I took the oath and quicker than you could say '*take that, Department of Defense,*' Kit Nelson promoted me to the position of Deputy District Attorney.

Pete took me to court with him so I could watch him put on a preliminary hearing. Civilian life held the promise of nothing but good times. It certainly started out that way. Jeannie became pregnant almost faster than I became a Deputy DA.

Eighteen

Daughter Kelly

"We need to save some money," Jeannie patted her *baby bump*. "The county's insurance doesn't have maternity coverage."

"Good idea," I said, not certain what she had in mind.

I found out she had in mind moving from a two-bedroom apartment complex that had a pool into one that didn't. But it did have cockroaches—lots of 'em. Many bug-bombs later, I shoveled out the corpses of those nasty critters, and we carted in our meager furnishings.

Jeannie went about establishing a nursery in the second bedroom. She subjected every nook and cranny, as well as second or third-hand baby stuff, to Lysol and Clorox scrubbings and re-scrubbings. No germ was going to get close to our little one.

Then—when I was at work—the doorbell rang, Jeannie told me.

How this guy knew is a mystery. But he knew.

I figure he said something like, "You want the best and safest for your new baby, don't you, ma'am? Well, this is it. It converts from a highchair to a stroller to a baby swing to a rocking horse to a spaceship—I was just kidding about the space ship part—with just the push of a few buttons and the flip of a few levers. Let me show you." So he did. And she bought the thing for what could have been the down-payment on a new home of our own. So much for saving money.

Thankfully, I was home when the Encyclopedia Britannica guy showed up. I convinced Jeannie we really didn't need the 100-year supplement package. I held firm at the 20-year package. Some of the volumes did come in handy for school projects as time went on, but mostly the books served as booster seats.

****

As Jeannie's pregnancy progressed in our new digs, she expressed concerns about our car situation. "Our family will be growing. We need to think about getting a bigger car."

My financial antenna went up. A bigger car meant bigger expense. But Jeannie had been the main provider for us the past four years, so I gave her opinion extra consideration. Not an easy task for a fiscal conservative. I consulted my father who came to the rescue in an unexpected way.

He said, "I have a friend in Oakland who has an Oldsmobile dealership. He gave me a great deal on what he called an executive demonstrator, one used to let potential buyers test drive. I'll see if he has something similar for you."

Before long, my pregnant wife and I boarded the train for Oakland to pick up an almost brand-spanking-new Oldsmobile Vista Cruiser. The price? $3,000, with 5% down and the rest financed over 24 months. What a deal!

The drive back to Bakersfield felt like we were in the proverbial lap of luxury. We shared the time behind the wheel.

She patted her expanding belly. "Let's go on a weekend fishing trip before I get too big."

"Good idea. We can sleep in the back."

I set about taking careful measurements of the contemplated sleeping area with the rear seats folded down and cut a four-inch-thick piece of foam rubber to fit. Jeannie made a zippered mattress-cover out of waterproof material. By the next weekend, we were ready to go. I don't remember buying fishing licenses or even if a license was required back then.

* * *

Friday evening, Jeannie had everything packed and ready to load when I got home. A quick change of clothes and off we went to terrorize the fish in the Colorado River. Several hours later, I pulled off State Route 62 and we prepared for the night. We had snacked along the way so all we had to do was zip our sleeping bags together and cuddle up.

The morning greeted us with an inch or so of new-fallen snow. We must have been at a higher altitude than I thought. A quick cold breakfast and visit to an even colder outhouse propelled us on our way to the lower and warmer reaches of the Colorado River. When we arrived, the warmth welcomed us, but fishing access proved difficult to find.

After a couple hours of searching, we came upon a spot that looked promising. The river must have been high, and water poked under a fence and up a gully next to a dirt road. We sat at the top edge of the gully and tossed our worm laden hooks and bobbers into still water. "Here, fishy-fishy," Jeannie said with her first cast. A couple hours later we gave up. She had landed one sunfish no bigger than the palm of her hand. She tossed it back. I caught zilch.

With such a paltry level of success, we needed to find more productive fishing water closer to home.

* * *

Not too many weeks later Jeannie said, "Feel," grabbing my hand and placing it on the taut skin of her watermelon-shaped tummy. I could detect the muscles tightening for a few seconds, and then relaxing. A few minutes later, the cycle repeated.

"You're going into labor?" I nearly jumped out of my skin.

"No, these are just Braxton-Hicks contractions. Real labor is much harder." She smiled blissfully. "This may go on for a few days."

That night, as I tossed and turned, picturing myself as a new daddy, I had no idea what the next week had in store. Ultrasound was a newfangled device not used to determine the sex of a fetus. Knowing the sex had to wait until the baby was born. The new father waited in a separate holding cell to find out later.

In the wee hours of the morning, my restless sleep came to an abrupt end. "It's time." Jeannie said as she shook my shoulder. "My water broke."

My eyes popped open. Outside the window, nothing but pitch darkness. The alarm clock said 3:30. Jeannie hopped around, trying to get dressed between contractions.

I was a bundle of nerves, giddy as a kid on a big swing for the first time. I jumped into my pants and slipped on some shoes, forgetting about socks, and fished a sweatshirt out of the closet. "Should I call Doctor Hubble?"

"No, they'll call him from the hospital . . . ooh, ooh, this is a big one."

Jeannie flopped back on the bed to wait out the contraction. When it relaxed, I checked my watch and helped her to her feet. The next big contraction came less than three minutes later. As soon as that one passed, we hurried to the car, and I drove fast—but with utmost caution—the mile and a half to the hospital.

In 1969, hospital doors remained unlocked even at that early hour. An attendant rolled Jeannie off in a wheelchair, leaving me to take care of the paperwork at the admission desk. Then I received directions to a little room—the holding cell—bearing the clever sign: *HEIRPORT*. Inside, two other gents sat silently in lightly padded armchairs. I waited for the black phone on the wall to ring.

When the phone rang an hour or so later, two of us went wide-eyed. Being closest to the phone, I answered. "Heirport."

The call was for the guy across from me, the other one who went wide-eyed. The third man barely raised his head.

I handed the phone across to Mr. Wide Eye. His face lit up. "It's a boy!" he said over his shoulder as he scurried out the door.

"This your first?" the remaining fellow asked me.

"Yup," I nodded. "You?"

"My fifth."

No wonder he looked so relaxed. When the phone rang again a couple hours later, I knew the call was for him. He was snoring.

It wasn't.

"Mister Brown, congratulations, you're the father of a beautiful baby girl. Mother and baby are doing fine. You can come to the nursery window and see your baby. When your wife is in a recovery room, someone will come get you."

I hung up the phone. The experienced dad appeared to be dozing, so I left quietly having no idea where to find the nursery window. The look of bewilderment on my face must have been obvious because a nurse in the hall gave me directions without me even asking.

I jogged down the hall to meet my Kelly. Jeannie and I had decided on names a few weeks earlier. Kelly for a girl. Matthew for a boy. As I turned the corner marked with a *NURSERY* sign, I saw some folks that I took to be grandparents tapping on the window and making faces at one of the six newborns, all wrapped up like burritos in either a pink or blue blanket. An empty burrito holder had the nametag *Brown* on the side and a nurse stood next to it wrapping a pink blanket around my little girl. I couldn't take my eyes off her.

But I also wanted to see her mom.

Nineteen

Hemorrhage

In 1969, Mothers and babies stayed in the hospital about three days, so Jeannie and Kelly came home on April 2. Kelly had lost a few ounces and now weighed less than six pounds.

"You can hold her. She won't break," Jeannie said, handing me this tiny little pink doll in a receiving blanket.

I took Kelly gingerly, not at all sure she wouldn't break. I held her like a piece of fragile porcelain for a few seconds before returning her to Jeannie's capable hands.

All that day, I watched Kelly's every move and expression and marveled at Jeannie's competence in caring for our baby.

I soon learned that when Kelly's face pruned up, something was being delivered to her cloth diaper. Disposables were kind of a new thing. And expensive. My job? To take the diaper-wrapped package to the toilet, dunk it several times while flushing, taking great care not to let go, then put the semi-clean cloth into the pail for recycling by the diaper service.

Meanwhile, Jeannie cleaned, powdered, and diapered our sweet little girl before stuffing her waving hands and kicking feet into a onesie.

Feeding was entirely up to Jeannie.

At night, Jeannie slept, if at all, with one ear open listening for any sound coming from Kelly's nursery. I marveled at how she could get up during the night and tend to whatever Kelly needed without waking me—until time for diaper-dunking duty.

* * *

In the early hours of April 5, I awoke to a pitiful sound. A low-pitched moan came from the side of the bed—Jeannie's side. But Jeannie wasn't in bed. The moaning grew louder and more urgent. I sat up. Jeannie's bedside light was on. She was standing next to the bed looking down.

"Ooohhh no. Ooohhh no," she cried, not loud, but in distress.

I scooted across the bed and looked at the floor. My sleep-numbed mind barely processed what I saw. A large circle of dark red surrounded her feet, growing larger by the second. It was blood! Two fist-size clots lay in the pool.

I needed to get Jeannie to the hospital right away. No time to wait for an ambulance. But what about Kelly?

I pulled up the bedspread, lay Jeannie on it, and bundled it around her. I threw on a pair of jeans, picked up Kelly out of her crib, and ran barefoot to the apartment next door. I pounded furiously on the door, not caring about the hour.

Marilyn, the neighbor who came bleary-eyed to the door, was herself a new mother with a six-month-old baby.

No time for explanations. I just said, "Please look after Kelly. I have to get Jeannie to the hospital."

The dear woman accepted Kelly into her arms, and with a jerk of her head sent me on my way.

I pulled our station-wagon from the garage and opened the back hatch. It still had the mattress we had made for camping trips. Jeannie was now sickly pale as I slid her onto the mattress. With the slamming of the hatch ringing in my ears, I jumped in behind the wheel and tromped on the accelerator. Barefoot and shirtless, I raced to Memorial Hospital. My heart pounded like a jack hammer. I wasn't going to stop, not even for a cop.

What to do when we get there?

My rattled brain told me to pull up to the Emergency Entrance and lay on the horn.

"What are you doing?" Jeannie's weak voice asked.

"They're coming." I jumped out to open the back hatch.

Thank God for an emergency room with a well-trained staff.

I told the man with a wheelchair what happened. He ran back for a gurney. We lifted Jeannie onto it. He pushed her inside where a nurse got an IV going. Off Jeannie went to where I couldn't follow.

I stood there breathless.

Someone directed me to a desk where I sat shivering, taking care of the admission paperwork.

"When can I see her?" I asked the clerk.

"It'll be a while. You have time to go home and get dressed. I'll call you."

I raced home, slipped into a shirt and shoes and hurried back to the hospital, not waiting for a call. The nice lady said, "She's in ICU, Mister Brown. Go down that hall and follow the signs."

When I found the ICU, a doctor took me aside. "It was touch and go," he said with his hand on my shoulder. "We expressed an additional liter of blood from her uterus before we could stop the bleeding. We're pumping blood into her as fast as we can."

"Is she g-going to be o-okay?" I asked.

"She's stable. Not out of the woods, but stable."

I barely began to breathe.

"Doctor Hubble is on his way. He'll take over when he gets here."

"C-can I see her?" I couldn't stop shaking.

This has to be a bad dream.

"Give us a little more time. I'll come get you."

A little more time. Right.

Each minute seemed like a week. I couldn't sit. I couldn't stand still. I paced and paced in the tiny ICU waiting room, all alone with my reeling fears.

Eons later, I heard, "Mister Brown?"

The doctor stood in the open door.

I snapped out of my dark thoughts and looked at him.

"You can see your wife now. Follow me."

Jeannie had an IV in one arm with a bag of clear liquid dripping into it. The other arm was receiving blood. She was pretty groggy, but looked up at the doctor and grinned. "It was pretty bad, huh?"

"It was. You went into hypovolemic shock, but you're gonna be fine," he said. "A piece of placenta didn't detach and was stuck in your uterus. That's what caused the hemorrhage."

Jeannie seemed to understand.

"How long before I can go home?" she asked.

"That will be up to Doctor Hubble. A few days at least, though."

Jeannie looked at me with the corners of her mouth turned down in mock-sadness. "You'll have to take care of Kelly."

My head wobbled at the realization I was being thrust into a position of trust and responsibility for which I was totally unprepared and ill-equipped—being sent up the proverbial river without a paddle—or a boat.

Jeannie gave me a list of things I needed to buy in order to feed Kelly: formula, bottles and nipples and a pot to boil them in, bibs, and a few other things. She told me how to heat the formula, test its temperature on my wrist, make sure air got back into the bottle, and how to toss a towel onto my shoulder and put Kelly up there to be patted until she burped.

* * *

The next four days of fear, confusion, fumbling, bumbling, and virtually no sleep proved to be wonderful days of bonding with baby Kelly. I fed, burped, changed, dressed, and bathed this precious little girl and learned that she really wouldn't break like a fragile glass Christmas tree ornament.

Giving her a bath proved to be the hardest, scariest, all thumbs part. I had no idea how a six-pound baby could have a seven-pound head and so many wrinkles, creases and folds that had to be washed, dried and powdered—or how to do any of it with only two hands.

By the time Jeannie was released from the hospital, I was no longer terrified—but tired. Being Mr. Mom was hard work, and I didn't like being able to only fall half asleep.

I delighted in having Jeannie home, pronounced recovered from the crisis but still needing to take it easy for a while. Little did we know that the hemorrhage had not finished taking its toll.

Twenty

PPD

During the three weeks following Jeannie's discharge from the hospital, she hadn't regained her fun-loving, chipper attitude. Pale, listless, prone to bursting into tears for no apparent reason, she had little appetite. I tried everything I could think of to cheer her up. Nothing seemed to work.

I called Bertha.

Jeannie's mom had a very direct and sensible way of looking at things. She was as smart as she wanted to be, but she loved to play dumb when she thought doing so was to her advantage. This wasn't one of those times for her to play dumb. "I think Jeannie is very depressed," she said. "I better come on out there."

"I'm sure she'd love to see you," was all I could think to say as I twisted the curly-que phone cord around my finger.

Hanging up the phone, I rejoined Jeannie in the living room. "I called your mom. She's concerned about you." I said.

"It's just the baby blues," Jeannie insisted. "I think it's because I can't get Kelly to breast feed." She was rocking Kelly slowly as she fed her from a bottle.

"She's coming out."

"What?" Jeannie knitted her eyebrows. "Why is she doing that?"

"She's worried about you. So am I." I stood beside her and massaged her neck.

"That's silly. I'll be fine. New mothers are like this."

Jeannie put Kelly on her shoulder and patted her back until she let out a good burp accompanied by a glob of formula. Tears began streaming down Jeannie's face and her body convulsed with waves of sobs.

"I . . . don't know why . . . I'm crying." She was able to get the words out between sobs. "Kelly's so sweet . . . such a good baby."

I knelt beside her. "You need more rest. It'll be good to have your mom here."

The County of Kern didn't provide *family* leave; I had to tend to my daily work duties at the District Attorney's Office. Neither of us had any relatives closer than several hundred miles. Mary Lewis came over from time to time, but she had two little ones of her own to deal with. Otherwise, when I was at work, Jeannie was pretty much on her own.

"Let me do that" was Jeannie's favorite phrase whenever I tried to take care of any of Kelly's needs. She seemed driven to be the perfect mother. I might be able to do it okay, but she could do it better. Whenever I got up in the middle of the night because I heard Kelly fussing, Jeannie instantly appeared beside me. "Let me do that. Let me do that." She wouldn't let me. Maybe she'd let her mom.

* * *

The next day, Bertha Maxine DuBois Ratliff arrived. Bertha was from a family of twelve children and knew more than a thing or two about caring for babies. More importantly, she knew how to care for her daughter, the one who needed and finally got some much deserved rest. But Jeannie's listlessness and crying spells continued.

After about a week, Bertha called me into the kitchen as she was fixing dinner. Jeannie was in the living room feeding Kelly a bottle. "She's getting worse," Bertha said. The look of worry on her face shouted the depth of her concern. "I want to take her back to Oklahoma City to see Doctor Morrison."

I had heard much about Dr. Morrison from Jeannie. If she had the power to do so, she would have made him a saint. He had cared for her entire family for years, including shepherding Bertha through two bouts of breast cancer, each involving a radical mastectomy and cobalt therapy.

I squeezed my eyes shut, trying to come up with an alternative, knowing I couldn't go to Oklahoma City with them. Nothing came to mind. "Let me talk to her."

I went into the living room where Jeannie sat in the rocking chair with Kelly. Jeannie stared off into space. There was no color in her cheeks. Still dressed in her bathrobe, she didn't seem to know I was there.

"Jeannie."

She slowly turned her head and looked blankly at me. "Yes."

I knelt in front of her and put my hands on her knees. "Your mom thinks it would be a good idea for you to see Doctor Morrison."

With no change in expression, she said nothing but "Okay" as the rocking chair came to a stop. She took the bottle from Kelly and burped her. No protest. No questioning why. No claim that she didn't need to. Just, "Okay." Then back to feeding Kelly.

I managed to book a flight for Jeannie, Bertha and Kelly departing two days later. I had convinced myself that seeing Dr. Morrison was the right thing for Jeannie to do. But the dark hole of being left behind for who knows how long frightened me.

What if something goes wrong? What if Jeannie doesn't get better? What if? What if?

* * *

Departure time came. In those pre-TSA days I went out to the plane with them, carrying Kelly. I tried to be upbeat and cheerful as I kissed Jeannie and Kelly goodbye even though moisture welled up in my eyes. I don't know if Jeannie saw it, but Bertha did as I gave her a hug.

"Everything is going to be fine. Don't you worry about a thing," Bertha said in her best Oklahoma twang.

"I'll try." I bowed my head and started to back away.

Bertha reached up her thumb and with a wink wiped a tear from the side of my nose.

I stood on the tarmac as the plane taxied to the end of the runway where it sat for several minutes before the engines roared and the wheels started to turn. My tears flowed freely, but I kept watch until the tiny dot of the silver plane disappeared into the blue of the morning sky. Loneliness descended on me with a rush.

Return from Oklahoma

While Jeannie was in Oklahoma being tended to by Dr. Morrison, the opportunity presented itself for a move from our dreary little apartment into a nice three-bedroom home. The house belonged to my father. He bought it in 1961 but a few years later he retired from the FBI and moved to Lake Tahoe. Since then, the house had been a rental. The most recent tenants had just moved out.

I called him. "Hey, Pop, how about renting your house to us?" He had made frequent complaints about being a landlord.

"Why don't you take over the payments and buy it?" He said.

The payments were cheaper than rent. How could I pass that up? Jeannie had visited there the summer before we were married and liked the house and the neighborhood, so I gave her a call. "My dad says we can buy his house by just taking over the payments. They're less than our rent."

"Great. I hated the thought of coming home to that apartment." She sounded good—much better than the last time.

A few weeks later, Jeannie and Kelly were ready to come back to Bakersfield. I met them when they got off the plane at LAX. Jeannie looked tired. She gave me a wan smile, set Kelly's baby carrier on the tile floor and gave me a big hug—no kiss. "Are we all moved in?" she asked.

"Yup. Everything's all set up."

I walked Jeannie to the baggage claim area with Kelly's carrier in one hand and my other around Jeannie's shoulders. Her arm was around my waist.

"How was the flight?"

"Fine."

"Did they feed you?"

"A little."

These short answers sounded unlike the Jeannie I knew. I decided to try one more time.

"Do you want something to eat or drink?"

"No. Let's just get our bags and go home."

When we finally got to the car and were on the road, she opened up a little.

"Doctor Morrison gave me a prescription that makes me feel weird. I'm not going to take it again."

"What is it?"

She told me the name of the drug. I don't remember what it was. "It's a mood elevator," she said.

"What else did he say?"

"If I get to feeling down, or start crying, I should run."

She got out her neck pillow, leaned her seat back and closed her eyes—a clear signal she wanted no more questions. She slept, or at least pretended to, the rest of the way to our new home.

I pulled into the driveway and got out to open the garage door. The house didn't have a pushbutton for the door to go up by itself.

Jeannie's eyes were still closed.

"We're home," I said as I was lifting Kelly's carrier out of the back seat. Kelly was out like a light.

Jeannie stirred and stretched. "That was fast."

"You get a good nap?"

"Uh-huh."

After we were inside, I set her bags down and gave her a wink. "Let me show you something. Follow me."

I led her down the hall leading to the bedrooms, opened a door between the hall and the den, then took her through the den and into the kitchen. I pointed to her bags where we started. "That's how we'll run laps."

She shook her head. "You're goofy."

*　*　*

Over the next several weeks we wore grooves in the floor running laps. Gradually, the need to run became less frequent until we didn't run together anymore. She might have run alone when I was at work but if she did, she didn't tell me.

What she did tell me was that she wanted to go back to work. "I talked to Mercy Hospital. They need somebody in pedes, and they have day care for Kelly."

"You sure?"

"Yeah." She continued rolling the chicken pieces in her special crust formula, dropping each coated piece into the hot oil.

The "I'm sure" didn't last long. Within a month of starting the job, her tune changed. "I can't do it. I feel like I've abandoned Kelly."

"Then quit." I liked her as a full-time mom and didn't want her depression to return.

"I have to give notice."

"You really don't have to," I said with lawyerly confidence. Then I saw the look in her eye. "But do what you think is right."

She gave notice.

Twenty-Two

Liver

If I had the chance to eliminate one food from the face of the earth, my choice would be liver. Liver makes me gag just to think about it. But it also makes me laugh.

Christmas vacation didn't come around for me in 1961, what was supposed to have been my senior year of college. It seems I had been suspended from the University of North Dakota for an indiscretion called a *panty raid*—wrongfully so in my case, but that's a whole other story. Here it is.

* * *

(October 1961)

I had taken the last of my six-week exams, but Jeannie had one more test the next day. She told me she couldn't see me that night, so I went to a movie with some friends. The night went all downhill from there.

After the movie, my friends suggested going to a watering-hole that catered to college kids—hardly ever checking IDs. We met some other guys there who had been drinking beer rather than watching a flick. Someone suggested we pick up a case of barley-malt and head south forty miles to see a friend who had transferred to Mayville State Teachers College. All anyone said they knew was that he roomed in a place called East Hall.

About midnight, eight of us (three in front, five scrunched in back) piled into an old Chevy sedan. The case of beer also rode in back. The town of Mayville posed no problem to find, nor did the college. Locating East Hall proved to be more difficult.

As I understand what happened, since I wandered elsewhere trying to find directions to East Hall, one of the fellows who hadn't gone to the movie walked up to a building that had East as part of its name and tried a door that opened into a girls' dorm. No girls were there. School was out of session for Teachers Convention Week. But the Dorm Mother remained there and must have heard the commotion in the hall with doors being opened and shut. She came out of her room, hair in curlers and some form of blue gel plastered on her face. I'm told she shouted, "What's going on here?"

I learned that the guy who led the troops into the dorm said something like, "Help! It's a monster." He then took the soda-ash fire extinguisher from the wall and doused the monster. Meanwhile, one of the other non-moviegoers came across a pair of panty-hose (a somewhat new invention at the time) that he kept as a souvenir. Hence, the application of the term panty raid to this misadventure.

I missed the action while finding directions to the real East Hall where we located our friend, fast asleep at one in the morning. All eight of us jumped on top of him as he lay startled in his bed. The bed collapsed. He was not happy. We left, deciding to continue on to Fargo rather than return to Grand Forks.

We didn't get far down Highway 81 before a red light came on behind us. Two deputies from the Trail County Sheriff's Office took seven of the eight of us into custody. Number eight walked across the highway and disappeared behind a tree while the officers removed what was left of the beer from the car.

The booking procedure at the Sheriff's Office proved to be rather informal. So much so that one of the remaining seven asked to use the restroom. He never came back. That left six of us to face the consequences. We were each given a notice to appear in court at a future date, a stern lecture, and permission to go back to Grand Forks.

The Sheriff's Office must have notified UND because all six of us were suspended for a year before we went to trial.

I appealed the suspension. The others didn't. After the trial, most of them took a vacation to Hawaii and never returned to UND. At my appeal hearing, my suspension was reduced from one year to the remainder of the fall semester.

Trial in the Trail County Justice Court later took place in a room that looked nothing like a courtroom. The judge, a local farmer, seemed to have no idea what his role might be. He sat behind a small desk and followed the instructions of the prosecutor (who coincidently went to law school with my father and was himself the father of a friend of mine who later married one of Jeannie's sorority sisters).

Other than the small desk for the Judge, the room held two folding tables and a few folding chairs. Most of us had to stand throughout the proceedings.

The first witness testified. Not the dorm mother. Not a deputy sheriff. Not even the friend whose bed we collapsed. This witness? The maintenance man from whom I got directions to East Hall. He identified me as the one seeking those directions and said I was very polite. So far, so good.

The prosecutor then called a few more witnesses, none of whom said anything about me, before telling the judge he had no others because "the crimes were committed under cover of darkness." He tied his closing argument to a couple quotes from the bible and told the judge to find us guilty.

The Judge finally spoke—sort of. He picked up a single piece of paper that had been on the corner of his desk the whole time and read his decision. "I find each of the defendants guilty of malicious mischief and fine them each twenty-five dollars. I also find each of the defendants guilty of minor in possession of alcohol and fine each of them an additional ten dollars."

He stumbled over many of the words while reading the decision and appeared to not know what to do next. The prosecutor bailed him out by announcing, "We're done now."

But there's more to the story.

* * *

As mentioned earlier, in 1963 I received notice from my local draft board to report to Fresno for a pre-induction physical. While there, I was required to fill out paperwork detailing any criminal record I had other than simple traffic tickets. I gave a detailed description of being convicted of malicious mischief and minor in possession of alcohol in Trail County, North Dakota.

That fall, I enrolled in law school. The State Bar of California also required information about my criminal record, even including any charge as to which I was exonerated. I provided the same details.

Upon completion of law school and applying to take the Bar Exam, I had to do it again. And was explicitly warned that the information better match what I had provided three years earlier.

When I was drafted in 1966, I had to divulge the same story a fourth time.

The fifth time was for my employment by the County of Kern as a Deputy DA.

Each time, I submitted the information under penalty of perjury.

Only the County of Kern bothered to check with Trail County, North Dakota. This was in 1968, less than seven years after the so-called panty raid and trial. The inquiry established the absence of any record of the above-described events. As far as the Sheriff's Office and the Justice Court knew, I didn't exist. They had no record of me having been arrested, charged, tried, or convicted of any offence whatsoever.

So, the only evidence of my criminal record is contained in the five documents filled out by my own hand (and now these pages).

* * *

(December 1961)

Having been removed from ATO housing due to the Mayville incident, my residence became a basement room in a home a few blocks up the street from the Delta Gamma house where Jeannie lived. My parental scholarship also disappeared. I was financially on my own, surviving on meager pay from a part-time job as a liquor store clerk and the snacks Jeannie provided when I made my nightly visits to see her.

Unlike your humble miscreant, Jeannie did get a Christmas vacation. She spent those two weeks with her roommate Mary (Black) Lewis' family in Fargo, 80 miles south of Grand Forks. While she was gone, I devised a plan for New Year's Eve. Having no more nightly goodies from the Delta Gamma kitchen, I decided to survive for a week on a loaf of bread and a jar of peanut butter. That way, I could save enough money to take Jeannie out for what I hoped to be a nice dinner.

On December 31, with the saved-up folding green in my pocket, I borrowed Rich Peterson's car and fought the blowing snow for about two hours before pulling up in front of the Black's home. After a welcoming kiss to make up for the time I'd gone without, off we went to a fine restaurant. Jeannie, red-carpet stunning, and I peacock proud to be with her.

I had reached the ripe old age of twenty-one, but not Jeannie. We confidently ordered drinks, hoping the well-dressed waiter had better things to do than ask for IDs. He didn't ask. When the drinks came, Jeannie raised her glass and said, "Cheers." We clinked and sipped, and I leaned across the small table for a smooch.

When the waiter returned to take our orders, Jeannie opened the leather-bound menu and her eyes lit up.

"I'll have the liver and onions," she said with the glee of a kid at a soda fountain ordering her favorite sundae.

My heart dropped so fast it bounced off the floor. My facial expression must have been horrible.

"What's wrong?" she asked, her eyebrows knitted. "I love liver and onions."

Words stuck in my throat. Aghast, sick, and heartbroken that the girl of my dreams was no longer perfect. She had a flaw—a big one. How could she possibly like liver, let alone *love* the nasty stuff? It made no sense.

"I can't stand liver," I said through gritted teeth.

"Oh, get over it. It's good. My mother made it all the time."

What did I order? I have no idea, probably Pepto Bismol. The rest of that New Year's Eve is a blur. I know we went to a party, but where or with whom remains a mystery.

* * *

My unexpected revenge for that New Year's Eve of nine years earlier came from out of the blue. Due to the kindness of her heart, Jeannie never ordered liver again. Out of the not-so-kindness of my heart, I agreed that chicken livers didn't count. She could order those if she promised to cook liver at home only when business took me out of town. Jeannie kept that bargain. Almost.

Kelly had reached the age to be introduced to small amounts of solid food, like bits of ground beef.

One evening I arrived home early. A putrid odor smacked me in the nose as soon as I opened the door.

"Phew," I said, waving my hand in front of my face as if it might do some good. "What's going on?"

"Calm down," Jeannie said, "I'm not going to have our daughter grow up to be like her father."

"Meaning?"

"I'm just going to mix a little liver with the ground beef."

Jeannie had fried up a piece of liver no bigger than the tip of her thumb and was mincing it into tiny fragments.

She stirred the chopped-up liver into the ground beef, making a mixture of about 5% liver and 95% good stuff. When it had cooled enough, she took it to the table where Kelly sat patting her hands on the tray of her highchair.

First Jeannie fed our sweet little girl a bit of Gerber's pureed whatever, scooping the dribbles from her chin. Then she offered the meat, cooing and making *num-num* sounds as she held the baby spoon to Kelly's mouth. Kelly liked ground beef, so she eagerly ate it.

Surprise! Liver!

Kelly's eyes bugged out, her face crinkled like a prune, and the liver, along with everything else she had eaten the past three days, flew across the table at me—an Olympic-size projectile vomit.

"That's my girl," I whooped, clapping my hands. The mess on the table, and on me, well worth it.

Jeannie didn't take it so well at first, but then she performed her specialty—she laughed until she cried.

Twenty-Three

Breast Cancer

Breast cancer ran rampant in Jeannie's family, on her mother's side. Not only did Bertha have her two bouts with breast cancer, several of her sisters also did, one dying in her mid-thirties. Jeannie said that she was at considerably more risk than the general population. So she paid strict attention to her self-examinations and visits to her gynecologist.

"I have a lump in my breast," Jeannie said one evening as I came in the door from work. "Doctor Hubble wants to do a biopsy."

I felt my face go hot. "What? When?"

"I don't want a biopsy. That just spreads the cancer." Her eyes began to mist over.

I didn't know what to say.

"I talked to my mom." She wiped her sleeve across her eyes.

"And?" My legs wobbled. I sat down.

"She wants me to see her surgeon."

"Why?" The thought of a radical mastectomy, removal of all the underlying chest muscle and lymph nodes put a vice -grip on my gut.

Jeannie sat down across from me, her eyes wiped dry and her speech clear. She took hold of my hand is if I were the one facing the ordeal. "He'll do the biopsy while I'm under anesthesia. If it's cancer, he'll go ahead with surgery right then. No risk of spread from the biopsy."

"Oh, Jeannie," was all I could say.

* * *

A few days later, I drove to LAX and once again said goodbye to Jeannie and Kelly. On the drive back to Bakersfield, terrifying visions floated through my head.

I parked in the driveway and turned off the engine, then said a silent prayer before going inside to wait for the call.

The thought of food made my stomach churn.

Should I run a few laps? No.

I tried reading the newspaper. The words blurred. Finally, the phone rang. "Hello." My voice sounded shaky.

"Collect call from Kelly Brown, will you accept the charges?"

They made it!

"No, operator, I won't." I hung up.

That was the way to get messages across without incurring long distance charges. When the call came, I knew they were safely at Bertha's house.

* * *

The next day Jeannie called to tell me she was to go to the hospital in two days, at 6:30 in the morning, 4:30 Bakersfield time.

I went to the DA's office the morning of surgery at 6:00 a.m. figuring at least an hour and a half for her to be prepped and ready for surgery. I tried to read some police reports. No luck. The words blurred. My mind was fifteen hundred miles away.

The clock ticked. I checked it often. Too often. The phone didn't ring. I walked to the door of the next office, standing where I could hear my phone if it rang. Another Deputy DA, Robby Robinson, was also waiting for a call. His jury was out in a robbery case. I knew the facts from handling the preliminary hearing.

"Anything?" I asked.

His feet were up on his desk, hands behind his head. "Nope."

"How long have they been out?" I didn't really care.

"Couple hours. Osborn sent 'em home right after instructions yesterday. Came back at nine this morning."

My phone rang. I jumped into my office and pounced on it. "Hello."

"It wasn't cancer." Jeannie laughed an exuberant, infectious laugh.

My heart started beating again—fast. "Wonderful, wonderful, wonderful." I was laughing too. "When can you come home?"

"A few days. It was a pretty big incision."

"I can't wait to see you . . . and Kelly. I miss you guys."

No sooner had I hung up when Robby's phone rang. He poked his head in and said, "They have a verdict."

I floated out of my chair, down the hall, into the elevator, into Department Two, and into a seat in the front row. I don't think my feet ever touched the floor. Elation and relief made me weightless.

The police officer who arrested the defendant sat to my right and the DA investigator to my left.

The bailiff brought in the well-dressed defendant, James Richards. The bailiff locked Richards' shackled ankles to the floor, but left his hands free. The jury came in next. That way Richards appeared to the jury to be a man cloaked with the presumption of innocence.

Judge Osborn then took the bench. "Let the record reflect that the defendant, his counsel and counsel for the people are present. The jury is present." He looked to the jury. "I understand you have reached a verdict, is that correct?"

"We have, Your Honor," the foreman said.

"Very well. Please hand the verdict form to the bailiff."

The bailiff took the form, handed it to the clerk who in turn handed it to Judge Osborn. He glanced at it briefly and returned it to his clerk. "The clerk will please read the verdict."

The clerk stood. "The People of the State of California versus James Richards. We the jury empaneled to try the above-entitled cause find the defendant, James Richards, guilty of . . . "

Richards leaped to his feet shouting "I didn't rob nobody! I didn't rob nobody!" He flailed his arms wildly as he ranted on. His lawyer jumped to his feet and backed away—fast.

The judge, his clerk, the reporter, the jury all seemed frozen in place.

Still floating with euphoria, I stepped over the rail, planted my shoulder in Richards' midsection, and took him to the floor.

I hadn't seen the blood.

Richards had the strength of a wild animal. In spite of his small size, I had all I could do to hold him down.

The bailiff's voice came from above me. "Somebody get that razor blade – somebody get that razor blade."

What razor blade?

I recognized the voice of the bailiff, not what he was talking about. I held tight as Richards thrashed about.

Judge Osborn then spoke. "Let the record reflect that the defendant apparently slashed himself with a razor blade and is being restrained by my bailiff and deputy district attorney Brown."

The judge was drowned out by Richards' lawyer screaming at Robby Robinson. "I hope you feel good prosecuting a crazy man!"

Robby stood far away from the action and shot back, "Then why didn't you plead insanity?"

I escaped the razor blade but not Richards' blood. He used a smuggled blade to sever the artery of his left arm just above the elbow. Others saw the blood spurting. I didn't. What I did see—later—was my suit and the courtroom carpet covered by it. No one thought of AIDS. It was another decade before the virus made its appearance in the United States.

All I cared about was that Jeannie didn't have cancer.

Twenty-Four

Santa Barbara

Jeannie deserved a special homecoming treat. Not having breast cancer called for something memorable, whether or not it broke the bank. I figured the Santa Barbara Biltmore might be just the ticket.

Before Kelly was born, Jeannie and I took a Saturday drive to the coast, visiting Ventura, Carpinteria and Santa Barbara. While exploring the coastline of Santa Barbara, we came upon the Santa Barbara Biltmore, a magnificent facility with its own private beach. "Wouldn't it be nice to be able to stay in a place like that?" Jeannie pulled out her little camera and took a picture.

Now, I intended for her to get the opportunity to do just that.

Once travel arrangements were made for Jeannie's return, I contacted the Santa Barbara Biltmore to see what they had available. A garden casita sounded perfect.

An interview of a witness in a burglary case who lived near Santa Barbara gave me the opportunity to stop at the Biltmore and make a reservation. Jeannie and Kelly were flying to LAX the next Saturday, arriving shortly before one o'clock. I needed the casita available in the morning for me to drop off Kelly's playpen and an assortment of Jeannie's clothes, including a sleek black outfit for dinner and dancing Saturday evening. I also needed a babysitter for Kelly. The Biltmore was willing to provide one.

On the drive back to Bakersfield, I congratulated myself for the wonderful surprise I had put together. I was pumped. Three more days to go. Saturday couldn't come soon enough.

I loaded the car Friday night so I could get an early start to Santa Barbara and have time to organize the casita before going to LAX. The next morning, I arrived at the Biltmore at ten o'clock and picked up the key. A paved drive led to a parking spot next to the casita, so unloading took less time than I thought. I hung up Jeannie's and my clothes, set up Kelly's playpen, put a vase of flowers on the coffee table, and dimmed the lights. Next stop, LAX.

In 1970, air travel did not function in the hectic manner it does now. Then, there was no TSA, no paralyzing traffic, no remote parking, and no restriction on meeting passengers as they came off the plane. I stood next to the arrival gate before noon, more than an hour early. My eyes drifted to the information sign above the agent's desk. "Delayed" Flashed next to Jeannie's flight.

I asked the agent how long the delay would be. She didn't know.

I found a place to sit and worry. An hour went by, then two. The sign didn't change, and the agent had no further information. Around four o'clock, the agent came over to tell me that the flight just left Phoenix and was scheduled to land in a little over an hour. I let out a breath of relief, but my plans for the afternoon and evening were in tatters.

When Jeannie came through the gate carrying Kelly, she gave me a wrinkly-face frown. "I'm sorry we're so late." She frowned, like it was her fault.

I took Kelly and gave Jeannie a one-arm hug, avoiding putting pressure on her surgical site. "I'm so glad you made it safely."

"Did they tell you what happened in Phoenix?"

"No. What happened?"

"A tornado." She took a tissue from her pocket and wiped some spit-up from Kelly's chin. "The weather was really bad, so we didn't get on the plane for a long time. When we did, and taxied out to take off, the pilot said there was a tornado touching down on the end of our runway. He told us he'd move if it headed our way. We sat there quite a while before he got clearance to take off. It was pretty scary."

"I'll bet."

By the time we picked up luggage and got it loaded in the car, the sun was setting on a lovely spring day. The private beach would have to wait for us until morning.

Jeannie was not the world's most astute navigator. I assumed it would take her a while to figure out that we weren't taking the usual route home. Not so.

"Where are you going?" A touch of annoyance sounded in her voice.

"I thought we could see the last of the sunset from the coast."

"I'm tired. I just want to get home take a shower and go to bed."

"This way won't take any longer." Not a lie. Santa Barbara was closer than Bakersfield.

How will she react when I reach the Biltmore?

Jeannie appeared to be sleeping when I drove up the path to the casita. Her head popped up as I pulled to a stop. "Are we home?"

"Sort of. Come with me." I opened her door and helped her out.

"What are we doing? Where are we?"

"I want to look in the window of this casita." I took her hand and tugged her up the walkway.

"Jim! Are you crazy? You can't do that."

I fished the key from my pocket and opened the door. "We're at the Santa Barbara Biltmore, our home for the night. Dinner and dancing await."

She put her hand on Kelly's playpen and looked around. "When did you do this?"

"This morning. I'll get Kelly. You get ready. I brought your black dress and an assortment of shoes. They're in the closet."

After laying Kelly, sound asleep, in her playpen, and putting on my suit and tie, I asked the front desk to tell the babysitter we were ready for her. I should have known better. The sitter arrived in a few minutes. Jeannie came out of the bedroom an hour later. She looked gorgeous. By then, Kelly was awake and playing with her toys.

Off we went to the Biltmore's restaurant. The dining tables formed a horseshoe around a dancefloor in front of a bandstand where five or six gentlemen in black suits produced big band music ala Glenn Miller, Tommy Dorsey, et al. A few couples occupied the dancefloor. Many more sat at tables, some still eating.

After the maître d' escorted us to a table, our waiter informed us that due to the late hour, our food choices were limited. I don't recall what we ate, but it was not liver and onions.

What I do remember is that we danced—sharing kisses before, during, and after each number—until the music stopped. Then we scurried, hand-in-hand, through the night chill back to the casita.

We slept in late the next morning before enjoying a delightful outdoor brunch under a canopy that shielded us from bright sunshine. From there, we stormed the beach, which we had all to ourselves. The California Coastal Commission didn't take away private beach ownership until two or three years later. Kelly played in the sand while Jeannie and I shared how grateful we were that Jeannie didn't have cancer, and that we could enjoy this once-in-a-lifetime experience at a five-star resort.

Far too soon, our late checkout time approached. When everything had been loaded into our station wagon, and Jeannie was busy feeding Kelly, I went to the front desk to settle our account. My BankAmericard took a mighty punch, but it was worth it. We had never before stayed in a motel with a rating above one diamond in the AAA book.

I jogged back to the casita where I found Jeannie loading cans of pop from the refrigerator into a brown paper bag. "What are you doing?" I asked more sharply than I intended.

"We've paid for this. I'm not going to leave them behind."

There were six cans. At the then going rate of one thin dime for pop from a vending machine, the sack held 60 cents worth of soda. I shook my head and carried the bag to the car.

* * *

The following Saturday, the mail included an envelope bearing the logo of the Santa Barbara Biltmore. Inside was an invoice. I chuckled and handed it to Jeannie.

"Three dollars! They're charging us for the pop?"

How can so wise a woman . . . ?

Twenty-Five

The Arrival of Brandy

Shortly before Christmas of 1970, Jeannie came to me with, "I think Kelly needs a brother or sister."

"Are you sure?" I picked up Kelly who was wandering close to our child-proof Christmas tree. We had removed all the lower branches so she couldn't reach the bottom ones. The thought of another pregnancy gave me pause, considering the problems that occurred following Kelly's birth.

Jeannie looked at me with her sparkling green eyes and took Kelly from my arms. "I'm sure."

In our discussions about family size before we got married, we agreed on four children. The draft had thrown a wrench into that plan. Those two lost years trimmed our target number to three—assuming Jeannie was up to it.

A mixed bag of thoughts—mostly medical but some financial—swirled around in my head. The cut in pay I had taken in moving from the District Attorney's Office to a private litigation firm made money pretty tight.

* * *

Not more than two months later, Jeannie greeted me with a big smile when I came home from work. "I went to see Doctor Hubble today. We have one on the way."

"For sure?" A tingle of joy skittered up the sides of my neck.

"Yup. Due in September."

She held out her arms and I gave her a hug, being careful not to squeeze too hard.

* * *

When she was four or five months along, Jeannie asked if I'd ever heard of Lamaze.

"No. What's that?"

"It's a natural childbirth program, how to deal with labor and delivery." She chuckled as she patted her expanding belly. "I'd like to go."

Her *I* meant *we*. So, *we* went. A Lamaze husband functions as the coach.

I learned about *dilatation* and *effacement* as well as how to help Jeannie deal with labor pains through breathing techniques, and something called *effleurage,* a form of light, circular massage she was to employ to ease the pain of her contractions. I also learned how to perform back massage in the event of *back labor.*

Jeannie quickly mastered the breathing techniques. She also learned something designed to help her deal with hard labor. She must establish a *focal point.* When her pain became severe, she needed to concentrate her visual and mental energies on some small spot on the wall as she performed her breathing and effleurage.

* * *

"It's absolutely the best bass lure ever." So said the man I regarded as the most accomplished fisherman around. I had to have one.

When I got home that night, I held my new purchase up and wiggled it in front of Jeannie. "Let's go up to Lake Success tomorrow and put it to work." We had discovered the aptly named lake after our ill-fated trip to the Colorado River a couple years earlier.

Jeannie, about seven months pregnant, pursed her lips. "You can use that thing if you want. I like purple plastic worms."

Saturday morning, we turned Kelly over to the babysitter and headed up to Lake Success, less than an hour's drive north. It was a cool fall day. Jeannie wore a bright orange sweat suit to cover her expanded belly and carried her supply of plastic worms along with her rod and reel. I had my special and very expensive lure.

We still had no boat, so we fished from shore. Three men in an aluminum boat with a trolling motor passed by shaking their heads at bright orange Jeannie sitting on the bank. I walked fifty or sixty yards further down the shore and cast my very-best-ever lure. It flashed and darted like nothing I had ever seen. This day promised to be mine.

Before I knew it, Jeannie's rod was bent and jerking as she reeled in a nice bass. The three men again shook their heads. Fish number two followed in short order. This time they didn't shake their heads.

Then came my turn. I felt a strike, set the hook, and pulled in a bass so small I could hardly tell which was the fish and which was the lure. I put the little fellow in my pocket.

The aluminum boat came by again. "Look at that old gal. She's got another one."

I spotted Jeannie running up the bank with her reel dangling off the rod. "Help. My reel came off."

I ran to help but arrived too late. She had pulled a five-pound bass out of the lake and it lay flopping in the grass. The men in the boat clapped.

Then everything changed.

Horrible sounds came from the highway a few hundred yards away —the screech of tires followed by a sickening thud and screams.

Jeannie took off running toward the highway. I picked up her gear and fish and followed.

A little Mexican girl, maybe seven or eight, lay on the pavement, not breathing. The driver of the car that hit her had tears in his eyes. "She ran right out in front of me. I couldn't stop in time."

The little girl's parents couldn't speak English and no one in the gathering crowd spoke much Spanish. Jeannie ignored the entire hubbub and set about giving the little one CPR. I don't know who or how word got out for the ambulance to come, but it did. There were no cell phones then.

Jeannie's CPR efforts got the little girl breathing and her heart pumping by the time the EMTs arrived. "She had no pulse and wasn't breathing when I got here," she told them.

The EMTs loaded the still unconscious youngster into the ambulance and drove off. We never found out how she did after that.

It was a quiet ride home.

* * *

Somewhere around her due date in mid-September, Jeannie returned from an appointment with Dr. Hubble. "It could be any time now. I'm three centimeters dilated, and eighty percent effaced."

By then, I knew what she meant.

Jeannie got on the phone and called her mom. Bertha had told us she wanted to be with Jeannie for the birth and to help her when she and the baby came home from the hospital. The way I recall it, Bertha arrived before Jeannie hung up.

Then things slowed to a crawl. The baby must not have wanted to leave its comfy home in the womb, so she held out for five weeks—five long weeks.

Each week Jeannie came back from her visit with Dr. Hubble with the same report: "Three centimeters dilated, and eighty percent effaced."

Most days in between doctor visits, Jeannie and Bertha went shopping. The goal wasn't to buy things. It was to do a lot of walking to speed things along. If, perchance, they stumbled on something one or both of them couldn't live without, it came home with them. Fortunately, that was the exception, not the rule.

September days in Bakersfield are hot, usually around a hundred degrees or so. Jeannie and Bertha walked the roasting sidewalks from store to store. They didn't waltz around in some air-conditioned mall. And they put in long hours. I usually got home before they did.

On one of those shopping days, they came in the door bedraggled and red-eyed. I recognized it as the *we laughed until we cried* look.

Bertha glanced up at me and cackled, "Oh, Jim, your little wife-."

They both burst out laughing.

Jeannie sat down at the kitchen table. Bertha stood there holding her hands to her stomach as if she were trying to catch her breath.

"Well, are you going to tell me?"

Bertha pointed to Jeannie. "She will."

Jeannie sat with her hands flat on the table and took a deep breath. "We went into the shoe store on Chester . . . more to sit down and rest than anything." She looked at Bertha and the giggling began.

"This nice young gal asked me what I was looking for, so I thought I might as well try something on." Bertha turned her back to us and made sounds like a car with a dying battery.

Jeannie grabbed a napkin and wiped her eyes. "I picked out a shoe and the gal went to see if they had it in my size. She brought back a pair, and I tried one on."

Bertha now cracked up and sat down facing away from us, I suppose in an attempt to help Jeannie keep her composure. If so, it didn't work. Jeannie was losing it between phrases.

"When I took it off . . . I held it up to look at it . . . and it stunk." Jeannie bowed her head. "So I told her . . . 'this shoe stinks. Do you have another pair?' . . . When she . . . brought out another pair. . . I tried one on and then took a sniff . . . 'This one stinks, too,' I said."

At this point, Jeannie and Bertha started laughing so hard I thought crying was on its way. But it didn't come. Jeannie pulled herself together enough to continue.

"When the little gal took the second pair back, I was putting my shoe back on. Then the odor hit me . . . It was my feet that stunk . . . not the shoes."

Bertha turned around, gasping. "I told her we had to get out of there before the clerk came back."

They both howled.

I figured if anything was going to shake the baby loose, this was it.

It wasn't.

I had to find out. "Well, did you get out of there before she came back?"

"Noooo." Jeannie held onto the word a long time. "We waited for her, and I apologized. She said she wouldn't tell anybody."

Bertha slapped her thigh. "I'll bet she told everyone the minute we were out the door."

* * *

On October 12 (then the real Columbus Day), Bertha came into the den where I was snoozing in front of the TV. "Jeannie's water broke." I could hear both excitement and relief in her voice.

Our new baby was on its way into the world. We didn't know if it was going to be a girl or a boy, Brandy or Matthew.

Jeannie came out from the bedroom carrying her pre-packed bag. "I called Doctor Hubble. He said to check in at Memorial and he'd be there in an hour or so."

Off we went. I mentally ticked off my coaching duties as we made the short trip to the hospital. Bertha stayed home with Kelly to await the news.

Admission went smoothly. I took care of the paperwork. A nurse led Jeannie to a wheelchair and rolled her off to a labor room and got her settled in bed. Dr. Hubble confirmed the onset of labor, and I assumed my coaching position at Jeannie's bedside.

Jeannie did her Lamaze breathing and tummy massage with each contraction. I timed the intervals and told her how well she was doing.

After a while, the contractions came closer together. Jeannie began using the Lamaze *puff, puff, puff, whhhh* breathing technique. She appeared to be handling the pain beautifully. Then she said, "I'm having back labor."

Time for the coach to do back massage.

The next contraction came almost on top of the one before, strong and hard. I had just started back massage when the nurse came in and needed to do something at my position by the bed. Jeannie grimaced and *puff, puff, puff, whhhed.* I needed to go to the other side of the bed to continue the back massage.

As I rounded the foot of the bed, a voice straight out of *The Exorcist* nearly blew me against the wall. "YOU'RE IN MY FOCAL POINT!" Those were the harshest words Jeannie had ever spoken to me.

Then, as if nothing unusual had happened, the nurse said, "You're ready to go," She turned to me. "You can wait in the heirport." My coaching duties had come to an end with Jeannie's words still ringing in my ears.

At least I knew what and where the heirport was.

I opened the door to the heirport, surprised to see no one else there. I picked out what looked like the most comfortable chair and eased myself into it. Not fifteen minutes later, the phone rang.

"Mister Brown?"

"Yes."

"Congratulations. You have a beautiful baby girl. Mother and daughter are doing fine."

Giddy, goofy, and relieved, I wanted to shout the good news—Kelly had a baby sister. But I didn't shout. Instead, I hurried to the nursery window, not knowing how long it would take to get Brandy Lea ready to go into her burrito blanket. When the nurse brought her in and wrapped her up, I stood there all alone and smiled through the glass.

"Hi there, little one. You fought long and hard not to be born, but when it was time, you sure came fast."

Twenty-Six

The Uncalled Four

Jeannie put her hand over the mouthpiece of the phone. "Mary invited us to come over for a hot dog dinner. Do you want to go?"

"Sure. Should we take Kelly or see if one of the Dommer girls can baby sit?" Andrea and Lanelle were two of our pastor's seven children, both eager to earn a little money. The Dommers lived just down the street a block and a half, so help was close by if the need arose. Jeannie accepted the invitation and then called Pastor Dommer. The girls wanted to come.

We enjoyed spending time with Pete and Mary Lewis. Jeannie and Mary not only shared a room at the Delta Gamma house at UND, but Jeannie performed matchmaking duties in getting Pete and Mary together. Pete and I had graduated from East Bakersfield High School the same year but didn't really know each other at the time, in large measure because I came to EB—my fifth high school—as a senior. Only after Pete transferred to UND as a sophomore and became a fraternity brother of mine did we become fast friends.

That evening, after chowing down on hot dogs, beans, and salad, washed down by a beer or two, Pete brought out his guitar. He played and sang well enough that some college girls had clambered for his attention. His good looks didn't hurt either. The four of us sang a few popular songs of the day. We must have been singing a little too loudly because Jennifer, Pete and Mary's little daughter, tiptoed into the room wiping sleep from her eyes. Mary got up to put her back in bed.

"Do you know Craig Jenkins or Ray Yinger?" Pete asked me.

"I know Craig, not Ray. Why?"

"Ray has a solo practice. Craig and I are going over to his house tomorrow to plink around. You want to bring your guitar and join us?"

"What time?"

"I'm going over about three. You want me to pick you up?"

I looked over at Jeannie. She gave me and Pete a smiling nod.

Jeannie had given me a child-size guitar during my military days, and I had taken a few free, on-post lessons, but I played it as if my fingers were bananas. And I sang like a rusty gate hinge. I found out at our first get-together that Craig and Ray both played and sang well.

* * *

At Ray's house we tried some Kingston Trio, Limelighters, and Gordon Lightfoot numbers. Ray had decent recording equipment, so we put a few songs on tape. Listening to ourselves on the play-back caused me to realize lip syncing might be the way for me to go.

Craig didn't discourage this but had some other ideas. "Rather than going with four guitars, I can bring my five-string banjo next time and Ray can break out his twelve-string guitar. If anyone has access to a stand-up bass, Jim could learn to play that."

Oh, great.

When I got home, Jeannie was playing with Kelly. "How did it go? Was it fun?"

"Yeah, but those other guys are good. Craig Jenkins is even better than Pete." I laughed. "Craig said I should learn to play the bass. My talent on the guitar didn't exactly overwhelm him." Then I told her about recording some songs and listening to the play-back. "I stink."

"No, you don't. I like your voice."

"Yeah. And you like liver, too."

She made a frownie-face. "Are you going to do it again?"

"We talked about next Saturday afternoon."

* * *

The next Saturday came and went. The get-together didn't happen. But Craig called me after a few days and told me he knew the owner of a local music store who had taken in a bass to be repaired. The customer abandoned it when he heard the repair estimate. Craig said the neck of the bass had broken loose from the body. We could buy it for fifty bucks and try to repair it ourselves.

As the only woodworker in the group, the task of making the repairs fell to me—along with learning how to play the dumb thing. The purchase went well. The repairs went well. The learning how to play it, not so well.

The neck on a stand-up bass doesn't have frets. How was I, with an ear several levels below tin, supposed to know where to put my fingers?

My undergraduate degree in engineering bore fruit. Harmonics depend on the length of the string. By making precise measurements, I determined where the frets went—if there were any—and drew pencil lines on the neck of the bass. Now all I had to do was figure out how to crane my own neck to see where my fingers were supposed to go—a slow and painful process.

* * *

When our get-togethers resumed, Jeannie asked if there wasn't some way the wives could be involved. "Maybe rotate houses and we could fix dinner while you guys practiced. Then after dinner, you could put on a show for us."

Mary, Penny Jenkins, and Dee Yinger liked Jeannie's idea, as did Pete, Craig, and Ray. And so it went. The first time we performed for this captive audience, they were somewhat reserved in their praise. They failed to reach the level of enthusiasm we had shown for their delicious dinner. Even so, they encouraged us to persevere in our efforts to make noises approximating real music.

We did indeed persevere. Our first almost gig took place on New Year's Eve 1969 at the home of a deputy DA who was hosting a party. Our invitations to the party didn't include a request to provide entertainment. We just brought our instruments along in case an opportunity presented itself. It did, as did a name for our group—The Uncalled Four.

How did we do? I don't know. 1970 had already arrived before we broke into song. By then, the revelers probably were ready to applaud a stick rubbing on a washboard considering the condition they were in. The best I can do is relate that a couple months later, the person assigned to come up with entertainment for the annual Law Day Dinner contacted me to see if we were willing to play a few numbers for the affair. He didn't have a budget to work with, but having heard us at the New Year's Eve party he thought we might provide a few laughs.

The thought of doing our thing in front of five or six hundred people—from a real stage—got our juices flowing. We agreed to do it. But Craig thought we needed to have our own sound equipment—speakers, mike stands and mikes—and he knew a fellow who built speakers as a hobby.

The sound equipment was ordered, and our weekly practices took on new intensity. Jeannie, Mary, Penny, Dee—and our baby Kelly—became our biggest fans. When it was "Show-Time" for the wives to critique a new song, Jeannie stood Kelly on an ottoman where Kelly bounced with the beat and clapped her approval.

"Why don't you be MC for the Law Day Dinner," Craig said. It wasn't a question. The job description included introducing the songs and hopefully providing some humorous patter along the way. I wasn't worried about introducing the songs but the humorous patter part caused me no small measure of anxiety. A large room filled mostly with lawyers and judges, and their spouses didn't provide an ideal audience.

* * *

The Law Day program listed entertainment provided by The Uncalled Four after dinner. So, when the servers began delivering dessert, we took the stage behind our new sound system, tapped the mikes to make sure they still worked, and launched into a rousing rendition of The Limelighters' *There's a Meeting Here Tonight.* People actually applauded when we finished the song. That felt good.

Then the time came for the MC to speak. I have no recollection of what I said that evening or what other songs we sang, but after we turned down a third encore, Jeannie made my day. "That was really good, and you were funny," she said.

I puffed out my chest. "But of course."

* * *

For the next few years, The Uncalled Four played at dinner and lunch meetings of service clubs and trade groups, at birthday parties or other private gatherings, and once at a political fund-raiser. Jeannie always went along. At the fund-raiser, our local congressman Bob Mathias, a two-time Olympic decathlon gold medalist, tried to hit on my personal groupie. Mary Lewis told me about it after we finished playing. "Jeannie was so cool. Mathias walked over to her and asked if she was there alone. She gave him a little smile and said, 'My husband is the bass player.'"

As time went on, we became professionals charging the outrageous sum of $50. But inevitably, like other similar groups—such as the Beatles and the Eagles—we broke up. First, Pete Lewis called it quits, saying it had become more like a job than just having fun.

Craig, Ray, and I continued for a while, still under the same name. My introduction then went something along the lines of: "We're The Uncalled Four." then looking at Craig and Ray I added, "We're lawyers, not mathematicians." For some reason, that always got a laugh—or a groan.

The highlight of our brief but stupendous career came when Pete was still with us. We appeared before an audience of over a thousand people attending the 1971 Farm Bureau Convention held in Bakersfield. Our final song that day was a satirical number we had collectively written about a fictitious local folk hero. My introduction was long. It went something like this:

> *Throughout American history there have been many folk heroes such as Paul Bunyan, the legendary lumberjack, Johnny Appleseed, the legendary applejack,* [small titter from the crowd] *and here in Kern County we have our own folk hero. I know that when you hear his name, a hoarse cry of recognition will well up in the throats of you all . . .* EDGAR SAVAGE! . . . [stone silence] . . . *So soon you forget.*
>
> *Many years ago, Edgar worked for one of the first pizza parlors in California. At the time, pizza was made with only a crust, sauce, and meat—no cheese. This bothered Edgar. He believed there should be cheese on each and every pizza. He felt this so strongly that he formed a union of like-minded individuals and called it The United Pizza Workers Organizing Committee—UPWOC.*
>
> *The pizza parlor owners across the state resisted, so Edgar called a strike. It was so successful there is now cheese on almost every pizza. Because of this, he earned the nickname "Cheeser."*
>
> *Here now is our tribute to Delano's own CHEESER SAVAGE!*

The Farm Bureau members in attendance had no trouble converting Cheeser Savage to Cesar Chavez, and they roared their approval. We were grateful, considering that each attendee had to chip in four or five cents to cover our exorbitant $50 fee.

The Uncalled Four (Pete Lewis, Craig Jenkins, Ray Yinger, & me)

Twenty-Seven

The House Hunter

In the early spring of 1972, my father decided to move back to Bakers-field and take up residence with us in *his* house, the one we thought we were buying from him. After three months or so of this living arrangement, Jeannie called me into the kitchen. "I think your dad wants his house back. We better look for a place of our own."

The search began.

Jeannie sat at the kitchen table. The classified section of *The Bakersfield Californian* lay open in front of her with circles around several listings. Pre-internet, the newspaper provided the best source of real estate information. "I'd like to find a two-story house in an older neighborhood. I don't like the new developments."

"That sounds good to me." I looked over her shoulder at the circled listings. One was just a couple blocks away.

I tapped on the paper. "Let's look at this one."

She smiled up at me with a mischievous twinkle in her eye. "I already called. We can see it tomorrow after you get home."

* * *

Three months and dozens of home visits later we were no closer to finding what Jeannie wanted than we were on day one.

Jeannie kept up the hunt. Unbeknownst to me, she managed to engage the services of five real estate agents, giving each of them a detailed list of the specifics she had in mind. No one had told her that proper house hunting etiquette involved only one agent at a time. And she never told any of the five about the other four.

With each prospective house brought to her attention by one of her fleet of agents, Jeannie packed up three-year-old Kelly and baby Brandy to go for a look-see. If the house held any promise, she told me we needed to go together for a second look. They all went begging.

One June day, Jeannie met me at the door with the paper in her hand. "Look at this. It sounds perfect. Old Westchester. Two story. Five bedrooms. Thirty-nine five."

I read the cryptic classified ad. It gave no address. Instead, it said it was on a dead-end street within walking distance from the Racquet Club, and invited anyone interested to respond to a box number at the newspaper.

"Well, let's send a letter to this box number," I said.

"I did. But how about going to see if we can find it." She pulled out a city map.

I located the Racquet Club and circled out from it looking for dead end streets. There was only one within reasonable walking distance. "It's got to be on this last block of 20th Street."

We packed up the girls and headed out.

The dead-end block on 20th Street had two, two-story homes directly across the street from each other. Neither gave any indication it was on the market. One definitely didn't fit the thirty-nine five price range—three times that much, maybe. The other could have been the one. In fact, it looked perfect. Since there was no address included in the ad we decided not to knock on the door.

"I guess we'll have to wait to hear back about your letter," I said.

She lifted her shoulders. "I guess."

No reply ever came. The ad must have been placed just to test the level of interest.

* * *

In late August, Jeannie called me at my office. "I've found our house. It's that one on 20th. You've got to get over here right away. All kinds of people are looking at it."

The excitement in her voice told me she was serious. I dropped what I was doing and drove to meet her at the house—barely a mile from my work. She was right. Real estate people and their clients were crawling all over the place. Jeannie was with John Garone, one of her many agents, who had called her as soon as the house hit the market.

We took a quick walk through the house. "I'd be happy living here the rest of my life," she prophetically said.

Within an hour it was ours—assuming we could come up with the down payment.

After cashing in all our chips and breaking open Jeannie's pink piggy bank, we scraped together just enough to close the deal.

We devoted September, October, November, and early December to getting everything ready to move in. Paint went on every downstairs wall after thorough scrubbing with TCP. Same with the ceilings. Spackle, putty, and paint became our evening ritual, often extending into the post-midnight hours.

Jeannie decided that four of the five upstairs bedrooms needed to be wallpapered, and that I had the job of hanging the paper while she painted the woodwork.

With my blessing, Jeannie picked out the wallpaper and the paint colors. Maybe not a great idea. The master bedroom walls became adorned with double-pasted, perfectly hung paper sporting pink and red roses. But she painted the woodwork blue.

Somewhere along the line, Jeannie announced, "I hate the carpet in the living room." *Hate* and *love* measured Jeannie's taste when it came to things. She didn't harbor much middle ground. Not so with people. *Love* ran by itself when it came to people, with a few—very few— exceptions.

Every downstairs room had hardwood floors. The pale green, cotton loop carpet covering the hardwood floor in the living room deserved her hate. We tore it out only to find ugly stains on the oak below. What to do? Jeannie had the answer but not the money. So, she negotiated a payment plan with a carpet company that allowed the water-stained wood of the living room floor to be covered by a wool floral carpet that suited her fancy. She *loved* it.

By Christmas, much to my father's delight, we were settled in.

It was just a house, but Jeannie made it into a warm and welcoming home.

Twenty-Eight

The Arrival of Matthew

Sometime in the summer of 1973, Jeannie presented me with a magazine article to read. It was about what a couple could do to influence the sex of their baby. It was not foolproof, but it sure sounded like fun.

We had long since given up on our plan to have four children, accepting three as the new goal. Jeannie wanted a boy to complete her nest. The article said the odds of having a boy could be increased to over 60% by following a few simple rules. The only one that stands out in my memory required increased sexual activity. I was good with that.

The rest of the rules, as I recall, fell into Jeannie's bailiwick—having to do with determining the precise time of ovulation and the like.

In any event, Jeannie became pregnant far too soon for my liking. I had become spoiled.

This pregnancy produced no complications or heightened anxiety. We took a Lamaze class again, and in it I learned the hospital rules had been changed to allow fathers into the delivery room. Good news.

* * *

On June 20th, 1974, our tenth wedding anniversary, Jeannie began to feel some mild contractions. They came every ten minutes or so. "They're Braxton-Hicks," she said. "They'll pass."

They didn't.

Over the next two days the contractions gradually became stronger and more frequent. By noon on the 22nd, they became painful enough for Jeannie to say, "It's time to go to the hospital."

I grabbed the bag she had packed many days before, and off we went. On the way, Jeannie did her belly-rub *effleurage* thing. I tried not to speed.

At the hospital, some woman gave Jeannie a quick evaluation and sent us home. "She's not ready to be admitted," the lady said.

No explanation. Just a gruff pronouncement and back through the door she went.

"That was weird," Jeannie said as we walked to the car. "Ooh, here comes another one."

I started to turn around. "Let's go back."

"No, no. Let's go home. I'll call Doctor Hubble." She pulled me toward the car.

The drive home took less than ten minutes. More contractions came. More *effleurage*. Some huffing and puffing.

I pulled into the driveway at home.

"My water just broke."

I backed out and this time sped to the hospital. I wanted to tell that woman she was about as smart as a sack of oats. After all, I had been to Lamaze—twice.

Instead, I focused on the idea of seeing the delivery of our hoped-for son.

At the hospital, a different lady evaluated Jeannie, put her in a wheelchair and off they went to the labor room. The hospital still had separate labor rooms and delivery rooms.

I stayed at the admissions desk a few minutes taking care of some paperwork before following the directions to Jeannie's labor room. When I opened the door, all I saw was the foot of her bed being pushed out into the hall leading to the delivery room.

A nurse handed me a pile of green things. "Put these on and follow me. She's starting to deliver."

I threw on the gown, pulled the hairnet over the few remaining strands on my head and hopped down the hall as fast as I could while trying to put the green booties over my shoes.

I skipped into the delivery room tugging the last booty over my heel just as Matthew made his appearance. The doctor—Dr. Davis, covering for Dr. Hubble—held Matt up by his heels and gave him a swat. "Tell Doctor Hubble that I'm the *boy* doctor."

All my hard work had paid off. Ha.

Jeannie just grinned and held out her arms to give her son a quick cuddling hug before he was taken off to be cleaned up, weighed and measured. Then she turned to me. "Well, we did it."

I wanted to try for another boy. Instead, I got a trip to the urologist for a vasectomy.

Twenty-Nine

Backpacking the Colorado Rockies

1975 brought with it a challenge. "How would you like to go backpacking in Colorado with Bill and Ruth and their family?" I asked Jeannie shortly after Matt's first birthday.

Matthew's first birthday

She shrugged her shoulders—neither a yes nor no.

Backpacking had become the outdoor sport of choice for many people. "What better place to try our hand at exploring nature than the Colorado Rockies? Bill and his family are willing to give it a go," I said.

Jeannie nodded. "Okay. Let's do it."

I detected less than outright enthusiasm in her voice. Nevertheless, I made a trip to Los Angeles to visit REI, the outfitting store of choice. REI emptied my wallet but filled my car with equipment and supplies. Jeannie rigged up a papoose-style pack in which to carry Matt. We figured the girls could carry their own sleeping bags and a change of clothes. Everything else needed to ride on my back.

With Jeannie's mini-school-bus-van loaded and filled with gas, we took off for Fort Collins, Colorado. Brother Bill had been charged with selecting the hiking routes and camping spots for two, over-night outings, each to a lake near timberline.

After arriving in Fort Collins, we filled our packs, avoiding as much weight as possible. Essentials came first, then desired items such as fishing gear and cameras. We opted for mostly freeze-dried food, but someone (I won't divulge who) packed a box of pancake mix. Bedtime came early, as did our morning departure for the trailhead.

When we arrived at our jumping-off spot and strapped on our packs, we lined up for a documenting photo.

Brandy, Kelly, Jeannie with Matt, Dan, Ruth, Meg, me, Bill, & Jim

Then we hit the path leading to our first destination. As the trail climbed higher, we encountered a swift stream that could only be crossed atop the trunk of a fallen tree. Most of us scooted on our butts—not brother Bill. He did his best imitation of a gymnast on the balance beam.

Jeannie, Brandy, & Bill on the log

Mid-afternoon brought us to an Alpine lake and the campsite Bill had chosen for our overnight stay. The kids threw stones into the lake while the adults set up tents and laid out sleeping bags.

Jeannie going fishing

Jeannie assembled her fishing pole and scrambled along the shoreline in search of a suitable spot to make her first cast—Matthew on her back and Kelly by her side. She returned with her head hanging. "No luck. I think the lake is sterile."

Dinner of freeze-dried goop and canteen water led to early bed-time. I tossed and turned trying to find a comfortable position in which to rest my aching back. The little sleep I got came between calls-of-nature for me, Jeannie, or one of the kids.

Daylight seemed to arrive shortly after midnight. The prospect of a pancake breakfast pulled me from the tent. In addition to the box of pancake mix, we had a single-burner camp stove and a fry-pan large enough to cook one large pancake.

At an elevation above ten thousand feet, pancakes don't brown-up very fast. With all of us to feed, one pancake at a time, breakfast lasted well past noon. Lunch would have to wait until we got back to the trailhead.

One pancake at a time

* * *

Back in Fort Collins, we discussed what improvements we might make for our second assault on the high-country. The kids chose cookies instead of pancake mix. The adults addressed the culinary merits of our assortment of freeze-dried food. Finding none, we chose beef stew as the least objectionable.

Jim, Meg, Brandy, Dan, & Kelly

After a couple days rest, we packed-up for a new adventure, this time on a trail without a river crossing but again near timberline. The drive over Rabbit Ears Pass took us to the trailhead. No documentary photo was taken.

The trail wound gently upward through the forest as the trees became more stunted and widely separated. Our lakeside destination soon came into view. As we approached the lake, I detected a slightly foul odor in the air.

second day backpacking

"Do you smell that?" Jeannie asked.

"I think it's coming from the lake." I walked to the water's edge. Unlike the lake from our first hike, this one wasn't sterile. Just the opposite. Inspection of a cup of the murky water revealed squirmy things living side-by-side with bits and pieces of who-knows-what. But as seasoned mountain people, having one trip under our collective belts, we came prepared. I had REI's best water filter plus purification tablets, Bill had his one-burner camp stove, and Jeannie had a bandana.

Since all our canteens were nearly empty, the (ugh) lake provided our only source of water for undrying the freeze-dried stew. First, we strained a potful of lake water, one cup at a time, through Jeannie's bandana. Next, we boiled the strained water before adding the purification tablets. After the boiled and purified liquid cooled, it went through my REI filter into something called a shower bag. Then it went back on the burner for a second boil and the addition of the freeze-dried stew .

When the stew was ready to eat, no one took even one bite. We threw it out and had cookies for dinner, saving a few for breakfast.

As the sun passed behind the mountain peaks to the west, Bill stood and pointed to the lake. "Look!"

The surface of the stagnant water swarmed with a cloud of mosquitos.

"Everyone in the tents. Hurry," Jeannie said. She picked up Matt and herded the girls to safety. I was right behind them and tied the outside flaps and zipped the inside netting as tight as I could. Still, a dozen or so of the nasty blood-sucking critters came in with us.

I've heard it said that the mosquitos making a buzz don't bite and vice versa. I don't know if that's true, but I do know that a lot of buzzing, biting, and slapping kept me awake most of the night. That and, "I've got to go potty." Jeannie's bottle of insect repellant was empty by daylight.

Morning found us hot-footing it down the trail munching on cookies and declaring that this would be our last backpacking adventure—ever!

Thirty

Bridalveil Fall

The summer and fall of 1976 brought a terrible draught to the Sierra Nevada mountains, reducing Yosemite National Park's Bridalveil Fall to a mere trickle. The water coming over the fall blew away or evaporated before reaching the ground 620 feet below. I wanted to get a picture of it with Kelly, Brandy and Matt in the foreground.

Kelly's Godparents had given us the gift of a weekend at Moore's Redwoods in Yosemite. I was in a lengthy trial. The evidence had concluded. Closing arguments were scheduled for Monday. We drove up to Yosemite Friday evening.

On the way, two-year-old Matt managed to get out of his seatbelt and take a tumble into the side door-well of the van. Jeannie picked him up and looked at the cut on his head. "He needs stitches," she said.

The sign for Saint Agnes Hospital in Fresno seemed to pop up out of nowhere on the side of the road. "We're in luck," I said. "That's the hospital right over there."

The door at the emergency entrance stood open and Jeannie took Matt inside. A parking place nearby allowed me to stay in the van with the girls and keep an eye out for Jeannie.

She wore a wry smile when she carried Matt back to the car and buckled him in. "They looked at me like they thought it was child abuse when I told them what happened."

"How many stitches?"

"Just a couple. Matt was a real trooper. He didn't let out a peep." She turned to look at Matt. "Don't get out of your seat again, Buster."

Darkness and semi-tame deer greeted us at Moore's Redwoods. We didn't have any handouts for the deer, so they wandered off. Jeannie checked over the cabin and got the kids ready for bed. After hauling in our luggage, I reviewed some notes for my closing argument.

Saturday morning arrived crisp and clear, perfect for my picture of Bridalveil Fall. I pulled into the parking lot for the viewing area, grabbed my camera, and lit out for the trail with the kids. Jeannie said she wasn't feeling all that well and wanted to wait in the van.

When Bridalveil came into sight, I spotted the perfect place for my picture. A large granite boulder sat at the side if the trail—on the other side of the guard rail. It had a natural bench in the rock for the kids to sit on with Bridalveil Fall in the background. I lifted Kelly over the rail to the bench and then put Matt up beside her. I wanted him in the middle.

Brandy held her arms out to be picked up. When I turned back, the world morphed into a slow-motion horror film.

Matt had scrambled to the top of the boulder and was toddling toward the edge. More boulders lay ten feet below.

"Matt, sit down!"

He took another step or two. Turned. And sat. With nothing under him but air.

I raced to the rail. Stretched out as far as I could. His little body skimmed my fingertips, headfirst.

A sickening thud drove a dagger into my heart.

I killed my son.

I don't know how I did it, but I went under the guard rail and made my way down to Matt. He was alive. I knew not to move anyone with a spinal injury. But I had to.

The next thing I recall is being back on the trail with Matt in my arms. My right hand cradled his head; blood oozed between my fingers.

At the van, Jeannie's eyes went wide. "What happened to Matt?"

I could barely tell her. My emotions were in shambles. "He fell . . . We need to get him to a doctor."

The Yosemite map showed a medical facility at the end of the loop road. Jeannie held Matt while I drove. The girls cried.

The next thing I knew, we were there—at the medical facility. The "doctor" was a medical student—a proverbial fish out of water.

He made a quick assessment of Matt. "This is more than I can handle. I can call for a helicopter, but if you think you can drive, that will probably get you to Fresno sooner."

Off we went. There is little in my recollection of the drive to Fresno. Matt didn't cry. Jeannie sang softly to him and told me his eyes were open. That's it.

At Saint Agnes Hospital, Jeannie took charge. The med-student at Yosemite had called ahead so they were expecting us. Matt went directly to radiology, Jeannie with him. Kelly, Brandy, and I huddled together in the waiting area, praying for Matt to be okay.

Jeannie returned with puffy eyes. "He has a double skull fracture. One of them is . . ." She swallowed hard. "Basal. That's the worst kind."

She should have screamed at me for being so careless. I deserved it. But she didn't. Instead, she hugged me. "He's being admitted for the night. Tomorrow, they'll arrange for a transfer to Bakersfield."

The girls joined in the hug. After a minute or so, Jeannie said, "Take the girls to the cabin and try to get some sleep. I want to stay with Matt."

* * *

When the girls and I got back to the hospital the next day, Jeannie looked surprisingly chipper. "I don't know how to describe it," she said. "I was overcome with such a sense of peace last night." The corners of her mouth tilted up. "I was sitting by Matthew's bed praying when the song *Amazing Grace* came on over the speakers. Somehow, I know he'll be all right."

"Is he still going to be transferred?"

"Yeah. Mercy's expecting him."

* * *

Sunday afternoon Matt was admitted to Mercy Hospital. Jeannie, his own pediatric nurse, stayed by his side.

Greta Rapp, an unofficial grandmother and neighborhood baby-sitter, agreed to look after Kelly and Brandy so I could go to my office.

Preparing to give my closing argument proved to be no easy task. The sights and sounds of Matt's fall kept my gut churning and my mind drifting to his plight. When I faced the choice between preparation and prayer, prayer won out. I did what I could to get ready for Monday morning, then headed for the hospital.

What looked like a miniature jail cell held Matt. A stout mesh ceiling topped the barred walls of the over-sized crib. Matt's eyes were open, looking at Jeannie as she sat close to his crib, reading to him from a children's storybook.

"How's he doing?" I gave Jeannie a kiss on the top of her head. "Can I get you anything?"

"No, I'm fine. Just look after the girls. I'm supposed to keep him awake. Doctor Ablin will be checking on him later this evening."

Dr. George Ablin, a brilliant neurosurgeon, took charge of Matt's care. A round-faced, nebbish of a man, Dr. Ablin was great with kids. Not so great with their parents.

* * *

Monday morning, my trial was about to wrap up with closing arguments and instructions to the jury. About 11:30 I stood up to give my summation when Craig Jenkins came into the courtroom and whispered something to the bailiff. The bailiff wrote on a notepad and gave it to the clerk who in turn handed it to the judge.

"Mister Brown, may I see you for a minute before you start?" the judge said. He held up his hand to stop the other lawyers from joining us—very unusual. He showed me the note.

Ablin wants to see you. There's blood behind the eardrum.

My throat went dry. From handling brain injury cases, I knew this was an ominous sign. Matt probably needed holes drilled in his skull to relieve the pressure.

My closing argument was brief—too brief—and disoriented. As soon as "thank you" was out of my mouth, I bolted for the door.

Out on the street, I ran the five blocks to Mercy Hospital. It would have taken longer to get my car and find a parking place. Huffing and puffing, I stepped into Matt's room where Dr. Ablin was talking to Jeannie. When he saw me, he turned from Jeannie. She made a scowling face, letting me know she wasn't at all happy with the good doctor.

"As you know, Jim, bleeding behind the ear drum is not good. But he's alert and showing no signs of inter-cranial pressure. We'll keep a close eye on him for now. No need to get the drill out yet." With that, Dr. Ablin pranced out of the room.

"That man makes me so mad," Jeannie said. He came in, saw me and made a beeline for the elevator." Jeannie shook her fist at the door. "He wouldn't talk to me. I had to chase him down the hall and put my foot in the elevator to keep him from escaping. I almost had to drag him back here. Then he said he wanted to talk to you because he's worked with you on brain injury cases before."

"He knows you're an RN."

"I don't know if he remembers me. He should. I had trouble with him back then, too. All the nurses did." Jeannie had worked briefly at Mercy Hospital before her pregnancy with Brandy.

The miniature holding cell sat in the middle of the room. In it, Matt lay on a mattress of fluffy pillows. A yellow plastic helmet perched on his head, secured by a strap under his chin. His eyes were fixed on Jeannie. "Sit. Read," he said.

Jeannie laughed. "That's all he wants." She returned to the armless chair next to the holding cell and picked up a book from the floor. "Do you remember where we were, Matt?"

"Jack threw beans out a window." He sat up and grabbed hold of the bars, not looking like he had a double skull fracture.

"Are you going to stay here again tonight?"

Jeannie nodded and continued reading. I headed back to court.

Plaintiff's counsel gave his rebuttal argument after the lunch break, the judge read instructions to the jury, and out they went to deliberate. This was nervous time for trial lawyers—nothing to do but wait and think about all the questions that weren't asked and all the things that might have been done differently. Not so for me this time.

There is a French phrase for it. I don't remember what it is, but it generally means *death on the sixth day.* A doctor used it once in a medical malpractice case, explaining that the most critical time for a patient with a severe head injury is the sixth day. The patient may appear to be doing well the first few days, then suddenly take a turn for the worse.

Jeannie knew this.

That evening I went back to the hospital. Jeannie was sitting in the same chair, a small pile of books on the floor beside it. Matthew appeared to be sleeping.

"I have to wake him up pretty soon—can't let him sleep too long."

"What about you?" I asked.

"They're going to bring me a cot for tonight. I'll be fine. How'd it go in court?"

"We won." I couldn't help but shake my head. "After the verdict, I talked to a couple of the jurors. They wanted to know what happened. They said I'd been making sense for two weeks and all of a sudden the judge talks to me and then I didn't."

"I'll bet Chevron's happy."

"Relieved is more like it. The other two defendants got hit. Not bad, though."

"Speaking of *relieved,* you better go relieve Greta Rapp . . . and pick up Happy Meals for the girls."

Soft breathing sounds came from Matt's holding cell. "Has Ablin been back?"

"No. He makes his rounds about seven." Jeannie held out a piece of paper. "Here's a list of things to bring me in the morning."

* * *

Matt made it past the sixth day, and then the seventh. Jeannie read him every book on the little bookshelf before he came home with his yellow helmet. He wore it the next five months.

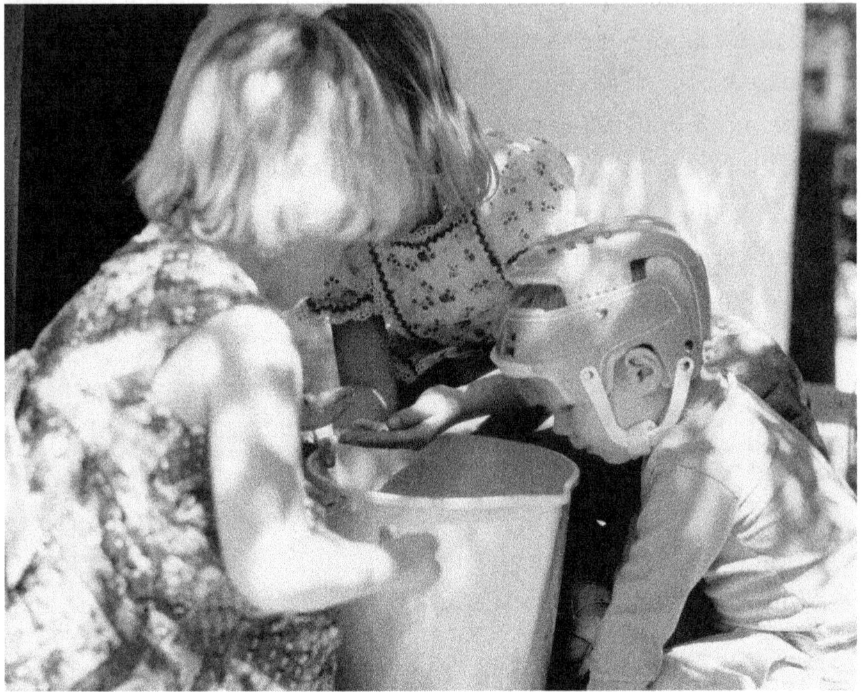

Thirty-One

Jeff

Jeannie loved birds, birds of all shapes and sizes from hummingbirds to bald eagles and wrens to great blue herons. She loved to watch them, feed them, and on occasion take nurturing care of them.

A near tragedy occurred when an old poplar tree toppled over in our Bakersfield backyard destroying our children's jungle gym. The tree had seen its better days and was rotting from the inside out. Fortunately, no one was injured except some newly hatched little birds whose nest was dislodged from the tree when it crashed to the ground. Two of the tiny hatchlings survived, one even smaller than the other. Jeannie named them Mutt and Jeff.

Her first instinct was to call someone with the Department of Fish and Wildlife to find out how to care for them. She said the person on the line told her to leave them where they were and see if their parents tended to the little guys. She went back outside to watch the nest from a distance.

Before long I heard a commotion.

"No! No! Get away. Get away."

I went to the door. Jeannie held the nest in trembling hands, her face red and her jaw clenched. "That stupid blue jay got Mutt. He's dead."

"What about Jeff?" I asked.

"I think he's okay." She looked out to the back yard. "I can't leave him out there." She carried the nest into the kitchen and put it on the counter next to the sink.

I took the remains of Mutt, wrapped in a paper napkin, to the far corner of the back yard for burial.

Jeff, a tiny lump of featherless pink skin attached to a wide-open beak, became Jeannie's special project. She got back on the phone and explained the situation. What could she do to save Jeff?

The news was not good. For Jeff to survive, he needed to be fed a special concoction every forty-five minutes around the clock until he feathered out. The recipe consisted of four ingredients, three of which were raw egg, cottage cheese, and milk. I'm not sure about the fourth. Perhaps breadcrumbs.

The mixture had to be poked into Jeff's open maw with tweezers, using a motion simulating that of his momma's beak. And the nest needed to be kept at Goldilocks temperature—not too hot and not too cold.

Jeannie feeding Jeff

The first several days, Jeannie fed Jeff every forty-five minutes around the clock without fail. While doing so, she talked soothingly to the teeny fellow and took great pains to keep him comfortably warm. When Jeff began to feather out, she held him in her palm, talking to him softly while stroking his neck and back with the tip of her finger.

Soon Jeff was able to scramble up to the edge of his nest when Jeannie came to feed him. It looked like he knew the ritual. First came the feeding, then the holding, cooing, and petting. She called him by name as she smoothed his new feathers and placed him carefully back into his nest.

The next step was to teach Jeff to fly. Jeannie moved him from his perch on the edge of the nest to her index finger, carried him to the living room, and sat down on the carpet. After the usual soft conversation and stroking of feathers, she began slowly raising and lowering her finger, gradually increasing the speed of the downward movement until Jeff flapped his wings.

After several of these sessions, Jeff was able to flutter down to the carpet. Then Jeannie took him outside.

The outside training began with Jeannie carrying Jeff on her finger into the backyard. She knelt by an azalea bush and coaxed him onto one of the lower branches by nudging the branch against his breast. He moved one foot and then the other to the foothold and clamped down tight. Once he did this, Jeannie backed away just a little and called for Jeff to come to her.

Before long, Jeff raised his wings and fluttered them but did not let go of the branch. Jeannie held her finger to his legs. He hopped on. She repeated the process, continuing to call him by name until he mustered up the courage to make a two-or-three-wing-flap flight to the grass and hop up to her waiting finger.

That first day outside, Jeff did very well flying down to the grass, but he had no ability to get airborne from there. Jeannie tried to get him to fly to her finger which she held just a few inches in front of him and slightly above the ground. No luck on day one. But the next day he made his first flight – maybe 6 inches. It was Jeannie and Jeff's own Kitty Hawk moment.

Over the next few days, Jeff became stronger and soon could fly from an azalea branch to Jeannie's finger as she was standing several feet away. He only did this when she called him to come to her. Later, she taught him to land on her shoulder, and he rode there like a little jockey as she puttered around the yard.

Along the way, Jeannie made sure Jeff became comfortable with each of our three children, and also with me. Any one of us could go into the back yard and call for Jeff. He'd fly from wherever he was perched and land either on a finger or shoulder.

Brandy & Matt with Jeff

Jeannie then faced the challenge of introducing Jeff to our dog Bridget, a toy French poodle getting on in years. As I watched in amazement, she convinced Bridget to let Jeff to ride on her back. Bridget strolled around the patio with her little passenger riding comfortably as if in a saddle.

* * *

Then one evening I came home late and found Jeannie distraught.

"I can't find Jeff." Tears welled up in her eyes.

She told me she had been sitting on the patio at dusk watching Jeff flit around in the bushes and trees. Out of the corner of her eye she caught sight of a darting blur—nothing more. After that Jeff didn't come when she called.

At the time, there were owls living in the neighborhood, and Jeannie was convinced that what she saw was an owl taking her little friend. The rest of the evening, and well into the night, we searched high and low for Jeff to no avail.

The next night, when I returned home from work, Jeannie stood in the kitchen sobbing, her hands cupped together. When I went to her, she opened her hands. I saw Jeff lying on his side with toes tightly curled.

"He's still alive," Jeannie said through her tears. "We have to get him to a vet."

A San Joaquin Valley dust storm lay in our path.

Jeannie carried Jeff in her hands as I drove through howling winds that peppered the car with dust and sand. Fortunately, the emergency pet clinic was less than a mile from our house.

As soon as we arrived, Jeannie and Jeff went back to the doctor's examining room. When they came out, Jeannie smiled weakly, her cheeks streaked with drying, dust-tinged tears.

"I think I was right about the owl."

She showed me a large, infected gash on Jeff's neck, now coated with antibiotic ointment.

Back at home, Jeannie took charge of her feathered little patient. Calling on all her nursing training and experience, she managed to get Jeff back on his feet and wings.

But as they say, every good thing must end.

Seventeen days after the poplar tree fell, our time with Jeff was over.

Jeannie, the kids, and I were in the back yard watching Jeff fly from one perch to another. Jeannie called him to her finger. She stroked his neck and talked to him with her bird-friendly voice before she tossed him into the air. He flew higher than he ever had, up and up over the roof of our two-story house, and out into a world he had never seen before.

He didn't come back.

Thirty-Two

Discovering North Idaho

In the summer of 1978, we took a long road trip from Bakersfield to Northern Minnesota for a family reunion. By then the kids were ages nine, six, and four. Matt no longer wore his helmet.

Kelly had done a school project where she wrote to the Chambers of Commerce of several smaller towns asking for information. Two of the towns were Pendleton, Oregon, and Sandpoint, Idaho. We laid out our route to pass through them. Of particular interest, at least to Jeannie and me, was the Pendleton Woolen Mill.

We spent the second night of the trip in Pendleton and took the tour the next morning. The kids weren't impressed with the tour, but they did like the car blankets we bought at the gift shop.

Sandpoint was a virtual unknown. I had made a motel reservation to spend our third night there. We had heard North Idaho was beautiful, but that was about it.

Near dark, we pulled into Sandpoint after nine o'clock. We couldn't see much of the town. The next morning dawned clear and spectacular. Breakfast in the motel restaurant treated us to a view of Lake Pend Oreille—huge and azure blue—stretching nearly to the horizon. It didn't take long for us to decide to scrap our planned return trip through the southwest desert in favor of coming back to Idaho.

From Sandpoint, we crossed Montana and North Dakota, passing through Grand Forks, where Jeannie and I met. We told the kids about our first evening together while I detoured through the UND campus. They didn't seem excited about that piece of history. All they wanted to talk about was the radio program we had listened to the night before as we drove into the early hours of the morning, a mystery-hour drama set in South America. The villains were vampire bats—big as crows— that sucked blood from the toes of their sleeping victims.

"Are there really vampire bats?" Kelly asked.

I couldn't help myself. "Oh, you bet." I looked at Jeannie. She wore a half frown, half smile, so I forged ahead. "The ones here in North Dakota and Minnesota aren't nearly that big. They're more the size of Jeff."

The conversation about bats went on for most of the next two hours before we pulled in at the reunion campground. Jeannie even stirred the pot with comments about how sneaky bats could be. The kids were atwitter, yakking back and forth about keeping their feet covered at night and what else they might do to protect themselves.

Sleeping assignments had already been made before our arrival. The kids shared a large bunkhouse with all the cousins. The grown-ups, by couple, got small, individual cabins.

Our three couldn't wait to tell all they'd learned about vampire bats as they scampered down to the lakeshore with their cousins.

* * *

By ten o'clock the last vestige of twilight had disappeared, and the campfire was down to its final s'more-making embers. The kids had been shooed off to bed and the grandparents were soon ready to call it a night. That left our generation to swap lies until we, too, felt our eyelids grow heavy.

When the time came, Jeannie and I crawled into a bed that was way too short for my nearly six-foot-four frame, and too narrow to allow much flopping room. Nonetheless, weariness from four days on the road coupled with a full belly sent me to dreamland.

Then I felt a thump on my back and heard Jeannie's urgent voice. "Jim. Jim. There's a bat in here. I can hear it."

My eyes popped open, waiting for her to pounce on me. She didn't.

I listened to pure silence. All I heard was a faint buzzing in my ears, coming from inside my head, until a loon-call echoed across the water.

I looked at the shadowy outline of Jeannie. "I don't hear anything."

"I heard it. A whoosh, whoosh, whoosh. It flew right over me."

Silence set in again. No whoosh. No anything.

"You must've been dreaming. Let's get some sleep."

A few minutes passed. "There it is again. It landed on the wall right above me." Her voice quavered. Moonlight reflecting off the lake came through the window and cast a pale glow on the wall above her. A calendar hung there.

I flipped back the covers, fumbled for my slippers, and groped for the light switch. When the light came on, I marched around the bed and thumped my finger on the picture of a beaver on the calendar. Adding, in my most authoritarian tone, "There's your stupid bat. Now, go to sleep."

Since I was up, I decided to use the toilet. It was separated from the sleeping area by a plastic shower curtain. I jerked back the curtain and . . . a black dive-bomber nearly parted the little hair still residing on my pate.

When I recovered from the shock of this sneak attack, the battle was on. Jeannie pulled the covers over her head, but I could hear her laughing. I scanned the room for a weapon. That fly-swatter won't do. Ah, there's a broom.

Whoosh, whoosh, whoosh. Swat, swat, swat. Jeannie laughing.

Finally—whoosh, swat, thud. Victory!

Jeannie kept laughing. She didn't cry. She just kept laughing. Neither the bat nor I did.

* * *

On the trip home, we retraced our route back to Sandpoint. We had three extra days of vacation to spend in North Idaho, but Jeannie didn't want to stay in a motel. She wanted to find a cabin (with no bats), preferably on a lake. We looked at a resort on Spirit Lake, about 30 miles southwest of Sandpoint. It was full-up.

"Have you tried Twin Lakes Village?" the proprietor asked.

"No. Where's that?"

"It's not on the map. Here, let me draw one showing how to get there." He took out a pencil and paper, talking as he drew. "Go back the way you came 'til you get to highway 41. Then go south about nine miles. There'll be a ramshackle place on the right called the Lightning Bar. Just past it, take the road to the right and that'll be it. They rent condos there."

The directions were perfect, and a one-bedroom condo with two pull-out couches in the den was available to rent. We fell in love with the village. It had a nine-hole golf course, tennis courts overlooking Lower Twin Lake, wild raspberries, and plenty of open lake frontage. Our three days there went by in a snap.

Before we left, Jeannie and I agreed to buy the condo above the one where we stayed. The owner was moving into a larger condo and offered us a deal that didn't require a down payment.
We could put the condo into a rental pool managed by Twin Lakes Village, but we first had to equip it to their specifications. Christmas vacation for the kids provided the perfect time to do that.

* * *

When vacation time came, we got a family room on the Amtrak from Bakersfield to Spokane, rented a car for the 40-minute drive to TLV, and shopped in Coeur d'Alene and Spokane for everything the condo needed. *Santa sacks* came with us on the train. We cut our own Christmas tree and decorated it with strings of popcorn and cranberries. The kids loved every minute of it, even the below zero temperatures.

Six years later, we were able to buy the up-and-down unit next to ours and tie the two units together by punching a hole in the adjoining wall. Grant Groesbeck, an architect and one of the founding partners of TLV, provided the materials and expertise for the job—along with much of the labor. Jeannie and I had met Grant and his wife, Nancy, on the TLV tennis courts and the four of us became fast friends.

Thirty-Three

Carden School

Jeannie scowled as if she was ready to punch someone—something she had never done. She pinched her lips so hard they almost disappeared. "That Miss Whitson makes me so mad. She didn't have Kelly read again today. I talked to her last week, and she promised she'd have Kelly read aloud every day. It's been a whole week and Kelly says she hasn't read a word."

A conference with the principal failed to produce a solution, but Jeannie didn't stop there. She went to the district office and spoke to a Dr. Something-Or-Other who suggested Kelly be tested for dyslexia.

"I'm going to take her to UCLA to be tested." Her tone told me the matter wasn't open for discussion.

UCLA confirmed Dr. Something-Or-Other's suspicion and produced a lengthy report outlining Kelly's learning limitations. Community college might be possible—on a limited basis—but nothing further.

Jeannie took that report to Dr. Something-Or-Other at the district office and looked none too pleased when she came home. "Guess what he told me. He closed the door and said, 'Don't tell anyone I said this, but the public school system isn't equipped to deal with her.' He recommended Carden School. It's way over in East Bakersfield."

I shrugged my shoulders. "Never heard of it. Have you?"

"No. But I'm going to check it out."

Check it out she did. Then she pulled Kelly and Brandy out of Franklin School and enrolled them in Carden. A couple years later, Matt joined them.

* * *

Putting the kids in Carden led to us meeting Bill and Avon Wonderly and their three children, Sally, Chandler and Anthony who also attended Carden. They were in the same grades as Kelly, Brandy and Matt, and they became good friends, as we did with Bill and Avon.

Despite the tuition payments Carden collected, a fund-raising lunch took place each year to keep the school afloat. The school administration had nothing to do with the lunch other than to take the proceeds. Parents organized the event, provided the food, served it, and cleaned up after.

One year, Avon and Jeannie took charge of putting everything together for the lunch. Avon enlisted her mother, Marie Amastoy, to participate. Marie was the proprietor of an eating establishment and watering-hole named, of all things, *Amastoy's*. She knew her way around food.

In Bakersfield, the menu for a fund-raising lunch is always the same: tri-tip, beans, salsa, salad, rolls and butter.

Jeannie volunteered to provide the beans.

When the time came for the lunch, Jeannie and her helper—me—drove to *Jake's Tex-Mex* to pick up the beans that the owner had generously agreed to provide. The pot must have been half the size of an oil drum. It barely fit in the back of Jeannie's mini-school-bus van.

The lunch came off as a complete success. The clean-up, not so much. Actually, the clean-up went fine. It was after everything was washed and dried that things unraveled. Jeannie picked up the serving ladle used to dish out the beans and put it in *Jake's* freshly washed pot.

Avon's mom—far from being a shrinking violet—piped up, "Where are you going with my ladle?" She pulled it from the pot.

"This is Jake's ladle. I got it with the beans." Jeannie grabbed the spoon end of the ladle.

The battle was on.

Marie gritted her teeth. "Do you think after all these years I don't know my own ladle?"

Jeannie dug in her heels. "I'm taking it back where I got it."

The ladle was at least two feet long. Marie had hold of one end and Jeannie the other. They pulled the thing back and forth with such force that had it been a lumberjack's saw, no log would have been safe.

Avon and I ducked for cover. "I'm afraid of blood," Avon said.

The test of wills raged on until Marie gave up.

Jeannie put her prize back into the pot, rounded up her cowering helper, and off we went to *Jake's Tex-Mex*. "Can you believe that? I wasn't about to not return their ladle."

When we arrived at *Jake's,* Jeannie hopped out of the van, popped open the rear door and pulled out the pot with the ladle rattling inside. She lugged her load to the door, pushed it open, and disappeared inside.

I waited in the van, certain she just had to tell the whole story to the owner.

A minute or two later, Jeannie came out with a look on her face that said, "*Oops, I made a big mistake!*" With shoulders hunched, mouth turned down, and eyes wide, she carried the ladle in her hand like it was a poisonous snake.

She opened the door and got in. "He said it isn't theirs."

Many smart-aleck remarks clambered to come out of my mouth. But in a rare fit of propriety, I resisted. Instead, I settled on, "What do you want to do?"

After a moment of silence, she said, "Let's go to Log Cabin. I can get a peace-offering."

I pulled up to the Log Cabin florist shop and waited while Jeannie went in to choose an appropriate gift. The ladle kept me company. Jeannie was not one to make her selection in haste. That gave me plenty of time to have an extended conversation with the ladle about what was likely to happen to it. It seemed happy to be going home.

* * *

We pulled up in front of Marie's house and parked at the curb. Considering what might take place, the presence of a witness was important, so I went to the door with Jeannie.

Marie opened the door and after Jeannie handed her the ladle and peace-offering, they both laughed. No fireworks. Marie invited us in. We had a nice visit and more laughs. When we left, Jeannie and Marie hugged. It was the start of an enduring friendship. From that moment on, Marie was no longer Marie. She was *Amachi*, Basque for grandma.

On many occasions thereafter, Jeannie and Amachi sneaked off to *Dewar's* ice cream parlor for a treat. Dewar's started making their own ice cream in 1909, and it's mighty good—as is their candy.

* * *

One fine spring afternoon I was sitting in my office, gazing out the window wishing I could play hooky and not deal with the work piled on my desk. Jeannie's van passed by. At least it looked like her van. A moment later our receptionist poked her head through the doorway. "Mister Brown, your wife is parked out front and wants to see you."

I couldn't imagine why she didn't come in like she had several times before. Our law firm was in a one-story building at the time – no security check or anything of the sort.

I walked outside and saw her parked at the curb with the passenger window down. As I approached, she slowly held up her left hand as a *stop* signal and pointed at her right shoulder.

There sat a hummingbird.

Jeannie spoke in a soft voice. "He's been riding on my shoulder since I left Carden. I think he's hurt. I'll see you at home." Then she raised the window and drove off with her little friend riding on her shoulder.

I double checked the work on my desk for any deadlines and convinced myself the work could wait. I wanted to hear the rest of the story. I told Saundra, my long-time assistant, "I've got to run home. I may or may not be back."

"Thanks. See you later."

The drive home took all of three minutes. I saw Jeannie's empty van parked in the driveway. I went inside and found her sitting on the couch, grinning. "Wasn't that something?" She let out a chuckle.

"How in the world did you get him on your shoulder?" I noticed that our large wrought-iron bird cage had been moved from the corner and stood empty with the door open. The cage had been home to a cockatiel several years earlier.

"I dropped the kids off at Carden and went to the office to talk to Mrs. Burger. I left the tilt-out side windows open. When I got back in the van, there he was, sitting on the back of the passenger seat. I thought he must be injured so I put my finger up to his legs – like I used to do with Jeff – and he hopped on. Then I put him on my shoulder and drove to your office. That's got to be at least six miles."

"Where is he now?"

"I put him on the swing in Scruffy's cage. He seemed to like it just fine until I closed the door. Then he went wild, buzzing around trying to get out. I was afraid he'd hurt himself, so I let him out and opened the front door. He flew right out."

"I wonder if he'll go back to Carden," I said.

"I hope he does. I'd like to see him again."

She never did.

* * *

When Sally Wonderly and Kelly graduated from Carden at the end of eighth grade, Kelly told us she wanted to go to Garces High School with Sally and several other Carden graduates. Garces is the Catholic high school in Bakersfield, geared toward college prep students. Admission required a prospective student to pass an entrance exam.

Jeannie waited until Kelly went to her room. "What if she doesn't pass? It'll break her heart." Jeannie most likely had the report from UCLA on her mind.

"Let's give her the chance," I said. "Running away from her dyslexia won't help."

We went up to Kelly's room and talked to her about our concerns. She wanted to take the test. She did. She passed.

We were then confronted with what to do about Brandy and Matt. The strength of Carden School came from the principal, Mrs. Berger, who unexpectedly passed away that summer. The Wonderlys decided to put Chandler and Anthony in Saint Francis, the Catholic grammar school in our neighborhood. Easy for them. They were Catholic. With Avon's help, Jeannie managed to get Saint Francis to accept our two Lutheran kids as well. Chandler and Brandy entered the sixth grade; Anthony and Matt the third.

Saint Francis was in for a surprise.

Thirty-Four

Jeannie's Introduction to the Catholic Church

Saint Francis School (and the Fresno Diocese) may think more carefully before letting another Lutheran family enroll their children. Matthew became the focal point of Catholic consternation that rolled up and down the San Joaquin Valley.

Martin Luther was about to celebrate his 500th birthday on November 10th of that year, a fact that was made quite well known at Our Savior's Lutheran Church where our family attended, and where Matthew was baptized. It was not an event of particular interest at Saint Francis School, or elsewhere in the Catholic community. Probably quite the opposite. Nine days before Luther's birthday, however, was All Saints Day.

To specially mark All Saints Day, Saint Francis School wanted each of the third graders to show up dressed as one of the Saints, wearing a placard bearing that Saint's name hung with a lanyard on their chest. Because of Luther's fast-approaching 500th birthday, Jeannie came up with the idea of Matthew going as Saint Martin Luther. She wasn't much of a student of church history. But she was a pretty good artist. The Saint Martin Luther costume she created was spot-on. So was the "Saint Martin Luther" placard with its purple neck-chord.

I did my best to dissuade her. "Probably not a good idea," I said. "I don't think the Catholic Church recognizes Martin Luther as a saint."

She squinted up at me from her sewing table where she was putting the finishing touches on a perfect Martin Luther hat. "He is too a saint. I called the pastor and asked him."

I shrugged. Not much I could do once she made up her mind—except look for cover when the fireworks went off the next day.

I should have told her to call Amachi.

Neither Jeannie nor I were there when the children marched into Saint Francis Church to pose for a class picture with Monsignor Leahy. But Jeannie got an earful when she showed up to help in the cafeteria at lunchtime.

"You were right," Jeannie told me when I got home. "They said the Monsignor almost blew a gasket when he saw Matt's sign. He made him black it out for the picture."

* * *

A month or so later, Jeannie came home from a shopping outing with a friend. "You'll never guess who I bumped into today . . . the principal of Saint Francis." She set down her bags and sat next to me on the couch. "He'd been at a meeting at the Fresno Diocese. Matthew was the big issue."

I suppressed a laugh. "The Martin Luther thing?"

"Yup . . . He told me about how the story made it to the Fresno Diocese where I guess it ruffled a lot of feathers. He thought it was the funniest thing to happen all year."

"He wasn't mad?"

"No. He was really nice. He said, 'Now we have a new Saint—Saint Blank.'"

After that, Jeannie became a quasi-celebrity at the school as she served lunches in the cafeteria and worked Bingo Night for the next five years. Every year on All Saints Day the story was retold with ever-increasing embellishments. She just smiled her coy, innocent little smile and went about her duties.

As the years passed, Saint Francis Church and its new pastor, "Father Craig" as Jeannie called him (even after he became Monsignor Harrison), played momentous roles in the lives and deaths that touched our Lutheran family.

Thirty-Five

Ski Boat

I may have mentioned earlier that Jeannie rarely expressed ambivalence when it came to how she felt about most things. "I love it," or "I hate it," often crossed her lips, especially when confronted with having to make a choice of color, style, or the like. She also had an innate sense of quality with respect to manufactured goods.

By marrying me, Jeannie had violated her iron-clad rule against taking a husband without a ski boat. Twenty years into our marriage, we had no ski boat, no rowboat, no boat of any kind. Not even a canoe. Things were about to change.

Elderly neighbors in our condo association at Twin Lakes Village had a boat they never used. For several years, it sat in their carport wearing a canvas cover. Another neighbor approached us with a proposal to buy the boat as partners. He and his family lived there year-round. He offered us exclusive use during our vacation. The rest of the year the boat was theirs. The price was right. And water skis came as part of the package.

Technically, the stubby thing qualified as a ski boat—if you considered the craft's age. When built, somewhere around the dawn of time, the designer equipped it with a post to which a ski rope could be attached. And the inboard engine generated enough power to pull a single skier. The tri-hull configuration gave it an English bulldog appearance and produced a ride akin to driving on a washboard road.

To Jeannie's delight, the kids learned to water ski our first summer as co-owners. She gave them all the tips they needed to get up, cross the wake, and turn back. Verbal tips, that is. She never got on a ski behind the ugly thing. In fact, the only time she water skied after our wedding came in the summer of 1965, pulled by her father's boat on a lake near Liberal, Kansas—and that was only once. Take that, Don Thorson.

* * *

Before we returned the following summer, our partners wanted to sell us their half interest in the yellow bulldog. They were moving to the Seattle area. The engine needed work, the man said, so he gave us a good price to buy them out. The engine needed work all right, work to lift it out of the boat and take it to a burial site. Jeannie and I then became the proud owners of a nearly powerless ski boat fit only to putt out to a fishing site or nap under its canvas cover.

Jeannie had never been a fan of its carpet and upholstery that proved hard to clean after landing a dozen or so trout. She wanted a fishing boat that could be hosed out. No carpet or upholstery.

Over the first winter of our boat partnership, while the engine still ran, Jeannie and I had visited a few boat dealerships in California. One was in Visalia, seventy miles north of Bakersfield. There we found a reasonably priced boat without carpeting. The salesman assured us the outboard engine had plenty of power to pull a skier. We said we'd think about it.

On the way out of the lot, Jeannie spotted a slightly smaller boat that looked totally different from all the rest. "What's that one over there?" she asked the salesman.

"A Montauk 17." He turned to me and shook his head. "It's way more than you said you want to spend."

"I'd like to just look at it," Jeannie said. She strode to the white boat with a center console and leaned over the side. "No carpet or upholstery. How much is it?"

He told us the price. More than double the cost of the bigger boat we'd been considering.

She raised her eyebrows. "Ouch, that hurts. Why so expensive?

"It's a Boston Whaler, Ma'am. Unsinkable. You can cut it in half and each part will float, even with you aboard."

"Will it pull a skier?"

"You bet. With this engine," he patted the outboard, "it'll pull two, no problem."

"How much for the engine?"

"Oh, no. It's included in the price I gave you. Same with all the boats."

She looked at me with longing in her eyes.

I gave her a *no way* shake of the head. "We'll think about that other one and get back to you." I shook his hand. "Thanks for the tour of the lot."

He didn't seem disappointed when we took our leave.

* * *

Throughout the winter and spring, Jeannie often brought up the subject of the Montauk. She *loved it.* I began looking for Boston Whaler dealers. I found one in Newport Beach, California, and one in Coeur d'Alene, Idaho. We took a drive to Newport Beach one Sunday afternoon to see if we could find a model in our price range. That was a mistake.

The Newport Beach dealership didn't mess around with piddly little boats like the Montauk 17. Now, if we were interested in a 27-foot Whaler with a cabin and twin 250 horsepower engines, they could help us. Or even an Outrage model like the Coast Guard uses. Ocean going vessels is what they carried.

Jeannie hooded her eyebrows and pinched her lips. "Maybe we can do better in Coeur d'Alene." Her *where there's a will, there's a way* persona came to the fore.

* * *

When we arrived at TLV to our fully-owned-but-nearly-engine-dead yellow ski boat, Jeannie spoke up. She pointed to the canvas covered hulk. "Let's see what Coeur d'Alene Marine will give us for this piece of junk in trade for a Montauk."

Our visit to CDA Marine earned us a demonstration ride on Lake Coeur d'Alene with the owner in his 27-footer like the one we saw in Newport Beach. He knew that this size boat was not what we had in mind. He just wanted to demonstrate how a Whaler performed.

When we were back on shore, he said, "Let me show you something." He took us to a storage building. In it stood a boat larger than the Montauk, equipped with every kind of electronic equipment then known to man. "I sold this to an executive at Sunshine Mine and outfitted it with all this gear. Then Sunshine went belly-up, and he couldn't pay for it. It's an Outrage 18, a foot wider and almost two feet longer than the Montauk 17. Much more stable and has more power than you will ever need. I can make you a good deal on it."

"We don't need all the electronics," I said before Jeannie could ask him 'how much?'

"I can take off anything you don't want."

"How much?" Jeannie got in her question.

He told her.

I gulped.

She furrowed her brow and made a bit of a prune face. "We'll talk about it."

Unless she held a winning lottery ticket in her purse, there was nothing to talk about. But talk we did.

I hauled the yellow bulldog down to him, told him the engine was shot, and asked what he'd allow in trade. He refused to lower the price but agreed to throw in a trolling motor with its own fuel system, mounted and ready to go.

Our vacation neared its end. Jeannie hadn't given up. "Can we buy it next summer?" she asked on our last visit to CDA Marine.

"If it's still here. Someone else will probably snap it up, though," the dealer said.

"What if we made payments over the winter?"

Somewhere along the line, he learned we lived in Bakersfield. "Here's what I can do. My son goes to college in LA. I'll be going down there in either October or November. If you can give me a down payment, I'll deliver it to you then.

Jeannie gave me *that look.*

"Will twenty percent down do it?" I asked.

He nodded, and I wrote the check. The next day, I dropped off the yellow bulldog.

* * *

Our new boat showed up in Bakersfield as promised, as did Jeannie's parents, Bill and Bertha. Since Bakersfield is not blessed with an abundance of boatable water nearby, we planned a Saturday trip to Bass Lake in the foothills of the Sierras for the Whaler's maiden voyage.

I hooked the boat trailer to Jeannie's mini-school-bus van which she had stocked with food for lunch and dinner along with various boating supplies. Bill, Bertha, Jeannie, Kelly, Brandy, and Matt climbed in the van. I double-checked the trailer hitch and we hit the road. The clear weather from Bakersfield to Fresno and up Highway 41 began to deteriorate near Coarsegold. A few flakes of snow greeted us before we reached Oakhurst. Then it began to snow in earnest.

With Bass Lake still a dozen or so miles away, and at a few hundred feet higher elevation, we needed a plan B. I found a wide spot to stop for a map-check and family conference. If we turned back, we could get to Pine Flat Reservoir by noon. The elevation there being much lower, we should be clear of the snow. Ayes all.

I reversed course and followed the winding road to our new destination. Rain accompanied us the whole way. At Pine Flat, we ate lunch in the van, listening to the rain pelting the roof. After I finished my sandwich, I donned a rain jacket, pulled the hood over my cap, and trudged down the steep boat ramp to what looked like an office where I could pay the launch fee. When I arrived, the door was locked and I could see no lights inside.

The climb back up the longest, steepest boat ramp I had ever seen convinced me not to back the boat all the way down. I could drive down to a wide, flat spot near the bottom of the ramp and then turn around.

Back at the van, I told everyone my plan and asked if they wanted to go boating in the rain. Ayes all again. I put the van in gear and crept to the top of the ramp.

"That looks awfully steep," Jeannie said. "Is it safe?"

Bill, an experienced boater, bailed me out. "That's what it's here for."

With my foot mostly on the brake, I inched down the slope to the turnaround spot. At the edge of the concrete ramp, a thin sheet of rainwater flowed by. At least it looked thin. A miscalculation of importance.

The front tires bounced through the supposed thin sheet of water, one at a time because of the angle of approach, but the back tires hit it together and didn't make it through the eroded gully. The van jerked to an abrupt halt with the trailer hitch resting on the edge of the concrete ramp. We were hopelessly stuck.

Bill got out, stepped on some slippery mud, and down he went, sliding halfway under the van. We pulled him out, all but Bill laughing at our seemingly dire situation.

I knew no one was in the office by the boat slips, but I recalled passing buildings less than a mile before we stopped to eat lunch. "I'm going to hike up the road and see if I can find a phone to call triple A."

"Good luck. We'll be here when you get back," Jeannie said. I had the feeling she wanted to say something else. Maybe, 'How'd you ever get so stupid?'

The buildings I remembered were closer than I thought. One was a bar and café. I went in and asked if they had a phone I could use.

"For local calls only," a sourpuss waitress said.

I put on my pleading face. "We're stuck at the bottom of the boat ramp. I need to call triple A."

A fellow at the bar turned around. "I have a four-wheel-drive pickup. I can pull you out."

"I don't know. It's pretty bad."

"Let's go take a look," he said.

"Yeah, let's go," said the lady next to him at the bar.

He led me to a four-door pickup with knobby tires and a stout trailer hitch. The guy and gal got in the front. I rode in the back. When he stopped at the top of the ramp, the fellow said, "I think I can get you out of there. We'll unhook the boat and I'll pull it up first. Then we'll see about what we can do with the van."

At this point, the woman embarked on a play-by-play commentary on everything he did, none of it complimentary. And none of it in language fit for church. She had the foulest mouth I had encountered since my days in the army. She disparaged him, his pickup, and every move he made. The air turned blue. He never responded. It was as if he didn't hear her. I felt so sorry for him.

I don't recall exactly how we got the trailer off the hitch on the van and onto the one on his pickup. But we did, and he hauled the boat to the top of the ramp where we unhooked it. The woman's off-color comments continued nonstop while he hooked up our van and pulled it free from the predicament I'd gotten it into.

When the boat, the van and his pickup were at the top, I got into the back seat of his pickup to express my thanks and to pay him for his wonderful help. He refused to take any money. "I'm happy I could get you out," he said. The passenger seat was empty so there were no vile comments coming from the gal.

I shook his hand. "You've been a gift from God. I can't thank you enough."

He then looked around and said, "Where's your wife?"

Jeannie was standing by the front of the van. "Over there." I pointed to her.

"Then who was that woman riding up here?"

My jaw dropped. "You thought she was my wife? I thought she was with you."

He roared with laughter. "No. I don't know who she is."

"You're a saint." I stuffed some bills into his shirt pocket and got out before he could give them back.

* * *

Long after dark, I backed the boat into our driveway and unhooked the trailer. Our new boat had to wait another day for her maiden voyage.

Sunday afternoon, we launched her at a local pond called Ming Lake. She did well. And no garbage-mouthed woman was in sight.

* * *

After the last payment on the boat, the time had come for Jeannie to have a car of her choosing. For more than a decade, she had driven a mini-school-bus van. Kelly and Brandy each had their driver's license and could get themselves back and forth from school. "Pick out what you want," I told her. "You're way overdue for the car you want."

Several months passed before she announced, "I found my car."

"Well, what is it?" I hoped for something other than a Ferrari or Lamborghini.

"I saw an article in a magazine at the beauty parlor about a car the Pope rides in called a Range Rover."

Until the day before, I had never heard of a Range Rover. Then, during a break in a deposition in Encino, I walked across the street to look at the showroom of a dealership that featured a Rolls-Royce Silver Cloud. I had never seen a real one, only pictures. After inspecting the British beauty, I walked across the dealership's lot on the way back to the deposition. In the last row of new cars, I happened upon one of the ugliest vehicles I had ever seen. What was the homely thing? I looked at the rear and said to myself, 'Hmm, I've never heard of a Range Rover.'

Now, Jeannie wanted one. That weekend, we took a drive to Santa Barbara to visit a Jaguar dealership that also sold Range Rovers. This being the first year Range Rovers were marketed in the US, I don't know if the dealership had actually sold any, but they featured one for sale. "I don't want that dark color. A white one will be a lot cooler in

Bakersfield," Jeannie said. Then sticker shock set in and we got something to eat and drove home.

The ugliness of the car had begun to grow on me, and I wanted to figure out a way to get Jeannie a white one (they called it *ivory*) for her birthday. She deserved to have her car. I placed a call to the Santa Barbara dealership. They could get an ivory one in six weeks and outfit it with a brush guard and protective grills for the headlights and taillights. Jeannie had shown me a picture of the guard and grills and said she *loved* the way they looked. Six weeks made it mighty close to her birthday, but it was worth the try.

I haggled the price down as low as I could and then paid a visit to my city league basketball teammate, George Barstow, who also happened to be our law firm's banker. George agreed to a finance package and I confirmed the deal with Santa Barbara, keeping Jeannie in the dark.

At four weeks the Rover hadn't arrived in Santa Barbara, and they had not been notified of a date for delivery. Same news a week later. Then, the dealer called. "We're supposed to get your car by Friday."

"Can you deliver it here by Monday afternoon at the latest?"

"If your car comes in Friday, we can make a Monday delivery." After a brief pause, he added, "But you'll have to come back for the brush bar and grill guards. They're coming in a later shipment."

"That'll work. My wife's birthday is Monday. She doesn't know about her present."

* * *

The surprise came off beautifully. At her birthday dinner I gave her the key in a little gift box, and she ran out to the parking lot of the restaurant to take a look. The add-ons came a week later. She loved her Range Rover for the next 19 years, driving up to Idaho and back at least 25 times, frequently pulling the boat. They looked like a matched ivory-colored set.

Thirty-Six

Oil Painting

In her mid-thirties, Jeannie decided to pursue something I knew had held her interest for a long time. She'd produced pencil sketches, more as doodles than art, for as long as I'd known her. But her painting had been limited to walls, ceilings, woodwork and the like.

"I think I'd like to learn how to paint," she announced out of the blue. "There's a senior citizen's class at Bakersfield College that meets once a week. Donna Rupert told me about it."

"You're hardly what I'd call a senior citizen," I said.

"That's what I told her, but she said it's for anybody. I'm gonna check it out."

The next week came and off she went. It was an evening class that met from six to nine on Thursdays, leaving me with kid duty.

About 9:30, Jeannie came in the door followed by a gust of chilly late fall wind and a few dry leaves.

"Well, how was it?"

Her face lit up. "I think I'll really like it." She set her notebook down and took off her coat. "It's just a handful of true seniors that sit at easels and paint while Donna walks around and gives comments. It's not really a class—more like an activity."

We went into the den where I had started the first wood fire of the season. Jeannie rubbed her hands together and held them palms out toward the fire and took a deep breath. "I like the crackle and the smell." She sat on the hearth and opened her notebook, then ticked off a list of items she needed before the next class.

* * *

The following Thursday, Jeannie loaded up her painting supplies and headed off to Senior Citizens' Art Class. True to her nature, she was supplied to the hilt. If the requisite talent went with her, she was equipped to paint the entire Sistine Chapel.

Jeannie's first painting

She returned that night with her first *masterpiece*. After clearing off a spot on the little table in the entry hall, she propped the painting against the wall. I recognized a blue bottle behind an apple and a banana. A blank background filled the rest of the canvas-board. For one of the few times I can recall, I did the smart thing my mother taught me. *If you don't have anything nice to say . . .*

Jeannie cocked her head to the side, chuckling to herself, as she studied the painting. "It's acrylic."

"What's that?"

"The kind of paint. I don't like it. Next time I'll use oil."

A not-so-kind thought ran through my mind. *I hope I don't have to hang that thing in my office.*

I didn't have to. But later my office walls held several of her magnificent oil paintings, as did most of the walls in our home.

Jeannie's talent grew, and also her collection of brushes, pallet knives, tubes of oil paint, easels, canvases, frames, books and magazines. She only attended Donna Rupert's class for a few months before Donna suggested she lash up with a group of true artists that got together in the back room of a local gallery. Jeannie followed Donna's suggestion and soon formed yet another group of friends. And her talent blossomed even more.

Because painting otherwise gave her an outlet for her creative talents without any commercial pressure, Jeannie tried all sorts of subjects and styles. One style she used is called *wipe-out.* This involved covering the canvas with a single color of oil paint, usually burnt umber, and then wiping away highlights until the subject appears. She finished these paintings by adding a few touches of color.

Butts & Putts

Somewhere along the way Jeannie saw a picture in one of her dozens of painting magazines that caught her fancy—three naked ladies (facing the other way) in a can-can line. The one in the middle was greatly broad of beam whereas the other two were slim and shapely. She thought a version of it with a golf motif fit the needs of the ladies' locker room at the Rio Bravo Golf Club. She titled it *Butts & Putts.* It still hangs there.

* * *

"I don't know what to do." Those were Jeannie's first words when she came home from playing in a golf tournament as a member of the Rio Bravo ladies' team.

"About what?" I said.

"Mr. Yu saw Butts and Putts. The girls were showing it around. Now he wants me to do some paintings for the clubhouse."

"That's great."

"No it's not. I hate painting on commission. I just like to paint for fun." She screwed up her mouth like she ate a bug. "He wants four… and he said he'd pay me five hundred dollars each."

That sounded good to me, but I didn't say so. "If you don't want to, don't."

She hunched her shoulders. "I didn't know what to say… but I kind of agreed to do it. I wish I hadn't."

Nonetheless, when all was said and done, those four paintings continue to adorn various walls of the facility. Here's one of them.

Rio Bravo 7th Hole

* * *

One summer in July or August, we were picking huckleberries at our favorite spot north of Lake Pend Oreille when Jeannie pointed up the slope and crouched behind the bush she had been picking. My eyes tracked in the direction of her finger-point and then I hit the deck, too. A bull and cow moose had stopped to munch on leaves and twigs no more than 25 yards from us. I could hear the chomp and chew.

We watched them for five minutes or so before their long legs carried them into a stand of fir trees and out of sight. I got back on my knees and with shaky fingers picked a few more berries.

"That was fun." Jeannie sat on the ground retrieving the huckleberries that had spilled from her bucket. "I want to paint one—a big bull moose coming out of the mist with some vegetation hanging from its rack."

"Why don't you? That Montana book the Kacks gave us has several moose pictures."

"I don't want to paint it from someone else's picture. I want to take it myself."

* * *

Jeannie's quest for taking a moose picture led to several outings, each to a location reputed to be moose habitat. One such adventure took us to the upper reaches of the Saint Joe River. No luck came our way during a long day of searching. We stopped at the grocery store on the way home to pick up something quick for dinner. One of our neighbors stopped us in the middle of an aisle. "You guys really missed it!" he exclaimed. "A big bull moose wandered down our driveway and took a nap right next to your back deck. He stayed there at least a couple hours."

"Just my luck," Jeannie said. She never painted a moose but the following pages show a few of her later works.

Farmers' Market

Navajo Boy (Wipe-Out)

Deer in the Woods

Clown

Hawk on one foot

Bull Rider (Wipe-Out)

Waves on Rocks

Brandy & Kelly Learning to Roller Skate with Pillows Tied to Their Butts

Jeannie's Great-Grandma

Thirty-Seven

No Slave to the Clock

"I'm sorry we're so late. It's all my fault."

I heard Jeannie say these words more often than I care to remember. Being late to social engagements was the norm for us. In the early years it tested my patience. I was ready on time. Why wasn't she? Tromping up and down the stairs didn't help. Nor did checking on her progress.

"Don't hover over me. I'll be ready when I'm ready." Her eyes remained fixed on the make-up mirror, eyebrow pencil or some other implement in hand. "The invitation said six o'clock."

"It's already quarter after six. It'll take at least fifteen to twenty minutes to get there." Most of the time I did my best to keep the irritation out of my voice. Most of the time.

"No hostess wants guests to show up right on time," she said. "It's best to be a few minutes late." Our definitions of *few* must have come from different dictionaries.

When all else failed, I retreated to my comfortable chair in the living room to wait for the sound of her footsteps coming down the stairs. Whatever the occasion, she looked great, and I made a point to tell her so. Sometimes through slightly clenched teeth.

"Are you ready?" It came from her lips as if she really didn't know I'd been ready since five thirty.

Then she followed with, "Did you lock the den door?"

"I did."

As years went by, my patience quotient reached the point where I bypassed tromping and hovering and went straight to my comfortable chair. Every once in a while, I even dozed off to be awakened by, "Are you ready?" and "Did you lock the den door."

People who knew Jeannie well, adapted in their own way, adjusting her invitation by thirty minutes to an hour. It was known as *Jeannie time.*

Attendance at school sporting events, particularly when our kids were in high school, suffered greatly. Not much in the way of parking spaces remained when we arrived after halftime. It made for a long walk.

On the bright side, I don't remember ever missing the end of any game.

The same can't be said for weddings.

One time, when son Matthew was a groomsman for a friend of his, we missed the entire wedding ceremony and went straight to the reception. It was well under way when we got there. Matt didn't seem the slightest bit surprised when he saw us come in the door.

Leaving on vacation presented two entirely different scenarios. Travel by plane fell into the same category as work. Jeannie was never late for work. And she was never late for a plane. Just the opposite. If the standard was to arrive one hour before flight time, she insisted on two. But travel by car allowed for open-ended flexibility.

* * *

Each summer after discovering North Idaho in 1978 we made a road trip to Twin Lakes. I gave Jeannie at least two weeks' notice of our departure date. "We're going to leave on the seventeenth (or whatever), bright and early," I announced with as much optimism as I could muster. As the date grew near, my ploy was to tell her I made reservations in Klamath Falls or Bend or wherever to give us a good day's travel.

By bedtime the day before departure, my hopes trickled down the drain. Jeannie sitting on the bed in the guest room sorting the clothes she might take drove me to the phone to cancel the motel reservation.

Sometimes the wheels didn't start turning until about six in the evening. One summer we pulled into the motel parking lot in Klamath Falls after sunrise.

Memories of the morning arrival in Klamath Falls caused me to grant Jeannie one full day for her final packing after the scheduled time to leave. That way we could get on the road *bright and early* the next day. Wrong.

My attempt at *Jeannie time* didn't work. Somehow, she dreamed up things that just had to be done around the house before we could leave. Whatever it was couldn't wait until we got back. I kept checking my watch. Maybe we can leave by ten. Then noon. Then two o'clock. Then *bright and early* tomorrow. *Bright and early* never came before noon.

One road trip to Oklahoma to visit Jeannie's parents set the record. We planned to leave Monday morning. That gave Jeannie the whole weekend to dream up projects for me to do that couldn't wait. None came. Instead, Jeannie worked on an oil painting to take to her mom and dad.

While Jeannie tended to her painting, I packed fishing gear, golf clubs, my stuff, the kids' stuff, and some of her stuff into her mini school bus van. Sunday evening came and Jeannie packed the rest of her things—or so I thought—and told me to put them in the car. I did. We were going to make it.

* * *

I got up early the next morning raring to go. Jeannie hadn't gone to bed. She stayed up all night redoing her painting. "You'll need to make a place for this to dry where nothing will touch it."

Out to the van I went and rearranged things to make a nice home for the painting. Ready to roll, I sat down on the back bumper to wait for Jeannie to bring out the newly painted canvas. Then I went inside to wait. Then I went back out to the bumper. Then it was noon and a carload of my partners drove by waving and making laughing comments about my early start to Oklahoma.

Sunset brought a cool breeze and a bit of chill after a nice warm day of waiting, so I went in the house. I didn't tromp or hover. I just asked, "What do you want to do for dinner?"

"Just go pick something up for you and the kids. I'm not really hungry." She was sitting at her easel, brush in hand.

I did as I was told, ate, watched a little TV, and went to bed. Jeannie kept at her painting.

The next day, Tuesday, played out like the movie *Groundhog Day*. I sat on the bumper. I sat inside. I went back to the bumper. My partners drove by waving and laughing. I got dinner for the kids and me, watched a little TV, and went to bed. Jeannie kept working on her painting.

Wednesday, Thursday, and Friday saw only changes to the painting, along with changes to the expressions on my partners' faces.

After dark on Friday Jeannie announced, "I'm done. Do you want to go to the Mexicali?" We sure did.

Saturday, at the crack of noon, we headed east to Oklahoma, a mere five days late.

Thirty-Eight

New York

"I have to take depositions in Missouri and New York next month. How about going with me?"

Jeannie looked up from the book she was reading. "I'd love it. But what about the kids?" They had two more weeks of school before summer vacation.

"Maybe your folks would like to come out and spend some time with them." Neither Jeannie nor I had ever been to New York or any of the New England states.

Jeannie put down her book and picked up the phone. I listened to her end of the conversation with Bertha. "I have a chance to go on a business trip with Jim to the East Coast. How about you and Daddy come for a visit and look after the kids while we're gone?" She turned to me with wide eyes and a big smile. "That's great. After we get back, maybe we can all go to Idaho and do some serious fishing."

I gave Jeannie a thumbs-up, and she went on talking to her mom about all sorts of other things.

Four weeks later, Bertha and Bill rolled in on a Friday evening with the same camper they had when we went fishing at Clear Lake 19 years earlier. The following Wednesday, Jeannie and I flew into Columbia, Missouri. Thursday's deposition went well and didn't take more than a couple hours to complete. That gave us plenty of time to explore the

University of Missouri campus, enjoy a leisurely dinner, and rest up for an early morning flight to The Big Apple.

We landed at La Guardia Airport Friday morning and soon found ourselves surrounded by a host of jugglers tossing various objects back and forth. They were in town for a jugglers' convention. Ducking the more dangerous missiles, we made our way to the ground transportation area and talked to a delightful young lady at a limousine desk. As true country bumpkins, we had no hotel reservation so we asked her advice as to where to stay.

"Rockefeller Center is good," she said. "It's right across from St. Patrick's Cathedral and close to Central Park."

We took her recommendation, and she called to reserve a room for us. We also took one of her limos which came with a tour-guide-like driver. The price was the same as a taxi.

Saturday, we visited St. Patrick's, ate breakfast at a sidewalk café and marveled at the towering skyscrapers.

Jeannie didn't like our hotel. "It's too plastic and chrome. Let's look for something more... I don't know . . . interesting."

After breakfast, we strolled up 5th Avenue to 59th Street, also known as Central Park South, peeked into the Plaza Hotel (where a small orange juice went for nine bucks), and browsed the hundreds of artisan tables lining the south wall of the park. Across the street from one of the tables was a hotel then called The Essex House. I recognized it from the *Ghost Busters* movie. When I pointed it out to Jeannie, her eyes opened wide. "Let's see if they have a room."

Dollar signs drifted across my vision when we stepped into the lobby. The place reeked *expensive*. I shook my head at Jeannie and motioned toward the door.

"We're here. I'll just ask." She marched to the reception desk. A minute or so later, she waved me over. "They have a weekend special. It's two nights for seventy-nine dollars, including a bottle of champagne and dinner for two at their restaurant."

We couldn't sign up for such a deal fast enough. The hotel got even when we decided to pass up our planned driving trip through New England in favor of staying five more days in the city.

During our time in Manhattan, we prowled the streets and avenues from Central Park to Time's Square. Rain showers came and went. Each time the drops fell, purveyors of umbrellas magically appeared on every corner. When it was dry, they tried to sell us knock-off Rolex watches. Street performers kept us entertained between visits to galleries and stores of all kinds.

Then Jeannie discovered the Metropolitan Museum of Art. She couldn't get enough of studying the works of the old masters. The day I took the deposition of the New York witness, we walked a few blocks to the museum. She went in and we agreed to meet there when I finished the deposition. The witness lived a short distance away, and the other lawyer and I had agreed to depose him at his apartment.

The deposition went long, not concluding until after 5:30, so I hustled to meet Jeannie. I found her sitting on the museum steps along with a few dozen other people watching performers on the sidewalk below. She waved me up, and I sat down next to her. "The museum closed at four," she said. "This has been going on ever since."

Together, we watched a mime and then a marimba player before a few drops of rain sent us on our way back to the hotel. The rain was coming down hard when we got to the lobby; a fine night to enjoy our free dinner, we decided.

With dry clothes and hearty appetites, we went down to the restaurant and dined as sheets of rain pummeled the window next to us. Our glasses clinked as we toasted our free dinner with free champagne. Unbeknownst to us at the time, about 450,000 people got drenched at the *Diana Ross Free Concert in Central Park* before lightning brought it to a halt. We had no idea the concert was taking place in the park right across the street from where we sat.

* * *

On one of our forays into the merchandise districts of Manhattan, Jeannie spotted a store selling oriental rugs. "I want to look at these rugs." The whole front of the store opened to the sidewalk. Rugs hung from tall ceilings and rolled up ones filled dozens of racks. One large hanging rug caught Jeannie's fancy, and she asked about it.

"Made in Iran. Every tuft tied and cut by hand. Only eight thousand nine hundred dollars," the proprietor told her.

"It's beautiful. But that's way too expensive for us," Jeannie said before turning her attention to another rug.

Over the next half hour, the man came back to her several times, lowering the price until his *final* ask was $1,800.

"We live in California. No way we can take it with us," she said. A picture flashed in my mind of the time in 1964 we climbed onto a bus carrying an $8 rolled-up rag rug on our shoulders to take to our Alameda apartment.

"I'll include free shipping." The man was now begging.

"We'll think about it." She took my hand, and we headed down the street.

I wonder if he'd take fifty cents and a Mickey Mantle rookie card.

That evening, we managed to get tickets to the Broadway musical *Cats*. Every time since, when I hear the song *Memories*, my heart does a little dance.

We were pooped when we stumbled into our room at The Essex House. The red message light blinked on the bed-side phone.

That's strange.

We hadn't told anyone we were staying there. In those pre-computerized days, I had to call the front desk to get the message. It was short: "Call Jermaine." No number.

"Do you know a Jermaine?" I asked Jeannie.

"What?" She was brushing her teeth.

"Do you know anyone named Jermaine?"

"No."

After we crawled into bed and turned out the lights, the phone rang. I answered. "Hello."

"This is Jermaine."

"Yes."

Pause.

"Are you James Brown?"

"Yes."

"From California?"

"Yes."

Pause.

"Are you associated with Richard Pryor?"

"No."

"I've got the wrong guy." Click.

Hmmm.

The rest of our New York experience included a concert at the Kennedy Center, huge sandwiches at the Stage Deli, an off-Broadway play, and being astounded by the number of diamond merchants on 47th Street.

When we got home, the kids didn't show much interest in hearing about our New York adventures—except for the call from Jermaine. Brandy went bug-eyed. Being a 12-year-old and the self-appointed president of the *Inter-Galactic Michael Jackson Fan Club*, she knew something we didn't.

"You talked to Jermaine Jackson! Really? You actually talked to Michael Jackson's brother?" she squealed. A one-on-one meeting with the President of the United States wouldn't have created as much excitement. "He was calling for *the* James Brown."

* * *

A few years later, business again took me to New York. This time Kelly went along. We stayed at the same hotel. When we talked to the concierge about tickets to a Broadway show, Kelly told her about the call from Jermaine.

"Oh yes, this is where James Brown stays whenever he's in New York," she told us.

A few days later it was time to check out.

As I was standing at the counter settling our account, I caught a glimpse of a large fur coat off to my left. I turned my head and there he was, close enough to touch, *The Godfather of Soul* himself. It took all my willpower to keep from blurting out, "James, call Jermaine."

Brandy's reaction when Kelly and I got home? "You should have!"

Brandy and Matt each had their turn to visit Gotham with me. They both rode the city's fastest elevator to the top of the World Trade Center and looked down on planes flying by.

After Matt's trip, I had no more business in New York, and didn't care to go back. *9-11* took away the luster.

Dr. John Young

I clicked the news on just in time to catch the sports. The lead story showed the UND logo.

"Hey, Jeannie," I called from the den.

"What?" She came in the room drying her hands on a dish towel.

"Cal State is playing UND this weekend. The winner goes to the final four."

We had to go. I stood in line to get tickets at the California State University Bakersfield (CSUB) campus while the three local TV stations interviewed excited students. When a reporter got to me, I had to admit my loyalty to UND. Boos echoed all around.

We arrived at the gym early—a rarity for Jeannie—but she wanted to prepare a small section in the stands for UND fans with green banners marking the four corners. Only Pete and Mary Lewis joined us—four UND faithful against the rest of the crowd. We didn't mind being outnumbered, cheering for each UND basket and giving the refs raspberries for each perceived bad call.

At half time, a man about our age asked if he could join the North Dakota rooting section. "I'm John Young," he said. We all shook hands with him and introduced ourselves. Before the game resumed, we learned that he was a doctor doing his residency at Kern General

Hospital. He not only had gone to UND, but he had also attended Williston High School shortly after Jeannie graduated.

UND lost. I blamed it on hometown refs.

* * *

Several years after the CSUB-UND basketball game, I had a bad case of the flu. Jeannie was convinced it had developed into pneumonia. "You need to see a doctor," she said.

I hadn't been to a doctor since the old guy I went to a couple times retired eight or ten years earlier. "I'll be okay." It was the manly thing to say even though I felt like I had been run over by a truck.

Jeannie took my temperature. "One-oh-two point five." She shook the thermometer. "I'm going to see if I can get you an appointment with that doctor we met at the basketball game."

A few minutes later, as I tossed and turned my sweat-soaked body, I heard the sound of her footsteps coming down the hall. "He's not taking new patients without doing a complete physical. They told me his earliest opening is next month. I had to use the Williston connection to get him to see you at five today."

Jeannie drove me to his office. Dr. Young did his physical exam—EKG, X-ray, blood and urine samples—the whole nine yards. He confirmed Jeannie's diagnosis of pneumonia, gave me a prescription, and said he wanted to see me in three weeks.

Three weeks later, I felt great. No need to go back to the doctor. Then a letter came from his office. He asked to see me in follow-up. I went.

"I wanted to feel your neck when you recovered—to make sure it wasn't from the infection." His fingers probed the front of my neck. "Yeah, it's still there. I'm going to call Darwood Hanse's office and set you up for a thyroid scan."

The thyroid scan was kind of an interesting procedure. I drank some form of iodine solution that the X-ray film showed as white dots in the thyroid. Dr. Hanse put the film on his view box and pointed to something in the white dots. "That's what we don't like to see."

"What is it?" My pulse picked up steam.

"Doctor Young will talk to you about it."

Whoa. I didn't like the sound of that.

What do I tell Jeannie? What do I not tell her?

I told her everything. The next day we went together to hear what Dr. Young had to say.

"There's a tumor in the right lobe of your thyroid," he said.

"What's the treatment?" Jeannie asked.

"Surgery."

"Is it cancer?" Her voice trembled.

"We won't know until it's removed and looked at under a microscope."

* * *

Our Idaho vacation took priority over a little knife-to–the-neck episode, so off we went with surgery scheduled the week of our return.

At age 46, my invincibility had taken a hit but I remained optimistic. Jeannie took it harder. "I don't think I can make it without you," she said as we packed for our return to Bakersfield.

"Everything's gonna be fine," I said. We hugged and then went back to packing.

* * *

Jeannie gave me a kiss before my gurney rolled down the hall to the surgery suite. The next thing I knew, a nurse was pulling a tube from my nose. "All done," she said. "You did fine. Doctor will be here in a minute."

My eyelids dropped back down.

The surgeon, who will go unnamed, must not have worn a watch. Either that or the nurse had no idea how long a minute is. More like an hour later, the doc came in wearing a pleasant smile. Jeannie was at my bedside looking at the dressing on my neck. The doctor didn't actually push her away—it was more like a nudge—so he could take a look.

"Pathology looked at a frozen section. It was benign." With that, off he went.

Jeannie watched him leave and then looked skyward. "Thank you, God."

After one night in the hospital, Jeannie drove me home. I sat in the den, watched a little TV and read the newspaper. Just before noon, the phone rang. Jeannie answered it and then held the phone toward me. "It's the surgeon."

"Hello. This is Jim."

The doctor's voice sounded subdued. "I just talked to the pathologist. He looked at the permanent slides and says it's cancer. He wants to send the slides up to Stanford."

"Why's that?" A lump formed in what was left of my throat.

"There's more than one kind of thyroid cancer. It looks to him like yours is a mix of two. He wants their opinion."

"How long will that take?" The lump grew larger.

"About two weeks."

"Okay." I gave the phone back to Jeannie to hang up.

"Well? What did he say?" I could see in her eyes she knew it wasn't good news.

"It wasn't benign. The pathologist says he thinks it's two kinds of cancer. He wants to send the slides up to Stanford."

She hung her head. "What do we do now?"

"Wait, I guess."

"How long?"

"He said about two weeks. My brain froze. I didn't ask him what else to do."

"Oh, Jim." Tears welled up in her eyes. She wiped them away with the back of her hand.

* * *

On Saturday, two or three days after getting the news from the surgeon, I drove to my office. Our library had a section of medical books. Scientists were still putting finishing touches on their invention of the internet, so this was the best source of information on thyroid cancer I could think of. I didn't like what I found.

A text containing a chapter on endocrinology listed three types of thyroid cancer. Two had good cure rates. The other was bad, usually fatal within a year or so. I dredged up what I could remember from my college statistics class. Only one chance in three I didn't have the bad kind. Reading a little further, the tightness in my chest eased up some. Of the three types, the bad one was the least common. I put my hope in that tidbit of information.

On the drive home, I rehearsed the order of information to relay to Jeannie. I hadn't told her what I was going to do at the office, just that I wouldn't be gone long.

She was out back watering the flowers and shrubs when I got home. "I have some good news," I said.

"Just a minute." She put a little more water on an azalea bush before shutting off the hose and joining me on the patio swing. "Well?"

"I looked up some information on thyroid cancer in our library. Of the three types, only one is bad . . . and it's rare." It felt like I was lying by omission, but I stopped there.

"How rare?"

"About two percent . . . and it usually hits people over sixty."

* * *

The report from Stanford provided welcome news. I had the two good kinds of thyroid cancer.

"We need to find a top-notch endocrinologist to tell us what to do now." Jeannie had lost all faith in the surgeon. He had suggested doing nothing.

"Okay," I said. "You use your resources. I'll use mine. Let's see what we come up with."

After a few calls to lawyers and doctors in the Los Angeles area, I found Dr. Andre Van Herle, the head of endocrinology at UCLA. By all accounts, he sat at the top of his specialty. With this little nugget in my pocket, I headed home thinking of Jeannie's hoped for approval.

She met me at the door. A smile lit her face. "I found the perfect doctor," she said, "Doctor Van Herle at UCLA. He can see us next week."

Forty

Goodbye Thyroid

The drive to UCLA to see Dr. Van Herle took longer than planned—an accident backed up traffic on I-5 to the foot of the Grapevine—so we had to forgo our stop at The Egg Plantation in Newhall, home of 101 different omelets. Fortunately, we arrived at Dr. Van Herle's office on time and spent only a minute or two in the waiting room.

With a slight Dutch accent, Dr. Van Herle got right to the point of our visit—what to do now? He examined my neck with fingers that seemed to have intelligence of their own. He then told us of a colleague in Georgia that did nothing but microscopically examine slides of the supposedly unaffected lobe of thyroid cancer patients. He found cancer present in over eighty percent of those cases. "There is no question that surgery to remove the remaining lobe is the most prudent option. Following surgery, I recommend radioactive iodine therapy to deal with any cancer cells that may have metastasized."

Jeannie looked at me with raised eyebrows. I just shrugged my shoulders.

"There's no urgency in getting it done. Both of your cancers are slow growing, and you need more healing time for the surgery you've already had." Dr. Van Herle closed my file. "Let me see you in a month. We can talk about it more then."

Jeannie and I agreed to follow Dr. Van Herle's advice but we didn't want the same surgeon. Once with him was enough. Again, we did our separate searches and came up with the matching results, Dr. Armando Giuliano, a surgical oncologist at UCLA. This choice received Dr. Van Herle's hearty endorsement.

* * *

"Try to get a room on the Wilson Pavilion," my partner Steve Clifford said when I told him of the upcoming surgery.

"What's that?" I asked.

"It's the 9th and 10th floors of the UCLA Hospital. All the Hollywood celebs and high-rollers use it. It has its own chef and fancy menu. You deserve it."

"Yeah, but how much does it cost?"

"I don't know. But I've heard it's worth it."

At the pre-surgery visit with Dr. Giuliano, I inquired about the Wilson Pavilion.

"Very hard to get," he said. "Usually booked up months in advance."

Bummer.

Dr. Giuliano then got down to his business. "Do you know if your surgeon saved a parathyroid?"

I had no idea what a parathyroid was let alone whether or not the surgeon saved one. Dr. Giuliano explained that usually there are two behind each lobe of the thyroid, each of the four about the size of a grain of rice. They control blood calcium levels.

"Thyroid surgery is a very bloody procedure which produces a lot of scar tissue," he said. "A parathyroid looks very much like scar tissue so it'll be hard to identify and save one from behind the lobe I'll be removing. What I'll do is take out everything and hunt for a parathyroid. If I find one, I'll mince it up and transplant it in your neck muscle, then we'll check your calcium every hour to see if the transplant took. You only need about an eighth of one to be okay. "

"What if you can't find one?" I hoped my voice didn't betray my nervousness.

"You'll be on daily calcium monitoring. If the calcium gets out of whack, your heart could stop. That's not good."

From Dr. Giuliano's office, we went to Admissions at the hospital to see if there was any chance of getting a room on the Wilson Pavilion. Lady Luck smiled down on us. A room reservation had just cancelled for the dates of my expected stay. The clerk checked my insurance coverage. "After what your insurance pays, your cost will be $80 a day for five days . . . payable up front."

That sounded like a good deal to me, so I gave her a check for $400.

From the hospital, Jeannie and I went looking for somewhere for her to stay. Directly south of the hospital, right across the street, we found a nice place that seemed perfect. It was clean and neat, had a kitchenette, and a comfy bed. And it was available. We reserved it.

Bertha came out to be with Jeannie while I was in the hospital. The facility where Jeannie was going to stay changed her room to one with two beds but no kitchenette. Here, the Wilson Pavilion came in handy. One of the perks it provided was food service for the patient plus one guest. Bertha could have the patient's meal. With a newly cut throat, I didn't think I'd be chewing much.

The hospital person who escorted us to my room on the 9th floor seemed pleased to let us know that the most recent patient in the room had been Rock Hudson. The two young men who came by shortly thereafter to take me for pre-op X-rays didn't seem quite so pleased to find a James Brown other than the *Godfather of Soul*. So goes life as a pseudo-celebrity.

* * *

The only thing I remember of the surgery is waking up with Jeannie at my bedside. "How does it feel to have a transplanted parathyroid?" She kissed my forehead.

"What?"

"Doctor Giuliano found a parathyroid and did what he said. It's in your neck muscle."

"Good." Then I went back to La-La Land.

Blood draws every hour to check my calcium levels were a pain in the arm, and then some. Sleeping in such short spurts, if at all, and watching Jeannie and Bertha chow down on lobster tail and prime rib got old fast. But after five days of it, Dr. Giuliano pronounced the transplant successful and said I could be discharged the next day.

On the way home, we stopped at a Marie Callender's, and I had a chocolate shake—my best meal of the last five days.

* * *

Our post-op visit with Dr. Giuliano introduced us to a cancer treatment I didn't know existed—a form of radioactive iodine called I-131. He told us that Dr. Young could arrange for it to be done in Bakersfield. Otherwise, he said I was doing fine. Then he added, "Several doctors volunteered to assist in your surgery . . . they wanted to watch a lawyer getting his throat cut." He patted my arm. "Just kidding."

Yeah, right.

* * *

Dr. Young set up another appointment with Darwood Hance who had done the thyroid scan that led to all this.

When I arrived at Dr. Hance's office, his receptionist showed me to a small, dimly lit room where the doctor sat behind a square table, about six feet by six feet. Next to the table, a metal chest much like an ice chest rested on a short stand that put the top of the chest at table-height.

Dr. Hance unlatched the lid of the chest. Dense fog flowed over the edges as he lifted the lid and reached inside with tongs that must have been at least two feet long. Up through the fog he extracted a lead cylinder and placed it near the center of the table. The whole scene reminded me of something from a Boris Karloff movie.

Again with his tongs, the good doctor picked the lid off the cylinder and removed a small cup. He placed the cup in front of me, reaching as far as his arm and tongs allowed. "Drink this," he said with no trace of a Transylvanian accent.

I wanted to run. But I drank it. It was cold-cold-cold.

Dr. Hance then gave me a pamphlet on I-131 and bid me good day.

* * *

"What happened at Doctor Hance's office?" Jeannie asked. She hadn't gone with me.

"It was strange . . . and scary." I handed her the I-131 pamphlet. She sat down to read it, holding up her hand, palm out, when I started to say something.

"You go up to the bedroom and stay there. Lock the door." It wasn't a request.

Trudging up the stairs it struck me as fortunate to be going out of town the next three days for depositions in Sacramento. The pamphlet said the I-131 would be excreted in saliva, perspiration, urine and feces over about a week. During that week, I was to double flush the toilet, do my laundry separately, stay away from children, pregnant women, and those who might be. And no kissing. The pamphlet said a lot of other things, but those stand out in my memory.

That night, Jeannie slept on the couch in the den.

* * *

In order to make good use of the travel time to Sacramento, I had booked a seat on Amtrak. I planned to prepare for the depositions during the six-hour ride. I knew nothing about I-131 when I bought the ticket.

Very few folks boarded the 6:00 a.m. train, none appeared pregnant or of child-bearing age, and there were no kids. I took a seat at the far end of the car and waved the conductor over. "I know you'll be picking up more passengers between here and Sacramento. Keep any women or children as far away from me as you can."

The look he gave me is hard to describe, so I won't try. Suffice it to say, I felt the need to hand him the I-131 pamphlet. He read it. Then he gave me a different look, one reminiscent of a drill sergeant glaring at a recruit who really screwed up. "Why are you on this train, mister?"

"I have to get to Sacramento."

He moved me to an empty baggage car.

The baggage car proved to be a good place—plenty of room to spread out my file material and no one to disturb me or worry about.

The train didn't go all the way from Bakersfield to Sacramento. It headed west at Stockton. The remainder of my trip was by way of an Amtrak van. My suitcase waited for me by the van where the conductor and the van driver engaged in an animated conversation. At one point, the conductor pointed at me with an extended arm and finger. "Get in the back." He really must have been a drill sergeant in a previous life.

Only one other person—I believe it was a man, but in any event not of child-bearing age—made the van trip with me. That passenger sat in the front.

The I-131 pamphlet stayed in my pocket for the next three days.

* * *

While I was gone, Jeannie double washed the bedding, towels, and every piece of clothing I might have touched—probably wearing gloves the whole time.

On my return, no welcome home kiss greeted me. The pamphlet may have said a week, but Jeannie didn't buy it. She gave orders to "double flush" and "double wash" for another week.

And "Stay away from the kids!"

Forty-One

Wife of a Trial Lawyer

I don't imagine it was easy for Jeannie to cope with being married to a lawyer who spent his career either in trial or preparing for the next one. But for me, she was a great asset—jury consultant, mock juror, cheerleader, and consoler.

"Don't you get nervous? My neck turns to rubber when I have to speak in front of a group, even my friends." She wobbled her head side-to-side to make her point.

"Not really. Certainly not like the first time I went to court when I worked for the Sill brothers."

Jeannie laughed. "That could have put you out of the lawyering business altogether, huh?"

* * *

During my last year in law school, while working for the Sill brothers doing legal research, investigation, and even fill-in secretarial duties, an unexpected assignment came from Lillian. When I arrived for work one afternoon, she told me the Sills' father had died unexpectedly in Pennsylvania and they were gone. "You'll have to cover a court appearance tomorrow morning for clients coming over from Nevada."

My socks almost caught fire. "I'm not licensed. I can't do that."

"It's okay. Robert will walk you through it. He asked me to call him as soon as you got here."

Robert Sill walked me through a land mine, one that could have—and should have—ended my hopes of ever practicing law.

I'm going to be disbarred before I'm even barred.

The risk felt out of proportion to the $1.75 an hour the Sills paid me. I told Jeannie what I feared might happen.

"Robert is the one to get in trouble. He's the lawyer, and *he* told you what to do." Jeannie opened her eyes wide and put on a plastic smile.

Clinging to that piece of wisdom, I left my seat unfilled at Hastings College of the Law and forced my feet to carry me into the Alameda County Court House and through the doors of Department 15. Lawyers—real lawyers—and their clients filled almost every seat.

Good. I'll get to watch what they do.

The bailiff called us to order, and the Judge entered. "Good morning," he said. Not waiting for the chorus of replies from the assembled throng, he addressed his clerk. "Call the first matter."

I couldn't believe my ears. My throat went dry. It was my case.

My briefcase increased in weight by about a hundred pounds as I lugged it through the swinging gate into the well of the courtroom and stood before the black-robed god.

The only snippet clearly in my memory from the rest of that ordeal is the comment the court reporter made when I addressed the judge. "Speak up, counsel," she said, not in a very friendly tone.

I'm not counsel. I'm just a lowly law student about to get into serious trouble.

I don't even remember meeting the clients. I must have because the judge ruled in their favor. And I wasn't arrested.

* * *

"Can I come watch you in trial sometime?" Jeannie asked me one day.

"I'd like that."

She hadn't come to watch any of my criminal trials while I worked for the District Attorney's Office, but after I went into civil practice—

and the kids were all in school—she wanted to and did. I treasured her feedback about the testimony of various witnesses and her assessment of the reaction of jury members to key facts.

Part of my standard trial preparation included giving Jeannie what I hoped was an unbiased overview of the case without telling her which side I was on. Sometimes I represented plaintiffs, sometimes defendants. She told me what she thought were the crucial facts leading her to her initial reaction as to who should win. Next came a series of *what ifs*. It might be, "What if this witness told a different story to (a friend, an investigator, the police)?" Or "What if the plaintiff didn't complain of injury until three days after the accident?"

The *what ifs* might go on for a long time before we moved to the *what abouts*. "What about the skid marks?" "What about prior complaints of the same pain?"

Then Jeannie asked me questions. These often opened my eyes to areas I had overlooked or thought unimportant. It's not unusual for a lawyer to develop tunnel-vision after living with a case for several months. Many-a-time I changed my approach to a trial based on what she thought needed to be addressed.

During trial, whether she came to watch or not, we discussed the events of the day. Trials have their ups and downs, good days and bad. No case is perfect. Jeannie could always tell how things had gone when I got home .

Good trial lawyers attempt to talk to jurors after a trial to find out how the jury came to its decision. I know I did and was amazed at how often Jeannie called it right on the button.

* * *

Jeannie was not fond of going to large gatherings of people she mostly didn't know.

One Christmas season, probably in the early '70s, the local Medical Society and local Bar Association decided to put on a fancy Medical-Legal banquet at the Bakersfield Country Club. It was not the kind of affair Jeannie felt comfortable attending, but the law firm I worked for represented the Medical Society, so as a young associate my attendance was pretty much mandatory.

Jeannie reluctantly agreed to accompany me.

My penance was to help select her attire. Whatever she was to wear must go with a pink knit shawl she dearly loved. "Do you like this outfit better, or this one?" I was absolutely no help, but proud of myself for not letting her see me checking the time. I knew how long it took her to get ready, and fashionably late departure time was fast approaching.

The clothing selection having been made, Jeannie began her hair and makeup routine, and I trudged down the stairs for what I feared was going to be a long wait. It was.

My patience in those years had not yet been fully developed. Jeannie viewed this as her long-range work in progress. In violation of an unspoken rule of patience, I casually walked upstairs and entered the bedroom. Jeannie sat at her makeup table, her hair up in pink rollers and an eye-liner pencil in her hand. "Don't hover," she said. "I'll be ready when I'm ready."

She went back to work with the eyeliner as I retreated knowing that we had missed the open bar and most likely the salad. But I held out hope for the main course.

Minutes raced by—the same minutes that at other times moved like tar—as I waited to hear her footsteps on the stairs.

"I'm ready." Then the click of heels on the wooden stair treads. "Did you lock the den door?"

"Yup." I hopped to my feet and told her how lovely she looked before hustling her out to the car.

Dinner was being served when we arrived. The hostess directed us to our designated places where full salad plates waited. There were probably eight or ten others at our table, only one of whom I knew. A server collected the empty salad plates from them. I nodded at the doctor I knew and introduced us to the others.

After dinner at this medical-legal affair, the master of ceremonies introduced the featured attraction of the evening, our guest speaker.

The distinguished looking gentleman was the Chief Justice of the Florida Supreme Court, or so we were told.

Jeannie listened to a few moments of what promised to be another painfully boring speech before she and another lady from our table excused themselves to go to the powder room.

While Jeannie was gone it became obvious this guy was no more the Chief Justice of any court than he was Superman. He was a comedian, a Don Rickles, only vicious—mean, not funny. At first, there was a polite ha-ha coming from here or there, but by the time Jeannie returned, mostly stunned silence filled the room, punctuated by an occasional gasp.

When Jeannie sat down, she had her hand over her mouth, sputtering through her fingers. Her shoulders were shaking. She shook her head back and forth as if trying to gain control. No luck. Finally she just burst out laughing in the stone-silent banquet hall. Silent, that is, except for the misguided attempts at humor by the "Chief Justice."

"What's so funny?" I whispered in her ear.

She didn't speak. Instead, she looked at the lady who went with her to the powder room. She was now laughing too. Jeannie opened her hand to show me a large, pink hair roller.

I shook my head, not having a clue what was going on. A man thing, I guess.

Jeannie managed to whisper, "When we got to the lady's room, she asked if I knew I had a roller stuck to my shawl. It dangled from the bottom like an ornament."

Jeannie survived the rest of the evening with only an occasional sputter, then laughed all the way home.

* * *

In 1990 the law firm was known as Clifford, Jenkins & Brown, comprised of around 18 to 20 attorneys. It was the firm's practice to give a special gift at the Christmas dinner to celebrate a lawyer having been on board for twenty years. My twentieth anniversary had come in June of that year.

Steve Clifford, the senior member and president of the firm, gave his usual welcoming speech and outlined the major accomplishments in the year coming to a close. He then looked at Jeannie and me.

"Jim Brown has been with the firm twenty years as of last June. We have a little gift for Jeannie and Jim. They are both avid golfers and neither of them have been to Hawaii, so this is for them" With that, he pulled a certificate from a large manila envelope and handed it to me.

I held it so Jeannie could read along with me. It said we could choose a week to spend at the Kapalua Resort on Maui and play six rounds of golf (two rounds at each of the three Kapalua courses) with all expenses paid by the firm. It also provided a car so we could explore Maui when not on a golf course.

He couldn't have chosen a better gift.

* * *

Our firm's Christmas dinner was an affair Jeannie didn't mind going to. The week at Kapalua proved to be even better than we could have hoped.

When we landed on Maui, collected our golf clubs and luggage, and picked up our rental car, we had no idea what our accommodations would be like at the resort. I think we both pictured a hotel room with entry from a hallway and maybe a small balcony. Wrong!

We were provided a villa overlooking the ocean with a large lanai complete with a hammock and lounge chairs. Lots of friendly geckos scampered around. None of them tried to sell us insurance. Our golf clubs and shoes were taken to the course we were to play in the morning. We asked for the earliest possible starting time to give us the rest of the day to explore the island.

At 6:30 the following morning, a driver took us to the Bay Course where our clubs waited on a golf cart. We checked in and were introduced to our playing companions, a nice couple from Texas. The beauty of the surroundings made it difficult to concentrate on golf, but we suffered through the morning—and five more days just as wonderful.

The Plantation Course, where the PGA kicked off each new year with the televised Sentry Tournament of Champions, proved to be the toughest—especially when the wind blew hard. The severity of the slopes can't be appreciated on a TV screen, most notably the 16th fairway.

Under the best circumstances, Jeannie was not to be trusted driving a golf cart. But she wanted to, so she did.

The first of the two times we played the Plantation course, we faced squalls of rain followed by blue sky and sunshine on almost every hole. By the time we reached the 16th, the grass was wet and slippery. Jeannie aimed the cart straight down the roller-coaster-like incline. We went faster and faster. She hit the brakes. The cart spun clockwise. Two and a half revolutions later we coasted to a backwards stop, facing uphill.

Here came the other couple. "Don't hit the brakes!" Jeannie cried. The wind swallowed her words. The man hit the brakes. Round and round they went, sliding to a stop facing us. Only inches separated the carts when theirs came to a stop. Stunned silence and deep breathing followed. Jeannie was the first to laugh. Then we all joined in.

I'm sure we finished the round. I know we rehashed the near disaster over cool drinks at the clubhouse, keeping our voices low so no one could overhear.

The week surpassed our wildest dreams—and foreshadowed another golf cart episode.

* * *

In truth, it was an accident—unintentional, or so I tell myself—that happened on the sixth hole of the Rio Bravo Golf Course in Bakersfield. Jeannie and I were playing as a two-some when a single golfer caught up to us.

Jeannie looked back at him. "Let's let him play through."

"Yeah," I said.

I drove the cart over to the side and parked behind some trees. We waved him up, and as he prepared to hit his shot I got out of the driver's seat, selected my club, and stood in front of the cart ready to walk out to my ball as soon as the other fellow passed by.

Jeannie, meanwhile, decided to operate the cart from the passenger seat. As she watched the ball of the other player land just short of the green and thinking I had moved—or so she claimed—she cranked the steering wheel and reached out her left foot to tromp on the accelerator.

BAM!

Down I went.

"Oh, no!" she shouted.

THUMPITY-BUMPITY-BUMP!

The cart bounced over my legs. My ankle cracked. My Mind raced. What in the world is going on? With what turned out to be a fractured ankle, I had to finish the next three holes on one leg.

"I was trying to hit the brake," she insisted—then, and every time she told the story thereafter.

I believed her, and I still do, even though I threatened to sue her for everything we were worth.

Forty-Two

Tennis

In 1973, a few months after we moved into our home on 20th Street, Jeannie signed up to be on the waiting list for membership at the family-friendly Bakersfield Racquet Club. None of us played tennis. Jeannie wanted to have a safe place for the kids to swim. The Racquet Club provided two pools, each with a lifeguard. One was shallow for smaller children. The other was deep and had a diving board.

More than three years later, her name made it to the top of the waiting-list, and we were in.

The first weekend of our membership, we took the kids on a leisurely seven-block walk to the Racquet Club so the little ones could enjoy the water while we checked out the adequacy of the lifeguard supervision. The lifeguards didn't disappoint. They kept on top of all the activity, blowing a whistle if someone violated the no running rule or otherwise misbehaved.

"Let's check out the pro shop," Jeannie said after the kids had splashed around a while.

"You go ahead." I had found a comfortable lounge-chair in the shade.

She went. An hour or so later she came through the gate to the pool area carrying a bulging sack. "They have really nice things in there." One by one, she pulled out her treasures and held them up for me to respond every time she said, "Isn't this cute?"

"But we don't play tennis," I protested at the sight of tennis outfits for each of us.

"I ran into Jack Cantrell in the pro shop. He said we really should." Jack taught our adult Sunday school class and coached the East Bakersfield High School tennis team.

After a couple second's thought, I said, "I'm game. Are you?" I didn't know how my recently repaired knee would hold up, but it was doing fine with jogging a mile or two each morning.

"Sure." She swung her arm as if smacking a forehand—a precursor of things to come.

Jack came into the pool area to say hello. He agreed to give us an introductory lesson Monday evening after I got off work.

Monday evening came. We donned our new tennis duds and headed to the club. Jack beat us there, waiting with two, old, small-headed racquets and a bag of practice balls. "Ready to go?" He held the racquets out to us as we walked to the lesson court.

Jeannie clapped her hands. "We're ready if you are."

For the next hour, Jack tossed balls to us, first to Jeannie and then to me. "Let it bounce. Then try to hit it back to me." After going through his bag of practice balls the first time with none coming back to him, he came around the net and showed us the proper way to grip the racquet. He then told us to pick up the balls that were scattered around the court—and a few that had sailed over the fence.

The second time through the bag, Jeannie nailed Jack in the chest with a wicked forehand. "Atta girl! See if you can do that, Jim." Jack rubbed his chest and tossed me a ball. I hit it into the net.

With that first lesson, we were hooked. Several times a week Jeannie and I took the kids to the pool and then hit the court to bat balls back and forth to each other. Eventually we tried playing real games. The one with the fewest double faults always won.

"I think we need lessons on how to serve," Jeannie said. "Let's talk to Andy."

If a finer man than Andy Davidson ever existed in my lifetime, I never met him. As the teaching pro at the Racquet Club, he had a way with newcomers—especially youngsters—his coaching inspired without criticism, including comments like, "We want to do this." He never said "No, don't do that." If a ball went flying over the fence out into the street, he'd say, "Whoops, the wind got that one."

His style worked exceptionally well. I later learned—not from Andy —that two boys and two girls he coached won multiple national junior tournaments and then went on to play professional tennis at the highest level. One boy later became the captain of the US Davis Cup team.

In spite of his coaching successes, Andy remained humble. He worked just as hard with a certain girl who couldn't manage to win a single match after playing in numerous novice tournaments. That girl was our daughter, Kelly.

In practice, Kelly had nice smooth strokes and hit the ball well. When confronted with an opponent in a real match, her strokes became tense and choppy. But despite losing every match for nearly two years, she kept a good attitude and continued to practice.

The summer after Kelly finished eighth grade, and we returned from our Idaho vacation, Andy called Jeannie. "I've found a girl Kelly can beat in the tournament this weekend." Jeannie signed Kelly up with Andy's assurance that her first match was against this girl.

As Kelly and her opponent, Tara, warmed up for their match, two things became obvious. First, Tara had never played a real match. And second, she moved like a good athlete.

The girls played what is called an *eight-game pro set*, meaning the first to win eight games, being ahead by two, won the match. If the score reached eight games to eight, the match was decided by a tiebreaker.

Even with her choppy and tense strokes, Kelly moved out to a six-games-to-one lead over Tara. Then things changed. Tara played better and better as the match went on. Kelly's lead shrunk to seven-games-to-six. If Kelly won the next game, the taste of victory awaited her for the first time. If not, it looked like Tara was on her way toward winning her first match and adding one more to Kelly's losing streak.

Non-stop cheering and coaching by Tara's parents contributed to my—and I'm sure Jeannie's—anxiety over the prospect that Kelly was about to snatch defeat from the jaws of victory. These folks, from a town forty miles to the north, obviously had not gone to *Etiquette Class for Tennis Parents* (ECTP). ECTP teaches that a parent is to remain silent during the match. The only exception is to politely clap for a winning shot by either player. Parents are never to clap or cheer for a bad shot by their child's opponent. Tara's mom and dad violated all the rules and were subject to being thrown into ECTP Prison.

Actually, there is no ECTP. Parent etiquette is learned by observation. Tara's mom and dad weren't very good observers.

Kelly slapped her thigh before each point of the crucial game and pulled out the victory after a tough battle. She came off the court beaming, a changed player. Her smooth practice strokes made their appearance and she won her next match, and the next, and then won the whole tournament.

Jeannie and I did our best to not act giddy around the other players' parents. As happy as we were for Kelly, I believe Andy felt just as much joy—and relief. He gave Kelly a big hug. "I knew you could do it."

The five years that followed Kelly's first win saw her play on four Valley Championship teams at Garces Memorial High School and a conference championship team at Bakersfield Community College. She also worked for Andy Davidson at several tennis camps, teaching little ones the game.

Thank you, Andy.

Kelly & her doubles partner Tina Pineda

Forty-Three

Kelly to Moscow

For years, Jeannie and I tried to plant seeds in the minds of our children that the University of North Dakota was *the place* to go after high school. Only weeds sprouted. Snow was suitable for skiing as far as the kids were concerned. Nothing else.

Next, we focused on the University of Idaho, hoping to find more acceptance of snow only two hours south of Twin Lakes Village. Several times on either our drive up or back from summer vacation we took them through the U of I campus. One of those times we stopped to visit the daughter of church friends from Bakersfield. Without our asking, she told the kids how much she loved the school, the city of Moscow, and the ease of making new friends.

Kelly maintained her resistance to leaving Bakersfield, let alone California. She had her heart set on returning to Bakersfield Community College and playing again on the tennis team. We still had a few more years to work on Brandy and Matt.

* * *

About the middle of August, our vacation neared its end. We decided to play a few holes of golf before pulling the Whaler out of the water for our trip home. Sometimes strange things happen on a golf course.

As Kelly prepared to tee-off on the second hole, she looked at Jeannie. "I don't want to go back to BC. I'd like to go to the U of I."

Jeannie raised one eyebrow. "Where did that come from?"

"I've been thinking about it for a while."

I had trouble believing what I heard. "It's a little late for this year. Maybe second semester."

Jeannie maintained her charter membership in the *Where There's a Will There's a Way Club* for just such circumstances. "Let's stop there tomorrow and see." She held her hands in a praying position.

We got off to our typical early morning start the next day—after 2:00 p.m.—making it doubtful the Admissions Office would still be open by the time we found it. At about 4:30 we spotted what looked like the right building. I pulled to the curb—which someone must have accidentally painted red. Jeannie and Kelly hopped out and scurried to the door. It opened. Jeannie turned, grinned, and gave a thumbs-up.

Fifteen minutes of anxious waiting at the blood-tinged curb caused me to suspect that progress was being made inside. It was.

Before long, Kelly came out with arms raised in victory. Jeannie followed clutching a fist-full of papers.

"Classes start in two weeks." Kelly clapped her hands before clicking her seatbelt.

Jeannie waved the bundle of papers. "There's a whole bunch of stuff we have to get done in a hurry to get her enrolled."

She filled me in on the way south toward Lewiston.

The easy stuff, transportation and payment, fell to me. Jeannie and Kelly would take care of the paperwork: application, transcripts from Garces and BC, medical clearance; and paring down what Kelly wanted to take with her. The last proved to be the most problematic. Commercial transportation couldn't handle what Kelly and her mom deemed essential.

Fortunately, the transportation chairman—me—had the solution. A client of one of my partners owned a twin-engine, six-place Cessna. He also had a stand-by pilot. The client wanted to sell the plane and the pilot as a package deal. My partner specialized in putting deals together. And he had a brother that wanted in on it and the resources to do it.

We could use the plane to move Kelly and her *essentials* to Moscow. In order to accommodate these essentials, the liquor bar that occupied the rear of the passenger compartment and two passenger seats needed to be removed. That space, together with the nose compartment, the two wing compartments, and our laps had to hold everything Kelly needed.

** * **

The day of departure came. Off we went into the wild blue yonder. All the way to Winnemucca, Nevada, where we stopped for lunch and to take on fuel. The added weight of the essentials didn't allow the plane to carry a full load of gas and still get airborne.

Onward we flew to the Moscow-Pullman Airport, surviving thermal bumps as we passed over mountain ridges. The U of I campus on the right, and the Washington State University campus on the left sparkled in the afternoon sun. The schools were only eight miles apart, with the little airport midway between.

The smooth landing—a *greaser* the pilot called it—released the tension in at least thirty white-knuckled digits. There may have been more on our toes. I didn't check.

With our feet safely on the ground, we loaded Kelly's essentials into a commercial van that met us on the tarmac. The pilot had arranged for the van to be there. From the airport we headed to the dorm. The van driver knew the way.

Jeannie, Kelly, the pilot, and I lugged the cargo up several flights of stairs to Kelly's room. The van driver took a nap.

The next day, we bid Kelly goodbye. Jeannie's eyes watered up but she didn't cry when promising Kelly we would be back for Parents' Day.

"That's just five weeks away. I'll be fine." Kelly gave her mom and me her usual bear hug, squeezing until ribs popped.

** * **

Any excuse to spend more time in Idaho was a good one, so Jeannie and I drove from Bakersfield to Moscow for Parents' Day, planning to spend the next few days at Twin Lakes.

As part of Parent's Day, the U of I provided a nice dinner along with an abundance of mostly useless information. Useless for us, that is, since we lived over a thousand miles away.

A couple from Idaho Falls shared our table at dinner. "We just got some terrible news," the mom said. "Our daughter at home got in an accident driving this one's car." She pointed to a blonde girl sitting in the new student's section. "She's furious . . . no one was hurt, just the car."

Jeannie looked at me and rolled her eyes. "Can you imagine if Brandy wrecked Kelly's car?"

Forty-Four

The Phone Call

Not long after we returned to Bakersfield from Parents' Day and a few days at Twin Lakes Village, I was at my office in the evening trying to clear my desk of work that had piled up while I played hooky.

My phone rang. The caller was a police officer who informed me that Brandy had been in an accident and was being transported by ambulance to San Joaquin Hospital. He had no other information. My heart sent a staccato pounding through my chest.

When I tried to reach Jeannie, the phone rang and rang with no answer. I double-timed to the elevator and punched the down button. The elevator came but took its sweet time in doing so. I prayed for no stops on the way down. My prayer answered, I hustled to the parking garage and jumped into my car. I tried to keep my speed and pulse to something under ninety on the short drive to the emergency entrance at the hospital.

The ambulance rolled up just as I did. EMTs pulled out a Stryker frame with Brandy strapped aboard and took her inside. Blood covered her face and chest, her head was secured by a strap, and a brace supported her neck. Other straps crossed her waist and legs.

Did she have a spinal injury? Was she paralyzed?

My legs wobbled. My throat grew cotton. Then I spotted Greg Pineda at the far end of the hall—Dr. Greg Pineda, a neurologist.

Greg's daughter, Tina, had played four years of high school tennis as Kelly's doubles partner. His wife Anne frequently teamed up with Jeannie as partners in women's events at the Racquet Club.

"Greg," I shouted, not caring what I might be interrupting. "Can you take a quick look at Brandy?"

He waved off the person he was talking to and jogged down the hall. "What happened to her?"

"Car wreck." Acid rose in my throat.

I stepped aside to give him room. He checked her eyes and mouth, had her squeeze his fingers with each hand, asked her to wiggle her toes, and then patted her on the knee. "You're going to be okay. You have a cut in your mouth and a loose tooth—and a broken toe."

Greg then turned to me. "All that red stuff on her is a mixture of tears and blood from the cut in her mouth. All her sensations are intact."

A long, slow breath escaped my lungs before I thanked him. He then went back to what he had been doing.

Jeannie still didn't answer the phone.

Brandy mumbled something about being sorry for wrecking Kelly's car.

Hospital personnel wheeled a gurney past us. On it lay the passenger who had been with Brandy. A few minutes later the driver of the other car rolled by on another gurney and disappeared behind a curtain. I could get no information about their injuries at the hospital. I had to wait until we were sued.

* * *

Although we called it Kelly's car, the title named Jeannie and me as owners. As such, we fell victim to the legal concept of *negligent entrustment*. To put it simply, if we allowed someone known to us to be a negligent driver to operate the car, we became legally responsible. If put under oath I couldn't deny my knowledge of Brandy's shortcomings as a driver.

The lawsuit came, naming Brandy, Jeannie and me. I knew the lawyer suing us. I didn't care for him all that much before he sued us and developed even less fondness for him after. He represented Brandy's friend who had been in the car with her. Perhaps *former* friend may be more accurate.

Brandy had been showing earrings she had just bought to her passenger and didn't see the traffic light turn red. She smashed into a car that had the green light. The driver of that car settled directly with our insurance company. Brandy's friend who really had no serious injuries should have done the same but decided to sue us instead.

Fortunately, the suit against us settled before either Jeannie or I were put under oath. Brandy still had to face the wrath of her sister.

Not too many weeks later, Jeannie greeted me at the door with a frown and two letters in her hand. "You'll never believe this." She handed the letters to me.

Both letters were from Allstate, our auto insurance carrier. The first one bore the signature of the president of the company thanking us for being 25-year customers. The second cancelled our policy. Something about the left hand and the right hand came to mind.

I called the head of Allstate underwriting and managed to gain his agreement to reinstate our policy (with an exclusion of Brandy as a driver). The fact that Allstate had recently retained me to defend about twenty of its insured drivers, and my suggestion that they think about transferring those files to a new attorney, might have played some role in his decision. Maybe not.

Forty-Five

Hair

In keeping with her long-standing desire to become an actress, Brandy devoted most of her time at Bakersfield Community College (BC) to theater related activities. "I'm going to be a star," she said—many times.

She had the lead female role in several plays, one of which had her on stage for the entirety of all 17 scenes. Jeannie and I attended every performance of each play she was in. I was a typical nervous parent the first time—for all of about two minutes. After that, I was hooked on her character, the one that made me laugh and made me cry. She was good.

Then came *Hair.*

It was the 25th anniversary of the Broadway opening of the love-rock "Age of Aquarius" musical. In 1990s Bakersfield, *Hair* remained controversial for its glorification of drugs and sex, but even more-so because of its full-frontal nude scene of the entire cast at the end of the first act.

When it was announced that BC was going to present a three-night performance, a moderate uproar ensued in town, fueled mostly by parents of theater-arts students. After an agreement was reached to eliminate the nude scene, Brandy joined the cast with our reluctant blessing.

Rehearsals went on for several weeks before Jeannie told me the theater-arts department reneged on the agreement. "They claim they're entitled to *academic freedom*," she said. My jaw and fists clenched. I wanted to punch them in their academic freedom.

Instead, I met with the BC President to get his take on the situation before I got myself in trouble. I left the meeting with my blood boiling more than ever. The President claimed his hands were tied, by what he couldn't quite explain.

Jeannie and I weren't alone in our anger. The former moderate uproar exploded beyond parents of BC students to the city at large. Criticism of the decision to include the nude scene dominated local talk radio. TV news covered it. Letters to the editor joined in. If any in the community supported the nude scene, their voices weren't heard.

In response to the growing opposition, the BC folks backed off a tiny bit and a new agreement was reached with the objecting cast members. Out of approximately twenty, all but Brandy and two others were fine with the prospect of appearing in their birthday suits. Brandy and the two other dissenters were allowed to lie on the floor, fully clothed, behind the riser holding the nude cast members.

Opening night came. All three local TV stations brought camera crews and reporters. BC officials barred the cameras from entering the packed theater. As the first act approached its climactic end, the stage went dark. Clothing was shed with a mild rustling sound in the otherwise stone-silent auditorium, followed by the pitter-patter of bare feet as the naked cast lined up. FLASH! The lights ignited the stage with an almost blinding brilliance for less than a second. Total darkness returned and the first act was over.

Jeannie, Kelly, and I went outside for intermission. Jeannie and Kelly sought out the powder room while I looked for a drinking fountain. On my way to get a drink, a reporter and her camera-man approached to ask me what I thought of the nude scene. "Totally stupid and unnecessary," I said. End of interview.

One-by-one, we made our way back to our seats. Jeannie leaned across Kelly and whispered, "I was interviewed by a reporter."

"So was I," Kelly said. "He wanted to know about the nude scene."

"That makes three of us." I shook my head.

After the performance, we hurried home to catch the late news, flipping from channel to channel. It turned out we were the only three interviews that were shown—maybe the only three actually interviewed. We all gave pretty much the same comment. None of us were asked if we were related to a cast member, let alone one of those objecting to the nude scene.

For the first time in Brandy's BC acting career, we skipped the remaining two performances.

* * *

Sometime during Brandy's third year at BC, the theater-arts students received notice of a mass audition to be held in Las Vegas. Brandy liked the idea of going to Las Vegas but had no interest in the mass audition concept. She declined to sign up. But one of her classmates needed someone to read part of a scene. She talked Brandy into going along and reading the part.

The whole gang from BC got on a bus and left Bakersfield in the dust.

At the first day of auditions, Brandy helped out her friend. Afterward, one of the BC theater-arts staff that went on the trip told Brandy the judges loved her and wanted to see her do something on her own. She was given a scene to memorize for the following day.

When Brandy got back from Las Vegas, Jeannie asked her how it went.

"I wasn't going to do it, but thought 'what the heck', so I did a scene of my own." She made a silly face and held up her hands. "I blew it . . . but I was the only one of our group to get a call-back."

"What's a call-back?" I asked.

"If they like what you did and want to see you do more."

"Who called you back?"

"The judges, I guess."

"Well, what happened?"

"I forgot my lines," she claimed. Nonetheless she received an offer from Timothy Busfield of *Thirty Something, West Wing, Field of Dreams,* and more to join his group of actors at the 'B' Street Theater in Sacramento. She also got an invitation from the theater-arts department at Cal State Fullerton. This reportedly included some form of scholarship.

Education was not Brandy's thing. The theater was.

Education was Jeannie's and my thing.

Conflict.

Forty-Six

Earthquake

Brandy's last semester at BC ended. "If I have to go to school, I'd rather go to Northridge. They have the best TV and film program."

Jeannie, Brandy and I drove down to the Northridge campus to look it over. We then stopped in at the admissions office to see if we could to get Brandy enrolled for the spring semester. We also asked about campus housing. Enrollment was not going to be a problem. Housing was. She had to live off campus. We were given a list of apartments on the school's "approved" list. Off we went to check them out.

Most of the apartment complexes we looked at either had nothing available for the spring term or were larger units meant to be shared by three or four students and priced as such. The only one bedroom apartment we found strained our budget, but we put down a deposit. It came furnished and clean. The owner agreed to a January 18 move-in date.

Things were moving way too fast. Our flighty, goofy, irresponsible daughter leaving home after taking three and a half years to complete her two-year Associate of Arts program at BC seemed unthinkable. But it would be happening in two days, after Brandy returned from a weekend with Kelly and two friends at Newport Beach.

On January 17, 1994, at 4:30:55 a.m. Pacific Standard Time, the earth had other ideas. A 6.7 blind thrust earthquake hit Northridge taking the lives of 60 people and injuring more than 9000.

According to news reports, the peak ground acceleration of the quake exceeded any event ever recorded in an urban area of North America. The apartment reserved for Brandy didn't survive.

Brandy and Kelly felt the quake in Newport Beach, almost seventy miles southeast of the epicenter. "It was scary," Brandy said. "The glass in the windows and sliding doors looked like jelly."

* * *

Because of the freeway damage, the girls had to take a long detour in order to get home. Traffic on the detour was horrendous, but they made it safely.

Cal State Northridge put its spring semester on hold.

What to do?

Jeannie came up with an idea. "What about Fullerton? Let's call down there."

I looked at Brandy. "They liked you in Vegas. You okay with that?"

She shrugged her shoulders. "I guess."

Rather than call Fullerton, I felt a personal visit might produce better results. Jeannie, Brandy and I made the long, circuitous drive over Tehachapi Pass, out through the desert, over Cajon Pass, and back west to Fullerton. After a bit of searching, we found the campus and then the admissions office. Even though it had been over a year since the Las Vegas auditions, the name Brandy Brown did the trick. The head of the theater-arts department remembered Brandy and still wanted her on board.

Housing with three other girls in that department came along as if it was meant to be.

Two and a half years later, Brandy graduated with a BA in Theater Arts but no job prospects. She had been a favorite of the director of the Master of Fine Arts program who had arranged several golden opportunities for Brandy—the kind that rarely come along to aspiring actors. Brandy shined them on, as they say. On one occasion, she didn't show up because she had to kiss a fellow other than her boyfriend. On another, she didn't follow up on an invitation to work with a day-time soap opera because she didn't think she was good enough.

What did she do? She took a job as a *serving wench* at Medieval Times in Buena Park. Medieval Times was set up much like an indoor rodeo arena where performers dressed as knights pretended to joust. And where rodeo fans would sit, diners ate Cornish hens with their fingers—hens brought to them by serving wenches.

Brandy worked at Medieval Times way too long for her parents' liking before finding the road home.

Forty-Seven

The College

In 1992, I received a letter from an organization called the American College of Trial Lawyers, inviting me to be inducted as a Fellow at the fall annual meeting to be held in Paris (France, not California). The price tag boggled my mind, so I didn't respond. Six months later another invitation arrived for me to be inducted at the spring meeting. The location escapes my mind. Again, I didn't respond.

The third letter came after several more months. I tossed it in the wastebasket. Then my partner, Steve Clifford, came to my office. "You didn't respond to *the College*. Why not?"

"I'm not much of an organization man. And the cost is through the roof."

Steve sat down on the opposite side of my desk. "You only get three chances. This is your last one. The firm will pay all expenses for you and Jeannie. Do you have the invitation?"

I fished through my wastebasket, pulled it out and handed it to him.

Steve shook his head. Then he walked out of my office with the papers in his hand. He came back a short while later. "You're all signed up to go to DC in September. You'll need to get a tuxedo. It's a black-tie affair."

Jeannie wasn't thrilled about going to the nation's capital for a gathering of lawyers—nor was I. I got more than my fill of lawyers through work. But then, things aren't always what we anticipate.

The College, as Steve called it, is unlike any other legal group I'm aware of. The fall meeting lasted three days, culminating with a black-tie dinner and the induction of new *Fellows*, men and women. Free time allowed for sight-seeing, making new friends, and a variety of activities—including golf. I drove the cart.

The biggest downer of the event came from learning we had passed up, by ignoring the first invitation, a dinner and induction ceremony held in the Hall of Mirrors at the Palace of Versailles.

In the years that followed, we attended meetings in a number of special places, two of which were Scottsdale, Arizona and London, England.

* * *

For two *road warriors* like Jeannie and me—and to save the firm a dollar or two—we decided to drive from Bakersfield to the spring meeting in Scottsdale rather than fly. Of course, we arrived on *Jeannie time*. The first evening featured a buffet dinner, live music, and socializing. By the time we made an appearance, the buffet tables contained slim-pickings.

Undaunted, we piled what remained on plates and hunted for a place to sit. The only table with two adjoining seats took the brunt of the band music blaring from speakers directly above it. Only three people sat there, a couple and the *sad little man* as Jeannie later referred to him. We had to nearly shout to make introductions, and neither Jeannie nor I heard the sad little man say his name. Brief pauses in the music allowed for a tiny bit of conversation during which we learned that our three tablemates hailed from Maine and Massachusetts.

The next morning, I attended an educational session while Jeannie enjoyed free time until lunch. The MC introduced the featured speaker that morning as the Chief Judge of the United States Court of Appeals for the First Circuit. On stage stepped none other than the sad little man. His presentation was magnificent, salted with wit and humor. He was neither sad nor little. I silently cursed the loud music of the night before.

When his presentation concluded, the judge opened the floor for questions. "They don't have to be about law," he said. "If you want to talk auto mechanics or lawn care, we'll do that."

The first questioner asked how he felt about being passed over by President Clinton for nomination to the Supreme Court. In response, the Judge praised President Clinton's choice, Ruth Bader Ginsberg.

At lunch, I told Jeannie that the morning's speaker had been her sad little man, and that he had been in the running for appointment to the Supreme Court. She seemed surprised and impressed. However, for her the highlight of the April 1994 Scottsdale meeting was the opportunity to play one of Scottsdale's finest golf courses. And she played well.

The next month, May 17, 1994, to be exact, we were driving through Southern California after visiting Brandy in Fullerton. The top of the hour news came on the radio. "Today, President Bill Clinton nominated Stephen Gerald Breyer to the United States Supreme Court . . ."

"Our sad little man!" Jeannie said. "Good for him."

* * *

A few years went by before we attended another meeting. The chance to visit London piqued our interest, so I signed up.

The flight from Los Angeles to London took more time than I care to remember. My assigned middle seat pushed my knees up to my chin. I spent most of the flight walking the aisles of the DC-10. Jeannie slept.

A fun ride in one of London's little black taxis got us to the hotel and we checked in 30 minutes before departure time to the evening's festivities. About a dozen busses lined the curb out front, engines running.

We needed to freshen up and change clothes. I was ready in 15 minutes. Jeannie wasn't.

"We have to hurry, Sweetheart. If we miss the bus, there's no other way to get there." The college had arranged to have exclusive use of King Henry VIII's Hampton Court Palace for the evening, and only the busses could enter the grounds.

When she announced, "I'm ready," we raced to the elevator, urged it to go faster, then dashed through the lobby and out to the sidewalk. One-by-one, the busses were pulling away. Then Jeannie saw them—not the busses—my brother Bill, the world's first photo-bomber, and his wife Ruth walking toward us, not more than twenty feet away. I was stunned.

"What in the world are you two doing here?" I asked, then looked over my shoulder and saw only three busses still at the curb.

"We're on a two-week walking tour of England," Ruth said. "We're staying at a B&B in Chingford."

Now only two busses remained, both filling up fast. The door hissed on the front one and it pulled away.

Only one bus left.

I gave Bill our room number and took Jeannie by the arm. We were the last two to board the final bus. But we made it.

Hampton Court Palace was spectacular.

* * *

The formal dinner and induction ceremony were held two nights later at the hotel. There, Jeannie and I—together with four or five hundred others—broke bread with the likes of Supreme Court Justices Sandra Day O'Connor and Anthony Kennedy. We were definitely out of our element!

When the conference ended, we took a short train ride to Chingford and spent a couple relaxing days with Bill and Ruth knocking around England. Four University of North Dakota grads on holiday.

I dreaded the flight home. With all the traipsing we had done with Bill and Ruth, the thought of walking the aisles again left a sour taste in my mouth.

At Heathrow Airport, I bit the bullet and asked for an upgrade to *business class.* No luck, all those seats were filled. On to the cattle call.

Halfway down the sky-walk, crammed between hundreds of other travelers wanting to get back to the States, I heard an announcement.

"Passenger James Brown, please report to the ticket counter."

Jeannie's face held a worried look. "Do you suppose something happened to one of the kids?"

"I'll see." Wiggling and squirming through a sea of packed bodies, I made my way to the ticket counter and identified myself.

"If I may see your boarding passes, please." The clerk held out her hand.

I gave them to her.

She handed me new ones. "We've changed your seat assignments."

I made my way back to Jeannie who was plastered against the sky-walk wall. "No bad news. We just got new seat assignments."

She scowled. "Why did they do that?"

"Don't make waves. The row number is very low." I showed her that we were now in row 2, seats A and B. Our other tickets put us in something like row 99, seats Y and Z.

On this 747, row 2 was not just in *first-class*; it was in a class by itself. The seats fully reclined. Even at six-foot-four, my toes didn't touch the back of row 1. Champagne flowed freely, unless other wine was more to our liking. We ordered food from menus fit for an upscale restaurant. Then a flight attendant asked, "Would you like a head and neck massage?"

Large, fold-away TVs at each seat popped up with the push of a button. An extensive list of movies to choose from appeared on the screen. The crew of attendants pampered us all the way to LAX. Neither of us wanted to get off the plane.

We never found out the reason for the upgrade and we were never charged for it.

Forty-Eight

Jim and Joanne Kack

A voice from the past greeted me when I answered the phone in my office. The caller said, "This is Jim Kack." Bells went off in my head. I hadn't seen or talked to Jim in twenty years, the last time being at UND Homecoming in 1976 when he received the prestigious Sioux Award.

Jim and I had been teammates on the track team, where we shared more laughs than medals. He married the former Joanne Schafer, one of Jeannie's DG sorority sisters, the one responsible for me meeting Jeannie at the Gravel Pits.

Why, after all these years, was he calling me now?

Jim explained that he had a legal question and was under the misguided impression that I was a knowledgeable attorney. He and Joanne were then living outside of Bozeman, Montana. I was able to refer Jim to a lawyer in Bellingham, Washington—born and educated in Bozeman—and the legal issue resolved to Jim's satisfaction.

Shortly thereafter, a package arrived at my office containing a beautiful fly rod and reel. Jim knew from our telephone conversation that I loved to fish but had never been a fly fisherman. He wanted me to give it a try.

I did. I was hooked.

Since that 1995 phone call, I have pursued the wily rainbow and cutthroat trout inhabiting dozens of rivers in Idaho, Montana, and Wyoming. Jeannie's knees didn't allow her to wade the rocky bottoms of these streams, but she was a drift boat queen, consistently bringing more and bigger fish to the net than I did.

Jeannie hooked into a good one with guide Tim Linehan

"Why can't we keep them to eat," she often complained when she put a nice one back in the water and watched it swim away. *Catch and release* made no sense to her.

The introduction to fly fishing by Jim Kack ranks high on the list of things I am thankful to him for. But at the top of that list is the renewal of our North Dakota friendship. Since Jim's out of the blue phone call in 1995, Jeannie and I have enjoyed many fun visits with the Kacks, some in Bakersfield, some at their Bozeman spread, and some at Twin Lakes. Laughter and wine always flowed freely.

On one of their visits to see us in Idaho, Jeannie came up with the idea to take them to Priest Lake and boat to the upper lake for a picnic. Warm sunshine greeted us when we took our boat out of Twin Lakes and loaded in the supplies for the day. A few puffy, white clouds drifted overhead on the hour-and-a-half drive to the boat launch at Elkins' Resort. The weather seemed perfect for a leisurely twenty-mile cruise to our favorite picnic spot.

I backed the trailer down the ramp and slid the boat into the water. Jeannie tied it to the dock while I drove to the parking area. On my walk back I noticed a few darker clouds moving toward the white, puffy ones, but the air was warm and calm. I untied the boat and joined the others on board. The engine fired up and off we went. As I turned the prow north, the puffy, white clouds were nowhere to be seen. The dark clouds must have eaten them.

The wind rapidly freshened and the temperature dropped a good ten degrees before we had moved a quarter mile up the lake. Then lightening flashed from a slate gray cloudbank ahead and the smell of ozone followed soon thereafter. I made a sharp U-turn and beat a hasty retreat to Elkins' covered boat slips, gliding in just as the first blast of pelting rain hit us.

"This will pass soon," we assured Jim and Joanne.

It didn't.

Morning turned to noonday with no letup in the deluge. We snacked on some of our picnic goodies in the shelter of a solid roof while Jim kept us laughing with one story after another. The afternoon teased us with a few hints of easing rainfall and calmer winds, but within minutes the storm continued as before.

Dinner time approached. We had long since abandoned any hope of making it to the upper lake. Now our wish was that we could get the boat back on the trailer, and us into Elkins' restaurant, before the lights went out.

We made it. The weather eased, and we had a delightful dinner before making the drive back to Twin Lakes.

An Upper Priest Lake picnic would have to wait for another day.

Forty-Nine

Wedding Bells

Kelly tried her hand at being an adult after two years at the University of Idaho. She shared an apartment with a friend, worked at a women's clothing store during the day, and waited tables at night. After six months of this lifestyle, she decided to give education a further shot.

"Kelly wants to come home and give college another try," Jeannie told me one evening in early January of 1991. "I want to go up there and help her with the move."

My stomach did a flip-flop. Jeannie had to fly to Spokane, take a little shuttlebus to Moscow, load the old blue van Kelly had taken up there, and drive home in the middle of winter. I feared Jeannie, one of the world's worst navigators, might wind up in either Canada or Kansas.

I got Kelly on the phone.

"If you go back to school, will you give it top priority?" I knew what her answer would be. The tone of her voice might tell a different story.

She promised, so I gave her a challenge. "Will you take a night class with me at Bakersfield College?"

"If *you* want to."

Jeannie made the trip to Moscow. I made the trip up the hill to BC.

Jeannie and Kelly loaded the van and prepared to head south—a good start. Then Jeannie backed into a parked car—not a good start.

She located the owner, had him look at the damage, and wrote him a check. Allstate never knew.

Meanwhile, I enrolled Kelly and her dad in an evening American history class and arranged for her to register for more spring semester courses. The first history lecture came while Jeannie and Kelly were still on the road, so I attended alone. When the class ended at 9:00 p.m., I gave them a call on one of those new-fangled cell phones.

Operation Desert Storm had started that night while I was playing student.

The next day, Kelly moved back into her old room in our house, registered for the spring term, and began a new chapter in her life. We attended every history class together, studied together, and celebrated our grades together—a great time of father-daughter bonding.

* * *

In the fall of 1991, Kelly transferred to Cal State Bakersfield. She majored in business, got good grades, and received her degree in June of 1994. She then embarked on a brief career in the area of interior design and decoration before the Spirit moved her toward becoming a teacher.

Another year of studies plus practice teaching led to her securing a teaching credential and a job educating fourth graders at

Kelly Graduating from CSUB

Pioneer Elementary. Jeannie delighted in helping Kelly decorate her classroom as "Miss Brown's Town."

Pioneer Elementary served a mostly Hispanic community. Many, if not most, of the fourth-graders Kelly taught spoke English as their second language. A large number of parents couldn't help their children because they had little or no formal education. So Kelly started an after-school parents' class.

The third year she taught at Pioneer Elementary, Kelly invited Jeannie and me to the school's Christmas program. We marveled at the number of students and parents who swarmed around Kelly, giving her big hugs and warm smiles. None of the other teachers received that type of welcome.

The principal came over to us. "We just love your daughter. She has brought so much joy to this school." My heart melted, and I'm sure Jeannie's did, too.

* * *

Then along came Bill Haines, romance, engagement, and a desired wedding date of August 8, 1998. Bill's lucky number 8 explains the 8/8/98 choice.

"Wouldn't it be fun if Pastor Shelley could do the wedding on one of the double-decker boats on Lake Coeur d'Alene?" Jeannie smiled coyly. She was revving up her wedding-planner juices.

By the time of the engagement, Jeannie and I had visited Tom and Harriette Shelley in Spokane Valley, Washington, where Tom was the pastor at Christ Lutheran Church. Tom served as our pastor at Emmanuel Lutheran in Bakersfield for many years before accepting the call to Spokane Valley.

I looked at the calendar. August 8 fell on Saturday. "Let's give him a call."

Pastor Tom agreed to do the wedding, sending Jeannie off and running so to speak. She reserved a banquet room at the Coeur d'Alene Hotel and one of their big double-decker tour boats. I started the process of refinancing our home. She then called back to the hotel and reserved the 16th floor honeymoon suite and arranged for the swank Beverley's restaurant to cater the reception. I called back to the bank.

This process repeated itself several times as the wedding day approached. A speedbump placed by Brandy required deft negotiation. That speedbump will be addressed in a separate chapter.

August 8 arrived. Lake Coeur d'Alene, the weather, and Kelly each said, "Mirror, mirror on the wall . . ." The mirror replied, "Kelly!" The lake and the weather tied for second. Both were beautiful. Kelly more so.

Eight months and 18 days later, Kelly gave birth to Spencer Kelly Haines. She never went back to teaching.

Fifty

The Miracle of Ryan

God works in ways often beyond our comprehension.

After Brandy's fling of carting Cornish hens at Medieval Times, she had returned to Bakersfield. Jeannie admitted her relief, as did I. Brandy moved back into our house but spent little time there. The social scene called. She answered.

And she actually sought out and found employment—three times. All three were befitting a young lady with a degree in theater-arts: hostess at the downtown *Mexicali*, an old-line, family-owned, Bakersfield restaurant; file clerk at a law office (mine); and server at *On the Border*, a chain diner.

I believe Brandy really did evening *work* at *On the Border* (after her substitute teaching stint), and maybe a little at the *Mexicali* and at our law office. I had no part in hiring her nor was I involved in ending her employment. Other partners in the firm took the blame and credit, in that order. Not to say that reports of Brandy's antics didn't make it to my door from time to time, mostly about how she made people laugh or her ability to thwart the romantic interest of one young associate.

* * *

In May of 1998, Jeannie pulled into the driveway and encountered Brandy who had a grim look on her face. "You look like you need a hug," She gave her a warm embrace.

"I'm pregnant," Brandy whispered.

Jeannie stepped back. "Well, that's not what I expected."

I knew nothing of this when I opened the door a few minutes later and saw the two of them in the living room located just to the right and one step down from the entry hall. It struck me as unusual for them to be there. Ordinarily, either the den or the kitchen served as the gathering place.

Jeannie sat on the couch with her arms folded across her chest. Brandy faced her from an old Cogswell chair that had been passed down in my family for generations.

"Brandy has something to tell you," Jeannie said.

News I didn't want to hear, no doubt.

At this point Brandy's recollection and mine differ as to how the words were conveyed. She says she wrote them on a piece of note paper. I recall them coming from her mouth. "You and mom are going to be grandparents." Her memory is probably the accurate one.

For some reason my mind went to Kelly who was engaged to be married in less than three months. That notion flew out of my head as fast as it flew in. The look on Brandy's face said it all.

I needed to sit down.

The rest of that evening and the next several days blend together in my memory. The sequence and timing of events are all stacked on top of each other, that is until Jeannie and Brandy left for UCLA.

Jeannie and I had a sit-down session with Brandy's boyfriend Marty, again in the living room. We had known him for a year or so. He willingly came to talk to us but seemed as nervous as a long-tailed cat in a room full of rocking chairs. The *A*-words, *abortion* and *adoption*, lurked in the background but remained unspoken. Marty acknowledged his responsibility and pledged to be supportive of Brandy whatever she decided to do. That's as close as it got. The subject of marriage didn't even get that close.

Later that evening, Jeannie came to me with eyes that looked like she'd been crying. "What are we going to do? You know Brandy's not equipped to be a mother. She's a 27-year-old *child*. We'll end up raising the baby until we're almost eighty." Jeannie was usually right.

Brandy and Marty met with our pastor, Milt Cole. He suggested the adoption route and recommended they talk to the folks at the Bakersfield Pregnancy Center. Later, Brandy told us she could never give up a baby for adoption. As best we could figure, that left two choices—we raise the baby or abortion.

Angst set in with all of us. Hours of debate over the morality of abortion led to an immoral and selfish decision. Jeannie contacted Brandy's doctor at UCLA, Jonathon Berek, who had several years earlier treated Brandy for what he called a pre-cancerous condition.

"He didn't really want to," Jeannie reported. "He only agreed because Brandy has been his patient."

The die was cast, so it seemed.

* * *

The trip to UCLA came quickly. Jeannie went with Brandy while I went to work.

Ha!

I could no more work than *leap over a tall building in a single bound* like The Man of Steel. I sat in my office and moved papers from one side of the desk to the other without accomplishing a billable minute. One hour passed, then another. Dark thoughts of what was happening at UCLA pushed aside any hope of being productive. Just as I stood up to head for the elevator and go home, my private line rang. It was Brandy.

"I chickened out. I'm sorry."

Those words lifted the elephant off my back. I felt weightless, like when Jeannie called from Oklahoma City to tell me she didn't have breast cancer.

Then Brandy said, "He wants me to come back in a week."

The elephant crawled back on my shoulders.

Then I heard Jeannie in the background say, "Tell him we'll be home in about half an hour."

Fifteen minutes after I got home, Jeannie and Brandy walked in the door. I gave each of them a long hug. "Tell me what happened."

"You know how big that UCLA Medical Center is," Jeannie said. "There must be a hundred elevators. We didn't know which one to get on, or even which building we were in." She held her hands palms up. "We got on the first elevator we came to and pushed three. Brandy knew Doctor Berek's office was on the third floor. We were the only ones on the elevator, but it stopped on two and a man got on . . . Doctor Berek. He and Brandy greeted each other like they were old friends."

Then Brandy told a bit of the story. "I asked him if it was murder. He said he just does what his patients want if they're not too far along."

My guess is that Dr. Berek thought the *murder* issue in the question was directed toward his role. I knew Brandy was asking about herself.

As the story went on in bits and pieces, I learned that Brandy began to cry, and after she was on the table with her legs in the stirrups, Dr. Berek thought it best to send in a social worker to talk to her. The social worker said she didn't think Brandy was ready and advised taking another week to think about it.

The three of us sat in silence, doing just that, before someone came up with the idea of calling Jeannie's mom to ask for her advice. Bertha had not been told that Brandy was pregnant. Jeannie put her on the speaker and explained the situation, then asked, "What are we going to do?"

Bertha simply said, "What are we going to do? We're going to have a baby. And it's going to be a beautiful baby." God's emissary had spoken. End of discussion.

Brandy was starting to show by the time of Kelly's wedding, raising the concern that her condition might take the focus off of her sister's big day. It didn't.

* * *

On January 29, 1999, Brandy's beautiful baby arrived. Jeannie, Kelly, Matt and I were there in the hospital, as was Marty.

Marty's parents were not.

When Marty's mom found out about the pregnancy, she lost her composure. She went to Marty's house and tore up all his pictures of Brandy and said some nasty things about her. Then she called Jeannie and ripped into her, saying their family would never have anything to do with ours and that Brandy was kin to Satan. I heard her voice even though Jeannie held the receiver tight to her ear.

Jeannie tapped her foot as she listened patiently before saying, "Maybe you should get some counseling."

The raised voice on the other end of the line snapped back, "Why don't you go on a diet, you FAT-ASS!" Then the line went dead.

Jeannie hung up the phone and turned to me with her eyes wide and her mouth turned down. "Well, she's right. I do have a fat ass."

* * *

Our new granddaughter Ryan Maxine—Maxine being Bertha's middle name—took up residence with Brandy in the north half of our living room. True to her pediatric training and experience, Jeannie had set it up as a nursery with everything a new mom and baby might need.

The day before Valentine's Day, Marty brought his parents over to see their 16-day-old granddaughter. Jeannie and I stood back while they fawned over Ryan a minute or two and then left, not taking the chill in the room with them. I can't remember them returning during the next several months.

Marty came every day from the moment Brandy brought Ryan home. He changed diapers, gave baths, held Ryan when she cried, made her laugh, and let her know how much he loved her.

To modify an old expression, time and Jeannie heal all wounds. By the time Brandy got over her

Marty, Ryan, & Brandy

insistence that she would not trap a guy into marriage by getting pregnant, Jeannie and Marty's mom had mended fences and became friendly grandmothers.

After several months of turmoil in her relationship with Marty, Brandy came around. Marty asked my permission to marry her. I gave it. Brandy said "Yes." And Jeannie again went into *wedding planner* mode. She had done wonders with Kelly's wedding on Lake Coeur d'Alene and expressed the desire for another Idaho wedding, this time at Priest Lake.

Marty, being Catholic, wanted a Catholic wedding. That was fine with us, but Jeannie's hopes for the Priest Lake setting landed on the rocks when the priest there refused to do an outside wedding. He would only do it inside his church.

Jeannie then set about planning a Bakersfield wedding.

Fortunately, a new priest was about to take over as pastor of the Saint Francis Parrish, a priest most of us knew from his time as chaplain at Garces Memorial High School when the kids were students there—Father Craig Harrison. He agreed to do the wedding—and a bit more. The date of August 28, 1999, marked the beginning of Brandy's married life and also the baptism of Ryan. It became the first of many times Father Craig touched the lives of our Lutheran family in special ways.

* * *

The wedding couldn't have been more beautiful. My heart pumped double time when I walked Brandy down the aisle. It beat triple time when Father Craig introduced Mr. and Mrs. Martin Starr. Brandy got her wish of becoming a *star*—plus an extra "R".

But Ryan, one day shy of seven months old, stole the show after she was baptized. Father Craig carried her around the church, presenting her to the assembled throng. Ryan, acting very much like a princess, held out her arm showing off the inscribed bangle Jeannie had given her. I gave Jeannie a hug while a shiver of relief coursed through my body over the thought of how close, how very close, Ryan had come to not being born.

I believe God smiled down on us that day. And I know he continued to bless the little Starr family that started out as a threesome but has since doubled in size with the addition of Joseph, Jonathan, and Cooper. Brandy, the girl Jeannie thought couldn't raise a baby, proved her wrong four times over. She is a magnificent mother. And Marty is a super dad.

Johnny, Cooper, Joe, & Ryan

Fifty-One

The Lot

All the hoopla about Y2K didn't prevent the year 2000 from arriving as scheduled. No mass disruption of the internet occurred. Commerce didn't collapse. The world didn't end. But my semi-retirement began. I had long pledged that if a year began with a "2", I was not going to work full time. Only two major cases remained on my trial calendar when Jeannie and I left for our planned three-month stint in Idaho. Unfortunately, the first of those trials had been rescheduled by the Superior Court in Fresno to begin smack-dab in the middle of those three months.

Jeannie decided not to go to Fresno with me. She wanted to stay at Twin Lakes. "What am I going to do in Fresno? I don't want to sit in a hotel for two weeks. I can set up my easel and paint while you're gone. Just call me every night and let me know how things are going in court."

That was fine with me. My client knew the only issue the jury had to decide was the amount of plaintiff's damages. She had suffered a brain injury in an accident caused by my client's negligence. This type of case we called a *how-mucher*. We thought the plaintiff wanted too much to settle. She thought we offered too little. The trial boiled down to a battle of medical experts.

Jeannie took me to the airport on the Friday before the trial was scheduled to start. "Remember to give me daily reports." I promised I would.

In Fresno, I stayed in a hotel across the street from the courthouse. My appetite leaves me when I'm in trial, so I subsisted on snacks and occasional deliveries from room service. I set the alarm in my room for 7:00 p.m. each evening for my call to Jeannie. As the trial progressed, she seemed to become bored with my trial reports. We talked more about other things until I needed to get back to preparing for the next day.

The evening before closing arguments, I got a busy signal when I put in my nightly call. I waited several minutes and tried again. Still the *bonk-bonk-bonk.* More than an hour later, the line remained busy. I knew that Jeannie sometimes had long talks with her mother or one of the kids. But by nine o'clock, my stomach had knotted up. I tried calling one of our Twin Lakes neighbors. No answer. One more call to Jeannie. *Bonk-bonk-bonk.*

I called the Kootenai County Sheriff's Office. After I explained my concern to the Desk Sergeant, he agreed to send someone out to check on Jeannie.

I sat clenching and unclenching my fists for half an hour before the phone rang. It was Jeannie. "That poor guy. I think I scared him half to death," she said.

"What happened?"

"I was upstairs in the old unit painting when the doorbell rang downstairs. It rang again while I was coming down. When I opened the door, I did my thing." She meant, making a high-pitched sound somewhere between the volume of a jet engine and the threshold of pain. A *thing* she did when startled. "I was shocked to see a guy in a Sheriff's uniform. All I could think of was something must have happened to you."

"I tried calling you for hours," I said, "kept getting a busy signal."

"Yeah. He told me that. I checked the phone. It wasn't squarely on the cradle. I hadn't hung it up right, I guess."

We laughed a while, both thankful the other was all right. "What's the trial report?" she asked.

"Only one witness today. The plaintiff's husband. He talked about how the accident had changed her. Then we met with the judge to go over jury instructions. Tomorrow, arguments in the morning, then to the jury in the afternoon. I hope they have a verdict by Friday, so I don't have to stay here over the weekend."

The verdict was read Friday morning. The plaintiff got less than half of what we had offered to settle. And I got to go back to Idaho in good spirits.

***

Jeannie picked me up at the Spokane airport. "I have a surprise for you," she said.

"What is it?"

"You'll see." A twinkle in her eye along with a subtle grin had me curious.

She resisted even giving me a hint for the next forty-five minutes. When I tried to pry something out of her, she changed the subject.

A mile south of the turn-off for Twin Lakes Village, Jeannie told me to close my eyes. I did. She turned left onto a road I wasn't familiar with. Then I felt the car turn right and stop a moment later. "You can open your eyes. This is the surprise. Come with me."

Nothing but trees occupied both sides of the road. Jeannie led me through the woods up a rise to level ground and a view of the lake. "This five-acre lot is for sale. Isn't it nice?"

"It's beautiful. But what do they want for it?"

She told me the asking price. I gulped.

For the past few years, we had been scouring the panhandle of Idaho and western Montana looking for a retirement home or the property on which to build one. Two places in Montana appealed to us. One was way out of our price range and Jeannie said the other was too remote for her comfort. Now, she found a perfect piece of property less than two miles from Twin Lakes Village.

After two weddings, I knew we didn't have the necessary funds. "Let's talk to the owner and see if we can structure a deal."

"I've talked to the realtor. He'll meet us here tomorrow and introduce us to the owner." She took my hand and guided me further toward the lake. "If we build a house right here, wouldn't this be a nice view? And there's waterfront where we can keep our boat."

We made an offer, received a counter proposal, and struck a deal calling for half payment up front and the balance in one year. Once we owned the land free-and-clear, we could explore our building options.

* * *

A short while after the girls' weddings of 1998 and 1999, and the resulting depletion of our financial resources, I had decided to embark on a program of prudent investing. IRA rules at the time permitted separate accounts for Jeannie and me, each could be funded up to $2,500 annually.

I committed to follow one principle in choosing how to invest these funds. That principle was: *Steady plodding brings prosperity; hasty speculation brings poverty* (Proverbs 21:5), a concept we had learned in *Crown Ministries*, a church sponsored guide to managing money. This verse of Proverbs flew in the face of my family's long-standing tradition that extended back many generations—*buy high, sell low.*

At the time, the New York Stock exchange listed well over four thousand stocks from which to select for *steady plodding.* It took me about a month to screen all four thousand and find two that had the right history, as I understood it, of Proverbs 21:5 compliance.

Jeannie said she wanted nothing to do with making investment decisions for her IRA. "You do it. I don't know anything about that stuff." So, I picked one stock for her account and the other for mine.

On down the road, she changed her tune a bit.

Neither of my astute stock picks turned out to bear any resemblance to *steady plodding*. Within about a month, my company's stock was bought out by a larger company leaving me essentially where I had started. Jeannie's stock, on the other hand, exchanged its plodding boots for booster rockets. Between galloping price increases and stock splits, the value of her account soared. In short order, I was able to sell a small part of her stock for the original investment amount. She was then playing with house money.

Day after day, her stock kept going up. I got nervous and sold half of her holdings at a staggering profit. Then, just before leaving for Idaho in 2001, I sold the other half for even more.

We stopped in Idaho Falls the second night of our road trip. Jeannie turned on the TV and up popped one of the financial shows with a so-called investment expert as a guest. He touted three stocks, Jeannie's now former stock among them, predicting growth of another 50% before year's end. She didn't know I had sold it all.

"Isn't that great? Let's celebrate at *Jaker's*," she said. Jaker's was our favorite restaurant in Idaho Falls, just a short walk from the motel.

I shook my head. "I sold the last of your shares before we left."

Her smile faded like she'd been shot. "Why did you do that?! He said it was going to go up fifty percent more."

I refused to wither under her glare, whether it was supported by a TV expert or not. "I got nervous. It was going up too fast. Plus, we have enough to pay off the lot."

Dinner at Jaker's lacked much in the way of celebration.

* * *

Fast forward one week. The stock didn't go up as the expert predicted —it fell off the cliff—dropping below the original purchase price. So, I became a financial genius in Jeannie's eyes, proving the old saying: *Even a stopped clock can find an acorn.* Or something like that.

In any event, we now owned the lot free and clear. Building something on it had to wait. Meanwhile, we had a grading contractor carve out a dirt driveway through the woods along with a path to the water's edge. I scrounged up enough rocks to build a fire pit for roasting hot dogs and making s'mores.

Jeannie found a tent-like enclosure designed to house a port-a-potty. I set it far enough into the woods to allow easy access and a bit of privacy. We shared our heavenly five acres with deer, racoons, rabbits, squirrels, and an occasional moose—none of which were allowed to use the port-a-potty.

Another seven years passed before house construction started. By then, because of everything that had happened in the interim, everyone but Kelly thought we were crazy.

Fifty-Two

Battle with the Scale

After giving birth to three babies, and raising them through their school years, Jeannie began a battle with the scale. Up and down. Up and down. At one point, she shrunk to 106 pounds. At other times she saw numbers showing she reached twice that size.

Jeannie with Kelly in Her Prom Dress

No commercial diet plan lacked her attention. She tried them all, and usually to a satisfactory level of success. She joined local support groups, read books and magazines, engaged in exercise programs, and tried various supplements, all in the hope of maintaining a healthy weight.

Jeannie with Jim

"I never feel full, no matter how much I eat," she said.

Playing tennis with a group of women at the racquet club had served her well until she suffered a stress fracture in her foot that put her on crutches for several weeks. During her time in a cast, she stayed too close to the refrigerator. One day when she opened it to get a snack, she looked at me with lips squeezed tight. "I think I could eat everything in there."

The weight elevator went up rapidly, down slowly. It went to the fifth floor, then down to the second, up to the sixth, then down to the third, and so on.

Jeannie went back to playing tennis, but the stress fracture recurred. In spite of it, she kept playing golf, even in a walking cast.

After her last elevator ride up the weight scale, Jeannie vented her frustration. She was walking with a cane, taking two blood pressure medications, and getting no real exercise. "I don't know what to do. I diet and get the weight off, but it keeps coming back—with friends."

A visit to Dr. Young in 2001 changed this cycle. Jeannie and I were sixty years old at the time. He suggested we attend a seminar put on by the Scripps Clinic on the topic of bariatric surgery. We went. The surgery sounded pretty drastic, separation of a large part of the stomach and part of the small intestine. It was called a *Roux-en-Y* gastric by-pass. The promised results, however, peaked Jeannie's interest in doing some further investigation.

The folks at Scripps put us in touch with a young lady in Bakersfield who had undergone the procedure a year earlier and was anxious to share her story. We met her at the Barnes & Noble café. Bubbling with enthusiasm, this gal pulled up her shirt and showed Jeannie her surgical scar, proclaiming, "I just love this scar! It's given me a whole new life."

The scar was long, wide and red. But she loved it.

She told us how much weight she lost in the year since her surgery. I've forgotten the number of pounds, but it was an astonishing amount. Except for the long, wide, red scar under her shirt, she looked good. Not fashion model skinny, just average size.

After this glowing endorsement, Jeannie wanted to meet one-on-one with the San Diego surgeon. A few weeks later, we drove down to see him in San Diego and get more specific information about surgical risks, recovery time, future potential complications, and so forth.

Jeannie liked the surgeon and what he had to say. She was ready to go. I had my doubts. She went for it—right before Thanksgiving.

After a brief period of recovery, her Thanksgiving feast consisted of one spoonful of mashed potatoes. In short order the pounds began to melt away. By the time we headed north the next year for our annual Idaho vacation, she loved her long, wide, red scar. I never saw her pull up her shirt to show it to anyone, but she loved it just the same.

Her blood pressure returned to the normal range, eliminating the need to continue her medications. Her knee pain almost completely disappeared. No more use of her cane. She didn't return to the tennis courts, but the golf course saw a lot more of her. She was pretty much a sixty-one-year-old ball of energy.

Fifty-Three

I Have Some Bad News

In the fall of 2003, shortly after returning to Bakersfield from our three-month vacation in Idaho, I was at my office continuing to wade through the mountain of paperwork that had stacked up while we were gone. I didn't think semi-retirement would expose me to so much mail.

Many times over the years Jeannie started out a phone call with, "I have some bad news."

Usually, it was something that was going to cost money, like the time she started her car and put it in reverse before closing the door. Then, one of those yellow critters she calls bees flew in, she panicked, the car rolled backwards, and the open door crumpled against a huge camphor tree that stood next to the driveway.

A call of that sort I called *another bug on the windshield of life.*

This call came through my secretary, Saundra, instead of to my private line. I can't remember another time Jeannie did that.

"Jeannie's on line one," Saundra announced over the com-line.

I picked up the phone, puzzled, and punched the blinking light for line one.

"Hi, Jeannie."

Silence for a second or two before she said in a halting voice, "I have some bad news." My heart stopped. This wasn't going to be about money. This wasn't going to be a bug on the windshield.

"I have ovarian cancer." Then more silence.

I felt like I'd been hit by a wrecking ball. I didn't know what to say. I didn't know what to do. I was totally helpless—numb.

"How do you know?" I stupidly asked.

Jeannie somehow managed to pull herself somewhat together. "Doctor Young called with the CA125 results."

I had no idea what she was talking about. I didn't even know she had seen Dr. Young since we got back from vacation. And I had no clue what CA125 meant. I learned much about that in the weeks and months to come.

"The normal range is something like zero to thirty," she said. "Mine was over eight thousand." She spoke in a halting voice. "John said he could see me right away."

"I'll be home in five minutes."

I jumped up and ran to the elevator, pulling the car keys from my pocket.

All sorts of crazy thoughts raced through my mind. *Is it terminal? How long does she have?* All I knew about ovarian cancer, the so-called *silent killer,* was that it had taken the life of Gilda Radner, Roseanne Roseannadanna of *Saturday Night Live* fame. She died in her early forties.

Miraculously, I didn't get in an accident on the short drive to our house. Jeannie met me at the door and we hugged and wept.

Then I drove slowly and carefully to Dr. Young's office.

As soon as we arrived, we were ushered into John's office. He gave Jeannie a hug and me a warm handshake. "We're going to get you the best help possible, Jeannie. Bakersfield has been blessed with the finest surgeon you could possibly hope for—Sergio Perticucci. He came up from LA a year or so ago to get out of the rat race down there. He specializes in the kind of surgery you need."

Jeannie furrowed her brow. "You don't think . . . UCLA?"

"No, I don't. Doctor Perticucci is as good as they come. Anywhere."

Dr. Young put his arms around us and said a prayer that brought tears to all our eyes. He then pulled some strings to get us in to see Dr. Perticucci the next day.

* * *

Daughter Brandy joined us at Dr. Perticucci's office. After a short wait, we were ushered in to see him. In his Italian accent, this small, grim-faced man, with Jeannie's records spread before him, said her situation was dire. The surgery he expected to perform involved her entire abdominal cavity and he expected it to last about six hours. The large tumor had grown without symptoms, as is the norm with ovarian cancer, and was pushing against the internal organs.

Dr. Perticucci pulled no punches. "I'll remove the uterus, tubes and ovaries. The bladder also appears to be involved as does the large intestine. I may well have to cut out part of the bladder and resect the colon. The right side of the diaphragm is pushed upward, and part of that may need to be removed also. I'll carefully inspect your abdominal wall and all its contents, dissecting every trace of tumor I find. One year later, we'll open you up again and perform the same inspection and tumor removal. Meanwhile, you'll undergo chemotherapy."

Jeannie listened with a stoic expression. My eyes were on her as I tried to digest those awful words.

"When can you do it?" she asked.

"Not for three weeks. I'll be in Italy. I can schedule you for the day after I return."

"Three weeks…" Jeannie's voice trailed off.

"You can't do it before you go?" I could hear the sound of begging in my voice.

"No. I'm leaving tomorrow." No trace of empathy for the agony we faced while he cavorted around Italy.

Jeannie and I walked silently to the car, neither of us wanting to vocalize our despair. I opened the door for her and closed it after she was seated. When I got in the driver's seat, her head was bowed with a tear ready to drip off her cheek.

I could barely hear her as she said, "I feel like I've been smashed in the face with a brick."

Fifty-Four

Perticucci Surgery

After receiving the devastating assessment from Dr. Perticucci, the drive home took only a few agonizing minutes. Brandy followed in her car and the three of us sat in the living room trying to come to grips with the three-week wait for Dr. Perticucci to return from Italy.

None of us knew what impact a delay in the surgery might have on the outcome, but deep in my bones lay the dread that Jeannie's life was soon to be snatched from her—and us—no matter what.

"Let's call Jimmy Brown and see what he thinks," Jeannie said.

That Jimmy Brown was and is Dr. James Brown, my brother's son and a urologist at the University of Iowa. He took the call and listened to our concerns. "I don't know how significant a three-week delay is, but the sooner the better." That put Brandy into high gear. "I'm going to ask Doctor Berek," she said.

In my memory it seems like no time passed before Brandy told us we could go down to see Dr. Berek the next day. This appeared to brighten Jeannie's spirits. Not mine.

I'm not one who kneels to pray. I pray in just about every other position—whatever position I'm in when my mind tells me prayer would be a good idea. This time was different. I climbed the stairs to our bedroom and dropped to my knees beside the bed. I lay my head on my folded hands and silently cried out to God. I begged him to spare Jeannie and take me instead. The girls, each with two little ones, needed her. She was their go-to person for just about everything.

By the time I finished praying, my hands and the bedding beneath them were drenched in tears. I was drained dry and barely able to stagger back down the stairs.

After Brandy left, Jeannie took my hand. "If this is my time, don't be sad. I've had a wonderful life, thirty-nine years of marriage, three fine children and four special grandchildren. You have been such a good husband. I couldn't ask for more."

I could—and did.

Brandy went with us to UCLA to see Dr. Berek. He was most gracious and generous with his time. The three of us vented our concerns about waiting for Dr. Perticucci to return from Italy. Dr. Berek checked his schedule and told us he could do the surgery the next week if Jeannie wanted him to. He said the operation would take about two hours. Jeannie looked at me with raised eyebrows. I read her mind as saying, "Perticucci said six."

Before we got home, Jeannie had made up her mind. "I'm going to stick with Doctor Perticucci. It'll be so inconvenient being in Los Angeles. And I think Perticucci will be more thorough. Six hours versus two is quite a difference."

* * *

The next morning, Jeannie called Dr. Perticucci's office to arrange for her surgery to be scheduled at Mercy Hospital's downtown location—less than a mile from our home. Living in the old downtown residential section of Bakersfield has some unexpected advantages.

"November 19, the day after he gets back," the nurse informed Jeannie. I was listening on a connected phone and gave her a thumbs-up.

"That'll mess up your birthday and Thanksgiving," she said.

I just shook my head. "So? What if it does?"

A short while later, Dr. Perticucci's nurse called back with a list of things Jeannie needed to have done to clear her for surgery. Most were routine, like x-rays, an EKG, and such. But one clearly didn't fit that mold.

Jeannie's abdomen needed to be drained of an increasing accumulation of fluid that resulted from her body's reaction to the growing tumor.

* * *

We went to San Joaquin Hospital on November 11 for this to be done. I went with Jeannie into the room where Dr. Cornforth, a radiologist, prepared her for the drainage. He had her sit with her bare back exposed and used some kind of equipment I knew nothing about to locate a spot for a large gauge needle to be inserted. I watched as he disinfected the skin and brought out the needle. Then I had to turn away. Needles of any size gave me the heebie-jeebies.

When I looked back, pink tinged fluid flowed through a tube into a gallon-size glass jar. The level rose higher and higher. I feared it might overflow. Jeannie didn't let out a peep. Dr. Cornforth periodically checked the flow rate. At one point, he patted Jeannie on the knee and said, "You are the bravest patient I've ever had."

She smiled. "I bet you say that to all your patients."

The doctor shook his head. "No, I really mean it."

* * *

November 19 seemed to take forever to arrive. But when the date did, along with it came Jeannie's sister Judy from Dallas and her mother Bertha from Houston.

Preparation for surgery went smoothly. Dr. Finberg, who had agreed to serve as assistant surgeon, stopped by to say "Hi" to Jeannie and give a final check of her medical chart. We knew him from the Racquet Club. He had also delivered our four grandchildren.

Soon it was time for Jeannie to be wheeled off to the surgery suite. Daughter Kelly, the family optimist, gave her a hug and said, "Everything's going to be all right, Mom."

I gave Jeannie a kiss and watched the gurney disappear through the double doors guarding the place where surgeons wield their scalpels. My heart was pounding ferociously against my ribs.

Our group of family and friends more than filled the surgery waiting room. It was a standing-room-only crowd, even as some departed and others took their place. Many brought goodies of all kinds to eat. I couldn't. My stomach was the size of a mustard seed. The clock on the wall tormented me with hands that didn't seem to move. By my reckoning, those six hours took at least six days before Dr. Finberg appeared with a smile on his face that broke my gloom.

"Jeannie did fine. Doctor Perticucci removed the tumor—about the size of a grapefruit—along with the uterus, tubes, and ovaries. He could find no evidence of involvement of the bladder, colon, or diaphragm. The tumor appeared to be encapsulated."

"Is that good?" someone asked.

"Yes. But Doctor Perticucci took at least a hundred biopsies to be looked at under a microscope to check for spread. There were cancer cells in the fluid Doctor Cornforth drained at San Joaquin, so we have to look closely for any metastasis."

"When can I see her?" I asked, not having the decency to thank him first.

"She's in the recovery room now. A nurse will come get you when it's time."

Only then did I have the presence of mind to say, "Thank you." The family all joined in with their thanks, and we gathered for a group hug.

Fifty-Five

Dr. Cartmell

The day following Dr. Perticucci's surgery, Jeannie was dozing in her hospital room. I kept watch as her chest rose and fell, the IV dripped, and the heart monitor traced a steady beat. The rhythm had almost put me to sleep when a *rap-rap* sounded at the open door and a thin, jaunty man stepped into the room. He removed his small-brimmed hat, took three or four quick strides, and sat down on Jeannie's bed.

Jeannie blinked a few times, then silently stared at this man who had leaned forward to put his face no more than a foot from hers. "Oh, Hi," she said.

"Hi, Barbara, I'm Alan Cartmell. I'm going to be your oncologist. How are you feeling?"

"Groggy."

"Not surprising. They've got you on some pretty heavy pain meds."

"I don't hurt. I'm just tired."

"Okay, go back to sleep. I'll see you tomorrow and we'll talk about chemotherapy." Dr. Cartmell stood and extended his hand to me. "You must be Mister Brown."

"Jim." I shook his hand. He had a good, firm grip.

"See you tomorrow." Off he went.

Barbara. I couldn't recall anyone calling her Barbara before. *Barbara Jean* was the name on our marriage license, her nursing license, her driver's license, the deeds to our house and condo, and our bank account, but everyone knew her as *Jeannie.* This day marked the start of her new identity.

* * *

The following evening, Dr. Cartmell returned as promised. Again, he sat on her bed and looked her in the eye until she spoke. We learned over time that this was his ritual.

"I don't think I want chemo," Jeannie said.

"Well, let's talk about that. Why not?"

Jeannie told him about what she learned in the continuing education course she had taken many years earlier. He listened without interrupting.

After several seconds of silence, Dr. Cartmell said, "Much has changed since then." He gently explained the procedure, the side effects, and the statistics supporting the benefits of chemotherapy.

Jeannie nodded along. When he finished, she looked at me. "What do you think?"

"Remember what we learned at Crown Ministries about seeking wise counsel?"

She turned back to Dr. Cartmell. "You really think I should?"

"I do. We won't start for about a month. You need a good amount of healing-time first."

Jeannie fiddled with her IV line, untangling it from under her blanket "Okay, if you think it's best."

"You'll be here another four days or so. When you're discharged, they'll set up an appointment for you to come see me and have blood work done. We can talk about it more then."

* * *

Our first visit to Comprehensive Blood & Cancer Center (CBCC) to see Dr. Cartmell was a surprise, to me at least. About forty people sat scattered about the spacious waiting area. The reception counter had two stations for receiving patients, both occupied. After waiting our turn, Jeannie presented her paperwork. "Barbara Brown to see Doctor Cartmell."

"We're running a little behind, Barbara. Have a seat and someone will call you."

Three doors led from the waiting area to the interior. Periodically, someone appeared at one of the doors and called out a first name. If more than one patient responded, the name-caller had to discretely identify the correct one. The first time *Barbara* was called, it wasn't for us. Later, we learned that the call for blood work or for patients seeing Dr. Cartmell came from a different door.

When the call came for Jeannie's *Barbara*, I was invited in but told to sit in one of the chairs in the hall while she had blood drawn. *Fine with me.* After the blood-draw, we were escorted through another interior door and down a long hall to one of Dr. Cartmell's exam rooms. His nurse had Jeannie sit on the examination table where she took *Barbara's* temperature and blood pressure. "Doctor will be in shortly." Off she went, closing the door behind her.

A few minutes passed before Dr. Cartmell came into the room dressed in a white lab coat and carrying a thin file folder. He placed the folder on the counter by the door and sanitized his hands. We said our hellos before he sat on a rolling stool and wheeled to a spot where he could look Jeannie in the eye. He said nothing.

Jeannie broke the silence. "How was my bloodwork?"

"You're a bit anemic, but your CA125 is down to 386. It was over eight thousand before surgery."

More silence.

"What's normal in your lab?" Jeannie asked.

"Zero to thirty-five."

"Do you still think I should have chemo?"

"Yes. What do you think?"

"I don't like the thought of it . . . but I'll do whatever you think is best." She gave him a wan smile.

"Let's give you a tour of the infusion room."

Several doorways and long halls led us to a spacious room with many windows granting views of outside greenery. The room held 15 to 20 plush recliners, most occupied by patients who had IV-poles beside them. Hanging bags dispensed what I presumed were chemotherapy agents. A half dozen or so brightly dressed staff appeared to be monitoring the patients' progress, some of whom were asleep.

"Your treatment will consist of eight sessions, three weeks apart. Each session will last about six hours." Dr. Cartmell rolled out an IV-pole from beside an empty chair. "You can take your medication with you to the restroom, or if you just want to take a walk."

"Will the chemo make me very sick?"

"I hope not. You'll get a dose of anti-nausea medication flushed in with a bag of normal saline before you leave. Also, there are several prescription drugs available to help with nausea. But the first week you probably won't feel like doing much after a session other than rest."

Dr. Cartmell then took us to the scheduling desk where Rachel set up appointments for the first infusion, pre-infusion blood work, and a visit with a physician's assistant.

A long and rough road lay ahead.

Fifty-Six

Chemotherapy

Jeannie put on comfortable clothes for her first session at the CBCC chemotherapy infusion center. Despite her lingering reluctance to welcome the poisonous drugs into her body, she crawled in the passenger seat and off we went—*ten minutes early!*

Let me get this out of the way. I alluded to it before. I'm a coward. I hate needles. I hide my eyes even when someone gets poked by one in a movie or on a TV show. When I knew a needle was about to be stuck into Jeannie, off I went to the vending machines until it was over.

The first order of business at each session involved a blood draw to make certain various blood levels were adequate to withstand the chemo agents to be administered. While waiting for results of these tests, an IV was started to give Jeannie medication to make her drowsy, and to provide a pathway for the cancer-fighting chemicals if the tests said she was good to go.

Jeannie's nurse went over the results of the blood tests with us. They showed some borderline anemia (normal for Jeannie), but otherwise everything fell in the acceptable range.

"Here we go," Jeannie said. A mock frown hid what I knew lay beneath it—apprehension and dread.

The nurse hung a bag on the IV stand, ran the flow-tube through the dispensing machine, set the flow rate, and connected it to a receiving port on Jeannie's IV line. I looked at the label on the bag but it was a waste of time. The chemical name meant nothing to me. I could have studied it for an hour and come away with no clue how to pronounce it, let alone know what it was or how to spell it.

For the next several hours, Jeannie drifted in and out of slumber. I kept watch as the nurse changed bags and reset flow rates. When Jeannie regained a bit of consciousness from time to time, about the only thing she said was, "I'm sorry. I just can't stay awake."

At long last the nurse said, "This is the last bag". She upped the flow rate and gave us a quick grin. "It's just normal saline. When it's empty, you'll be ready to go." Jeannie perked up some and gave me a weak smile before heading back to pay a final visit to the sandman.

The *last bag* must be related to a *watched pot*. I had to look away for the bag to empty. When it did, the nurse took out the IV. "Check out at the scheduling desk," she said.

"Where is it?" Jeannie asked. Her voice sounded like it came from far away.

"I'll take you over there." She marched us down a short hall to a counter that looked as if it belonged in a bank. The nurse knocked on the counter and a lady looked up. "This is Barbara Brown," the nurse announced, "Doctor Cartmell's patient. She just had her first infusion."

The lady behind the counter filled out several cards and handed them to Jeannie. One was for the next chemo session, another scheduled a blood draw to check Jeannie's CA125 level, and the third scheduled a visit with Dr. Cartmell's physician's assistant.

On the drive home, Jeannie asked, "Can we go by Starbuck's?"

"Sure. What do you want?"

"I'll tell you when we get there."

About half a dozen cars filled the drive-through lane when we arrived. "I'll have a Grande, Mocha Cappuccino Light, with whipped cream," Jeannie said when we finally pulled up to the post holding a box covered by a grill. A voice came out of the grill giving a name and work title followed by, "What can I get started for you?"

Never having been to a Starbuck's before, I had forgotten what Jeannie wanted, so she leaned across me and gave her order with heavy emphasis on *with whipped cream.*

About five minutes later, we pulled up to the product dispensing window and a young girl handed me a plastic cup and took my money. I handed the cup to Jeannie. She handed it back. "There's no whipped cream."

The young girl gave me my change. I gave her the cup. "There's no whipped cream."

She looked at the sticker on the cup and disappeared into the dark recesses of Starbuck's. I know the driver behind me wanted to honk—or worse—but he didn't. A few minutes later, the young girl reappeared with a bubble-topped cup loaded with whipped cream. A wide-eyed smile lit Jeannie's face when I held the cup out to her. She removed the wrapper from her straw, stuck the straw through the hole in the bubble-top, and sucked in some whipped cream. "Thank you. Did you leave a tip?"

"No. Was I supposed to?"

"Of course."

"How much?"

"Fifty cents."

"I'll get her next time."

The cup holding the Grande, Mocha Cappuccino Light, *with whipped cream* was empty by the time I pulled into our driveway. Jeannie was starting to nod off. I don't know what Starbuck's puts into its Mocha Cappuccino Light, but it's no match for what CBCC gave her.

I guided Jeannie into the den and onto the couch. "Do you want me to turn on the TV?"

She shook her head and closed her eyes.

Nausea set in the following day. At first, Jeannie said it wasn't too bad. Her assessment changed a day later. Anti-nausea pills helped but not much. As the second chemo date approached, she said she felt better except that she didn't look forward to the cycle of nausea repeating many times over the next several months.

Hair loss seemed to impact Jeannie even more than nausea. We had been told when to expect her hair to start falling out so the shedding of some in the shower didn't come as a surprise. Then one afternoon, I heard, "Aaah! Oh, no!" coming from her bathroom. She opened the door holding a fistful of hair. "It's coming out in clumps."

This started the wig hunt.

A local organization—the name of which escapes me—provided loaner wigs to ladies going through chemotherapy. Jeannie tried a few, even wearing one for her driver's license photo, before deciding she wasn't a wig person. She was a hat person. After all, she had worn a hat for our wedding. Her collection of head coverings grew like mushrooms. Floppy hats, ball caps, knit caps, straw hats, you name the style and she had some.

"I don't mind being bald so much. What I really hate is not having any eyebrows. I didn't know I'd lose those too." Eyebrow pencil in hand, she attempted to recreate an arc of hair above each eye. "Linda says they'll grow back."

Jeannie and I met Linda at CBCC, and true to form Jeannie had made another friend—but not for long. Linda also had ovarian cancer and Dr. Perticucci had been her surgeon. Her attitude toward fighting cancer inspired many patients, Jeannie included. She always had a smile on her pretty face as she shared her Christian faith with seemingly everyone she encountered. And she never wore the same wig more than once.

Less than a year after we met Linda, we attended her memorial service. Jeannie cried all the way home.

* * *

The three-week circular path of Jeannie's chemotherapy continued with interspersed visits to CBCC for consultation with Dr. Cartmell. Frequent blood draws checked the CA125 level as well as her red and white blood cell counts. After each trip to CBCC, the next stop was Starbuck's for a *Grande Mocha Cappuccino Light with Whipped Cream.* The whipped cream part might appear to defeat the "Light" part, but that's the way Jeannie wanted it. Sometimes the cup came with whipped cream, sometimes without. If without, back it went for the foamy white stuff to be added.

After about the fourth infusion session, we learned a new word—*thrombocytopenia*—a problem of low platelets, the little blood thingies needed for coagulation. Chemotherapy is a frequent cause of thrombocytopenia, in which case a reduction in the dosage of the chemo agents is often called for. Jeannie experienced this problem, and the dosage for her next session was cut in half, thereby extending the overall length of her chemotherapy treatment. This in turn delayed our planned Idaho vacation.

The next new word we learned was *neutropenia,* a low count of neutrophils often the result of strong chemotherapy. A neutrophil is a type of white blood cell that fights infection. Because Jeannie's blood work showed she had developed neutropenia, Dr. Cartmell put her on a course of daily (weekends included) injections of Neupogen at the CBCC Injection Clinic. Neupogen stimulates bone marrow to produce more neutrophils. Starbuck's then saw us daily. Soon whipped cream appeared as regularly as sunrise.

"I can give myself these shots," Jeannie said as we walked out of the injection clinic one day. "But I still want Starbuck's."

She checked with Dr. Cartmell. It was okay with him, and I was okay with making solo runs to Starbuck's. That way, I didn't have to hide from watching Jeannie stick the needle in.

Things progressed fairly well except for the increase in both the intensity and duration of Jeannie's nausea. The anti-nausea medication she had been taking wasn't doing the job, so Dr. Cartmell wrote out a prescription for a new medication.

When I stopped by the pharmacy to fill the prescription for twenty pills, the clerk looked at her computer screen and her eyes went wide. "Do you know what the co-pay is for this?"

"No," I said, figuring the co-pay might be a little more than the usual $25 for most prescriptions.

"It's thirteen *hundred* dollars"

Yikes! Now *I* was getting nauseous. For 20 pills, that was $65 a pill. Co-pay.

I pulled out a new credit card and left with the golden pills. I hoped they would work (both the credit card and the pills). They did—on Jeannie's nausea at least.

Dr. Cartmell had a smile on his face when we met with him about a week after the last of Jeannie's all-day chemotherapy sessions. She had begun to feel a bit perkier before we left the house to drive to CBCC. Dr. Cartmell's words lightened her spirits even more.

"Your doctor is very happy, Jeannie." (He had learned that she didn't go by Barbara.) He patted her on the knee as she sat before him on the examination table. "Your CA125 is almost down to the normal range, and I expect it to go even lower over the next couple weeks."

"That's great." She leaned forward and gave him a hug.

"We'll check it monthly for a while and see how it goes."

Jeannie scrunched her face. "When can we go to Idaho?"

This question led to a nice solution. Dr. Cartmell contacted a doctor at the Kootenai Medical Center in Coeur d'Alene and arranged for Jeannie's bloodwork to be done there with a copy of the results sent to CBCC.

It didn't take long for Jeannie and me to pack and hit the road. No kids or grandkids—just the two of us. Before we left, Jeannie got a month's supply of Neupogen syringes for her self-injections while we were gone.

In Idaho we played a little golf and did a little fishing. But mostly we just relaxed and breathed the clean, cedar-scented air. It was autumn. The leaves had turned color—especially beautiful in the older residential areas of Coeur d'Alene. Life was good with Jeannie's chemotherapy behind her even though darker days might lie ahead.

At the scheduled time, we went to the cancer department at Kootenai Medical Center for a CBC (complete blood count). More blood was drawn to check Jeannie's CA125. We had to wait until we saw Dr. Cartmell to find out the results when we got back to Bakersfield.

Fifty-Seven

Blood Test Results

During the two-and-a-half-day drive back to Bakersfield, neither Jeannie nor I brought up our concerns about what the blood tests might show. Later, we discovered both of us avoided the subject for the same reason. Fear.

We got our usual early morning start—about two in the afternoon. Instead of talking about what was forefront in our minds, we talked of everything else and worked crossword puzzles. Jeannie loved to do them on long trips when I was driving.

"What's a word for (whatever)?" she asked.

"How many letters?"

"Seven."

"Do we have any of them?"

"Blank, blank, O, blank, blank, blank, T."

"I have no idea." Sometimes I did, but usually not the right one.

When we were stumped by something like *Genus of the blue-throated African garden toad,* and the crossword *Field hockey great Lambert,* Jeannie turned to the back of her puzzle book and gave me the answers. Information I quickly forgot.

On the last day of our drive, one of the kids called to see if we'd be back in time for the Mexicali. It had long been our tradition to have a family dinner at the Mexicali the night we returned from Idaho. Jeannie asked me for our ETA so a reservation could be made.

We pulled into the Mexicali parking lot right on time—the first of our family to arrive. A table for 11 had been set up in the back room. Matt came in right behind us. Kelly and Brandy then had two little ones each. Ryan and Spencer were five. Mason and Joe were two—Kelly and Brandy again having been pregnant together—so their tardiness was forgivable. Before Jeannie and I had very many chips and salsa, the kids and grandkids trouped in and the whole family was together. Jeannie got big hugs from them all.

The next day, we went to Jeannie's appointment with Dr. Cartmell. "I'm scared," Jeannie said as she got out of the car.

"Me too." I took her hand for the walk to the building that seemed to have become our third home.

We had just taken our seats in the waiting room when "Barbara" was called to the lab for a blood draw. I didn't go back for that. I stayed in the waiting room and stared at a page in an old magazine—not reading a word.

A few minutes later, Jeannie waved for me to come back to Dr. Cartmell's office. She sat on the examination table where Dr. Cartmell's nurse took her temperature, pulse, and blood pressure. "The doctor will be right in," the nurse assured us before the door closed behind her. Jeannie gave me her look that said, *I don't like this at all*, lips tight and brow furrowed. I patted her knee and gave it a squeeze.

Dr. Cartmell knocked, opened the door and peeked in, then entered with Jeannie's file under his arm. The file was by this time a couple inches thick. He rolled his stool in front of the examination table and silently stared into Jeannie's eyes. She knew he was waiting for her to say something. He didn't have long to wait.

"What was my CA125 from Coeur d'Alene?"

He smiled. "Near the bottom of the normal range."

Jeannie leaned forward and gave his neck a long hug. When she leaned back, her face could have lit up a football stadium.

I unclenched my fists and feeling began returning to my fingers.

* * *

Life went back to near normal except for anxiety leading up to appointments for blood draws at CBCC and meetings with Dr. Cartmell every three months. Jeannie kept close tabs on her CA125. At one visit she expressed more than a little concern. "My CA125 has gone up the last two times. Does that mean the cancer is coming back?"

When Jeannie was first diagnosed, I read an article on the internet that said ovarian cancer always came back. Recurrence wasn't a matter of if but rather a matter of when. I never mentioned that article to her.

Dr. Cartmell opened Jeannie's file and flipped through a few pages. "No. These are small variations we see all the time. Even though your last two were a little higher, they're still in the low part of the normal range."

Jeannie looked relieved. She confirmed her relief on the way to Starbuck's for her *Grande Mocha Cappuccino Light with Whipped Cream.* "I feel really good. Makes me want to work in the garden."

For more than thirty years Jeannie had labored to create and improve a street-side flower garden that ran across the entire front yard. My main contribution had been digging holes for azalea bushes and other larger plantings, mainly in places heavily invaded by roots of a large Liquid Amber tree. I had also installed a brick border between the lawn and her garden. "No straight lines. Graceful curves only," had been my instructions.

The brick border, then covered with moss, marked the territory for Jeannie to work her magic between the bricks and the curb. I knew the names of some of the flowers and shrubs such as Iris, Azaleas, and Roses when she planted them. Others I now remember from her instructions not to harm them. Agapanthus and Ranunculus among them. The perennials pretty much remained in place. Annuals varied from year-to-year depending on her whim and available nursery stock.

Neighbors and folks just out for a walk frequently stopped by to marvel at the beauty of the blooms and to see if anything new had been planted. If Jeannie was out there working, a lengthy conversation might ensue. It's one of the reasons people in the neighborhood got to know and love her.

Fifty-Eight

Wild Rice

In the summer of 1997, I went on my first guided fly-fishing outing. Just me. Jeannie loved to fish, but her knees didn't let her wade mountain rivers. I had arranged for a guide, Tim Linehan, to introduce me to a small stream I had heard about while in Montana on business that spring. It was the start of a long friendship with Tim and his wife, Joanne.

Joanne had prepared a wonderful lunch that Tim spread out on the bank of the stream after we had fished a few hours. Included in the lunch was a salad as good or better than any on the planet—Joanne's special wild rice salad.

When I got back to our condo in Idaho, I raved to Jeannie about it. "It was the best salad I've ever tasted. Wild rice, chopped vegies, and a delicious dressing. You should have been there just for that."

"What was the dressing?" Jeannie looked up from the oil painting she was working on as if really interested.

"I don't know how to describe it other than it wasn't creamy."

"You're no help." She went back to her painting.

Eight years later, we decided to host a family reunion at our Idaho condo for our kids and grandkids as well as my brother and his tribe—an assembly of 22 Browns, Starrs, and Haines. After more than forty years of marriage, Jeannie had perfected a few dishes she planned to prepare in advance and freeze. One of her specialties was spaghetti sauce that if we had taken it commercial could have made us fabulously wealthy. It took her all day to make a big pot.

"We'll have spaghetti the first night and you can make your Italian (she pronounced it *eye-talian*) salad."

My eye-talian salad was about as special as the Tuesday newspaper.

Before we headed north for our summer vacation and family reunion I received an email that contained the *LOC Newsletter.* LOC stands for Linehan Outfitting Company, Tim and Joanne's. In the newsletter was the recipe for Joanne's Wild Rice Salad.

I made a beeline for the guest bedroom where Jeannie was sorting clothes to take to Idaho. "You'll never believe the email I just got."

"What was it?" Jeannie was going through her annual ritual of taking just about everything out of her several closets to decide what to take to Idaho. She usually decided to take it all—almost.

"The recipe for the wild rice salad."

"Really?" Her eyes sparkled. "Did you print it out?"

"Yup." I handed her the print-out.

She forgot about her clothes—for a while—as she studied the list of ingredients. "Be sure to take this with us. We'll have wild rice salad with the spaghetti."

I did, and we did. Almost.

A problem greeted us when we arrived in Idaho. The deck behind our condo, where we were going to feed everyone at the reunion, was a disaster. Over the winter a tree had fallen and smashed the rails and most of the floor. The deck was old and starting to rot anyway, but the tree put it out of its misery.

Jeannie took a quick look. "You take care of getting the deck rebuilt. And make it bigger. I've got to focus on the food." I had my marching orders.

The troops were due to arrive from California, Colorado, and Georgia in less than a week.

I found someone who claimed to know how to build a deck, but he couldn't start for two days. So I removed the fallen tree, dismantled the old deck, and measured out the corners for the new family-reunion-size deck.

Meanwhile, Jeannie started her hunt for wild rice. She didn't want the kind mixed with regular rice. She wanted the real McCoy, 100% Minnesota-grown wild rice. She learned of some but had to order it and hope it arrived on time. It did—all three pounds of the stuff.

When I got back from the last dump run disposing of the old deck, the construction had started. Jeannie furrowed her brow and crooked her finger at me. "Did you see what they're doing?" She peeked out the back window and pulled me over.

The old boy I hired was putting in the footings where I had marked them. "Yah, he's putting in the footings. What about it?"

"Just wait."

About that time, a small lady, sixtyish, appeared from around the corner of the building. She was wearing high-heels and nice clothes. On her shoulder was a 16-foot length of two by twelve. I couldn't believe what I was seeing. She put the two by twelve on a pile of other lumber and went back for more.

"She's been hauling that lumber all the time you've been gone. In heels!" Jeannie began to giggle.

I shrugged and went out to help.

The rest of the day, Jeannie worked at her job of cooking up two huge pots of spaghetti sauce while the deck construction plodded along. She sliced, diced, pureed, and seasoned with her artist's touch. The following day, she worked on another of her treasures, albondigas soup, which took regular rice for the meatballs.

"Hurray," she whooped when the wild rice delivery came. Guests were arriving the next day.

The rest of the salad had to be fresh, but she prepared the wild rice and put it in the fridge. She scheduled tomorrow's dinner to be yummy spaghetti, garlic bread (if someone else watched the oven to make sure it didn't burn), and *Joanne's special wild rice salad*.

Gathering day came. In between greeting folks as they pulled in, Jeannie sat in her tiny kitchen preparing the bevy of fresh vegetables for the salad, a glass of her favorite wine at her side. Two pots of sauce simmered on the stove-top. The delightful aroma filled our little condo. Kelly, Brandy, and Matt, did their usual; they each scooped sauce into a bowl and wolfed it down, claiming they were *sauce testers.* Then they went back for more.

Later, the kids took charge of setting up picnic tables on the new deck, covering them with bright red and white tablecloths, and putting out the place settings.

Jeannie told everyone about *Joanne Linehan's wild rice salad* that I said was the best ever.

When all was ready, she rang the dinner bell, and the feast was on. It was delicious. And it was nearly ten o'clock our time, midnight for the Colorado folks, and one in the morning for those from Georgia.

The late hour, travel fatigue, and full bellies brought on the need for our guests to get a good night's sleep in their rental condos. Soon, Jeannie and I were alone taking care of the clean-up duties.

"Well, you did it again, Sweetie," I said while rinsing off a stack of plates to go in the next dishwasher cycle.

"Do you think they liked it?" She always worried about that.

"Are you kidding? They loved it." I gave her a mock spanking.

* * *

The breakfast plan for the morning was strawberry waffles, bacon, and mimosas. Jeannie headed downstairs early to start the bacon and slice the strawberries. No more than a minute went by before I heard a shriek coming from downstairs followed by peals of laughter, laughter of the intensity I had never heard before.

I bounded down the stairs two at a time and found Jeannie sitting on the kitchen floor in front of a wide-open refrigerator. Tears rolled down her cheeks amidst a combination of laughs and wails and sobs.

I couldn't figure out if she had fallen and hurt herself, or what. "Are you okay?"

"No. look." That's all I heard before laughter overtook her again. She pointed to a large glass bowl in the refrigerator. Wild rice—all three pounds of it.

She didn't stop laughing and crying for a good long while. When my brother Bill, a real wild rice aficionado, came in the door, Jeannie was still on the floor gasping for breath.

Bill looked shocked. "What in the world?"

Jeannie looked up at him. "I didn't put . . ." She couldn't finish before more laughter erupted.

I explained what happened.

"I was wondering about that," Bill chuckled. "You know how I like the stuff." He pulled the bowl out, lifted the plastic wrap and took a long sniff. "I kept poking through my salad thinking she must not have put much in there."

How could so wise a woman . . . ?

Fifty-Nine

Lumpectomy

Shortly after our annual return from Idaho in the fall of 2006, Jeannie dropped another grenade when I arrived home from work. "I have breast cancer."

"What?" I felt like I'd been gut-punched.

"I had my mammogram today. Doctor Finberg said there's no doubt it shows a cancerous tumor in my right breast." Her eyes began to fill with tears. "I reminded him of the surgery I had in Oklahoma and that the lump they took out was benign. He said this tumor is different."

I hugged her while the world spun out of control. Tears ran down my cheeks while hers made wet spots on my suitcoat. "What do you want to do? Oklahoma? UCLA? Here?" I asked.

She sniffed. "I don't know. Doctor Finberg recommended a Bakersfield surgeon that we can talk to later this week."

Filled with apprehension and knots in my stomach from my experience with a local surgeon twenty years earlier, we went to see the recommended doctor. He explained the option of a mastectomy versus a lumpectomy. "Many studies have shown virtually no difference in long-term outcome," he said.

Jeannie shook her head. "What about a radical mastectomy? My mother had two of those, forty and forty-five years ago, and she's doing fine."

The doctor ruled out the radical surgery, leaving Jeannie with the choice between removing just the tumor or the whole breast. She told him she had to think about it.

"What do you think?" Jeannie asked me at dinner.

I knew she had consulted everyone she could think of and had prayed about the decision between a lumpectomy and a mastectomy. I didn't think my input carried much weight. So, I bailed out. "Whatever you're most comfortable with."

"That's no help." She shook her fist at me. "I've always said I'd never have chemotherapy, and I'd never have a lumpectomy. But the chemo seems to have worked. And everybody I've talked to and everything I've read supports what Doctor what's-his-name said about the long-term prognosis being the same."

"Which way are you leaning?"

"I don't know . . . probably the lumpectomy. It's less invasive. Either way, he'll take lymph nodes from under my arm to check for spread."

* * *

The day of surgery came. Jeannie had decided to go with the lumpectomy.

"She did great," the surgeon reported. "The tumor was about one inch by half an inch. I could see no evidence the cancer has spread. I removed lymph nodes from under her arm to be sent to pathology. We'll have their report in a couple days."

Kelly, Brandy, Matt, and I all thanked him, and I began to breathe normally again.

The doctor shook my hand. "She's in recovery now. A nurse will come get you when you can see her."

At the time, it seemed that Jeannie had made a good decision to go with a lumpectomy. Two days later she was home when the surgeon called about the pathology report on the lymph nodes from under her arm. They were good—no cancer cells were identified.

* * *

Chemotherapy, as dictated by the size and type of the tumor, started about a month after surgery. Part of the chemotherapy cocktail had to be carefully administered by a nurse using the *push* method. "We call this the *red death* because if it infiltrates, you could lose your arm." The nurse handed Jeannie a Popsicle and held up a syringe about the size of a basting tube filled with a bright red fluid. "It takes about ten minutes for me to slowly push this into your vein."

"Will she get it every session?" I asked, feeling a bit queasy.

"Unless Doctor Cartmell changes his order."

I decided to watch the ten minutes of push, hoping not to do something stupid, like pass out.

The nurse provided a running commentary as she went through the process. "We have to use your left arm because lymph nodes were taken from under your right arm. No blood pressure, no IV, no blood draws, and no injections on that side."

The needle went in smoothly as a lump the size of a baseball made its way down my throat.

"First, I'll withdraw the plunger a little bit to get what we call *blood return* letting me know the tip of the needle is in the vein." Dark red blood soon mixed with the bright *red death*. Then the ten minutes of *push* began. "Let me know if you feel faint or hot. Sucking on the Popsicle will help. It'll also help prevent blisters in your mouth."

When the ten minutes were up and the *red death* was roaming around inside Jeannie's body looking for cancer cells to kill, I went for a short walk to calm my nerves. Jeannie was sleeping by the time I got back. The rest of the chemo-cocktail drip-drip-dripped into the IV line.

Jeannie stirred when the last bag was hung on the IV stand, normal saline to flush the remaining chemicals from the lines into her vein. She looked up at me with a smile. "Can you get me another Popsicle?"

I tracked one down and gave it to her to suck on while we waited for the bag to empty. When it did, the nurse took out the IV, cleaned the injection site, and applied a little pressure bandage. "You're good to go, Barbara."

Off we went to Starbucks for the first post breast cancer chemotherapy *Grande Mocha Cappuccino Light with Whipped Cream.*

Sixty

Gene Testing

Jeannie's hair again fell out, including her eyebrows. Her collection of hats and caps grew. She didn't try wigs this time. From time to time she took her hat or cap off so the grandkids could laugh at their bald Amma.

The veins in Jeannie's left arm took a beating from the blood draws and IVs as the chemo sessions progressed. Finding a good vein became harder and harder for the nurses to start an IV, or so I was told.

At one infusion session, three nurses tried unsuccessfully to start an IV. "You'll have to come back tomorrow when our IV guru will be here," Jeannie's nurse told her. We went to Starbuck's.

***

The next day, I could see Jeannie's recliner at CBCC from my position at the vending machines. The *IV guru* pulled up a stool and sat next to Jeannie's left side. She seemed to spend a long time getting ready, turning Jeannie's arm this way and that, slapping here and there, before cleaning a spot with alcohol. I stayed at the vending machines, taking a quick peek now and then to see if it was safe for me to return. When I saw the guru walk away, I headed back, half-eaten snacks in hand.

Jeannie shook her head. The guru returned, carrying and armload of bags to be hung.

"She had to poke me seven times before she got into a vein," Jeannie said when I returned from my cowardice trip to the vending machines. "The vein kept rolling. Finally, she had to use a smaller needle, so this session will take longer."

Later that day, the nurse asked Jeannie if she had thought about getting a port. "What's that?" Jeannie asked.

The nurse said the placement involved a minor surgery just below the collar bone. A needle connected to a short tube would be inserted into the subclavian vein. A port connected to the other end of the short tube, and protruding through the skin, could then be used in lieu of an IV. It could also be used for blood draws.

A patient in the chair closest to Jeannie must have been listening. After the nurse left, she looked over. "Don't do it."

Jeannie furrowed her brow. "Why not?"

The lady unbuttoned the top of her blouse and exposed her left-upper chest. "This is what happened to me." Her skin—all of it we could see—was one ugly dark purple bruise. "They had to take it out."

On the way to Starbuck's after that session, Jeannie laced her fingers and twisted her hands. "I don't think I want a port. Too much risk of infection."

After seeing the lady's bruising, I couldn't disagree, even though it would eliminate the need for my escapes to the vending machines.

* * *

Jeannie didn't complain about anything—other than losing her eyebrows—as the months of chemotherapy ticked by. She treated the infusion sessions, the injections to bolster her blood levels, her nausea and weakness, and her appointments with Dr. Cartmell like they were just part of everyday life. However, she did smile more on the way to Starbuck's than she did on the way to CBCC.

The first time we saw Dr. Cartmell after the last chemo session, Jeannie wanted to know what her blood tests showed. More results were now involved. Along with the CA125 for ovarian cancer, her blood was tested for tumor markers related to breast cancer, CA15.3 and CA27.29.

"They're all in the normal range," Dr. Cartmell said. "But there's something else I think you should do."

"What's that?" Jeannie's voice sounded shaky.

Dr. Cartmell patted her on the knee. "There's a lab in Utah that does genetic testing looking for mutations that signal greater risk for certain cancers, including ovarian and breast cancer. These mutations are hereditary. Because of your family history, I think it's wise for you to have that done."

Jeannie nodded. "What about Kelly and Brandy?"

"Actually, Matt, too," he said. "It's not common, but men can also get breast cancer. If you have that mutation, each of them has a fifty percent chance they inherited the mutation from you, and they should get tested. It's quite expensive so wait for your results first."

"How expensive?" She looked at me with wide eyes. We knew that each infusion session cost around $10,000.

"I'm not exactly sure . . . several thousand dollars though. I'll see if your insurance will agree to cover at least part of the cost."

"Let's do it," I said.

Jeannie shrugged her shoulders. "I guess."

* * *

Dr. Cartmell convinced the insurance company to pay part of the genetic testing and CBCC sent a blood sample to the Utah lab. Not many days passed before the results came back. They weren't good.

Jeannie did have a mutation of what was called the BRCA gene. Good news came when the girls were tested. Neither Kelly nor Brandy had inherited the mutation. Matt declined to be tested.

While we were waiting for the girls' results, we talked to Dr. Cartmell about the chances of Jeannie having recurrence of breast cancer. He thought it was worthwhile for us to meet with Dr. Mai Brooks at UCLA, a specialist dealing with breast cancer problems of this sort.

CBCC was associated with UCLA and Dr. Cartmell spoke highly of Dr. Brooks—but he didn't give us a hint about her appearance.

****

At the huge UCLA medical center, we parked several levels down in the underground parking facility and took the elevator to the main floor of one of the three buildings and began our search for Dr. Brooks' office. Luckily we were in the right building and showed up early for Jeannie's appointment. While waiting in a small conference room, I conjured up an image of what Dr. Brooks might look like.

The person who came through the door wasn't Dr. Brooks. No way. She must have been a school child, lost in the labyrinth of hallways—maybe in seventh grade, and small at that. "Hello, I'm Doctor Brooks," the pretty child said.

After the shock wore off, it became obvious that Dr. Brooks knew her stuff. And she didn't pull any punches. Bilateral mastectomy with or without reconstruction provided the best protection from more breast cancer, but not one hundred percent protection. If Jeannie wanted reconstruction, Dr. Brooks suggested a consultation with Dr. James Watson, a colleague of hers at UCLA. It might be possible for the mastectomy and reconstruction surgeries to be done at one time.

Jeannie said, "I'll think about it."

When we got on the parking garage elevator, neither of us could remember which level our car was on. I guessed at which button to push. Ten minutes or so of wandering around hitting the panic button on my key fob eventually produced a faint honking sound coming from somewhere below us. We walked the long way around to get to the lower level and found our ride.

I backed out of the parking space to Jeannie's sputtering giggle. "You should have seen the look on your face when she said, 'I'm Doctor Brooks.' It was priceless."

"Well, what did you think when you saw her?"

"I thought she was very pretty, but tiny."

"She must stand on a stool when she does surgery."

Sixty-One

Bilateral Mastectomy

Dr. James Watson, the reconstruction surgeon recommended by Dr. Brooks, came to CBCC one day a week so we didn't have to travel to UCLA to consult with him. He discussed with us the various alternatives of reconstruction, from silicone or saline implants to methods of transplanting Jeannie's own tissue. It was a lot of information to think about.

The most complex surgery Dr. Watson talked to us about, called a *free flap* procedure, intrigued Jeannie. "I can get rid of fat from my thighs to use as implants."

Once Jeannie made up her mind about going with the *free flap,* the next step required a visit to Dr. Watson's office at the UCLA Medical Center. I had to wait in the reception area while Jeannie underwent evaluation.

More than an hour passed before Jeannie came out to get me for a joint meeting with Dr. Watson. "We won't be able to do the reconstruction at the same time as Doctor Brooks does the bilateral mastectomy," he said. "With both breasts involved, and two donor sites, it will have to be done about a month later."

"How long will I have to stay in the hospital?"

Dr. Watson was rather noncommittal. He said something about a few to several days. My bet was on *several.*

We left with a fistful of papers and headed to the elevator. "You were sure gone a long time. What all did they do back there?"

"Mostly marking the donor sites on each side. He had to locate arteries providing blood to the tissue he's going to transplant. He used some kind of listening device to hear the blood pumping. When he does the surgery, he has to connect those arteries to ones in my chest." Color rose in her cheeks. "Before that, he took pictures of my breasts and asked me how I wanted him to make me look. I said I didn't want to look like a sixteen-year-old. I want to look like me."

* * *

The bilateral mastectomy performed by Dr. Brooks took place in early January 2007, a great way to ring in the new year. The surgery went well, and I was able to bring Jeannie home in a few days. On the drive to Bakersfield, Jeannie came as close to complaining about her bouts with cancer as she ever had. "I guess I'm no longer a woman. They've taken my uterus, my tubes and ovaries, and now my breasts."

"You're still the most beautiful woman I know." My reassurance probably didn't have much effect—but she squeezed my hand and said I was sweet.

The reconstruction by Dr. Watson hung like a dark cloud a month away. In the meantime, we had another visit with Dr. Cartmell to go over the pathology results of the breast tissue removed by Dr. Brooks. "A small cancerous tumor was found in the right breast, so the decision to have both breasts removed was a good one," he said.

"Why didn't the chemo kill that?" Jeannie asked. I wondered the same thing.

"There's no way to know for sure. It was so small; it may have developed after your treatment ended."

* * *

Dr. Watson recommended spending the week before his surgery at a high elevation. This would allow Jeannie's body to adjust to making more efficient use of oxygen needed to withstand the surgery and facilitate recovery. A week in the mountains sounded good. We thought of a place in the Sierras but it was snowed in for the winter.

"What about Flagstaff?" Jeannie asked.

I checked the elevation of Flagstaff. "It's nearly seven thousand feet. That's high enough."

Jeannie loved Flagstaff ever since she met—quite by accident—a Hopi carver of kachina dolls during an overnight stay there. As usual, she had made another new friend, and before he went on his way, he invited us to come to a Hopi ceremony at Second Mesa, a Hopi settlement north of Flagstaff. At the time, we were heading to Oklahoma City and couldn't accept his invitation.

For our week in Flagstaff, we found a motel online that could accommodate us without breaking the bank. After packing some winter clothes, we hit the road east. Ice and snow don't seem to go with Arizona, but Flagstaff had plenty of both when we arrived.

From time-to-time, I'm sure Jeannie thought about what lay ahead. I know I did. But mostly we browsed the shops and searched out eateries that locals patronized, finding some good ones. We also took a few day-trips to higher elevations such as the Arizona Snowbowl ski area and the San Francisco Mountains.

Dr. Watson had arranged for Jeannie to receive injections of some kind every other day at the Flagstaff Medical Center. I waited in the car, claiming I wanted to keep it warm until she got back. She knew better. Coward that I am.

The week sped by and before long we were on the road back to Bakersfield. A few miles west of Flagstaff a near blizzard slowed traffic to a crawl. The blowing snow continued until the elevation dropped a couple thousand feet somewhere between Seligman and Kingman. We had clear sailing from there.

The next morning, we arrived at the UCLA Hospital before 6:00 a.m. Even at that hour, the LA traffic was fierce. Jeannie was taken down to the surgery prep area. I sat with her as the IV was started—looking away, of course. The anesthesiologist stopped by to give the usual *informed consent* spiel: "Complications could include bla-bla-bla and even *death*." It's always nice to hear that last part.

A nurse started the pre-op medication and Jeannie was about to be wheeled off to surgery when a young doctor assisting Dr. Watson flipped through Jeannie's chart. He held up his hand stopping the orderlies from moving the gurney. "I have to talk to Doctor Watson about this." He took the chart, pulled back the curtain and left.

The young doctor came back in a few minutes with Dr. Watson in tow. Dr. Watson looked grim as he said, "You've had more chemo since your last heart work-up, so we can't do the surgery today. You need to have an echocardiogram, a nuclear stress test, (and one other heart test, the name of which I've forgotten). The echocardiogram we can do here this morning. If it's within normal limits, the other two can be scheduled later in Bakersfield."

When Jeannie was going through chemotherapy for breast cancer, Dr. Cartmell had her see a cardiologist for a battery of tests. They were all normal, and her chemo continued. Those were the tests that found their way into her chart at UCLA. So, our week in Flagstaff accomplished nothing from a medical standpoint, but we each found something to buy—another kachina doll for her and a fly-fishing gizmo for me.

The surgery was rescheduled for early March. We didn't go back to Flagstaff.

Jeannie's new heart tests returned normal results so she and I again made the early morning trek from Bakersfield to UCLA. As before, Kelly, Brandy, and Matt also made the drive.

The same pre-op procedures were completed, and Jeannie was wheeled off to surgery at 8:30. I went back to join the kids in the auditorium-size waiting room. We knew it was going to be a long wait. But we didn't know how long.

A voice periodically came from a speaker calling the family of patient so-and-so to come to the information desk. Lunch time came without a call for the family of *Barbara* Brown. Dinner time was fast approaching when I made an unsolicited visit to the information desk. I hadn't eaten breakfast or lunch, and I had no appetite for dinner either. The only thing I learned was that the surgery was still in progress.

That evening, one of the kids struck up a conversation with a couple whose son was undergoing brain surgery due to a serious auto accident. It turned out they were from Newport, Washington. Newport is a small town about thirty miles from Twin Lakes Village. We prayed together for his surgery and Jeannie's to go well.

Time rolled on. It seemed every family in the waiting area except ours and the folks from Newport had been called to the information desk. Another unsolicited check produced no new information. My empty stomach did roll-overs as I thought about the final words of the *informed consent* warning given by both Dr. Watson and the anesthesiologist, "*and even death.*"

At nearly the exact stroke of midnight—fifteen and a half hours after Jeannie was taken to the surgery suite—Dr. Watson appeared at the entrance to the waiting area and looked around the nearly empty space. The kids and I raced the hundred or so feet to get to him.

"Everything went well and she's now in recovery." He was still in his surgery scrubs. "I'd like to talk more, but I have to take over as assistant surgeon in a very delicate brain surgery." Off he went to help take care of the boy from Newport.

Sixty-Two

Paddy-O

"I look like a Christmas tree." Jeannie was headed to the den bathroom to empty the balls attached to the four drainage tubes poking through slits in her modified housedress. The four balls, one on each hip and one on each side of her chest, were nearly full of red fluid.

"Christmas in March isn't such a bad idea," I said.

"I can't wait to get these drains out. Kelly says we need a dog."

"What does a dog have to do with it?"

"Nothing. Kelly thinks it will help keep me from becoming depressed."

Dogs had been part of our family almost from the beginning, starting with a Toy French Poodle named Bridgett given to us by Jeannie's mom in the summer of 1964. Bertha raised Toy Poodles as a side business, one actually becoming a national champion. After Bridgett died at age 13, our succession of dogs included Dolly (a Golden Retriever), Natasha (a Siberian Husky), Tex (another Toy Poodle), Max (a Boxer), and Dozer (a Rottweiler).

Jeannie with Natasha

Putting Dozer to sleep in the spring of 2006 was a heart breaker for us all. She had lost the ability to walk on her own, so Jeannie found a sling to go under the feeble dog's belly. When one of us hoisted her up with the sling, Dozer could shuffle her feet to get outside to do her duties. When she couldn't even do that, our vet said, "It's time."

Labradoodles had recently emerged as a new, popular mixed breed. Kelly and Jeannie scoured every resource they could think of, looking for one at a price that was not totally obnoxious. No luck. Plus, Jeannie didn't think she was quite ready to take on a new pet. Then Kelly found a lady that had a litter of eight-week-old pups, Golden Doodles, not Labradoodles, and she went with Jeannie to check them out— Christmas tree ornaments and all.

"They are sooooo cute," Jeannie said. "They have all their shots. One of them came right up to my feet, sat down and looked up at me. I just wanted to pick her up and hug her. But I told the lady I'm not ready." Jeannie's mouth turned into a pout.

"How much?"

"Three hundred. Do you want to go see her?" Now she was smiling.

We went. And they were cute, especially the one that again came up to Jeannie and sat by her feet.

Jeannie told the lady she really needed to get her drains out and wait for the incisions to heal. She didn't want to risk infection. The lady said she understood.

A few days later, the lady called and talked to Jeannie. "She said something told her I was the right one for that puppy and she wanted to give her to us as a gift. What do you think?"

"You still have your four ornaments."

"I'll be careful."

It was Saint Patrick's Day, my mother's birthday. She had been gone nearly 47 years—the length of her life. I was sitting out on the patio thinking about her when Jeannie made her decision. "Kelly is going to take me to get the puppy. You can stay here and come up with a name."

A name? I waited for inspiration, a process I use that seldom bears fruit. This time it did—but when Jeannie took a bite, would she spit it out?

When the little ball of black fur arrived at her new home, Jeannie brought the puppy out to the patio where I was still sitting. She set the little girl down to let her explore her new surroundings. "Well?" Jeannie asked.

How to explain it?

"Here's what I've been thinking. It's Saint Patrick's Day so an Irish name might be fitting. It's my mom's birthday, and most folks called her Pat for her middle name of Patricia. And we're out on the patio. I think her name should be Paddy O'Brown—Paddy-O for short."

Jeannie laughed. "I like it." So Paddy-O became the newest addition to our family.

Then a thought that had struck me when I first saw the litter of puppies came back to my mind. "Why are Golden Doodles black?"

"They can be a bunch of different colors," Jeannie said. Paddy-O's father is a black Standard Poodle, and her mom is a Golden Retriever."

* * *

Paddy-O grew in wisdom and stature—much more in stature than wisdom. What she did pick up in wisdom came from Jeannie's relentless devotion to obedience training. But no amount of training could cure Paddy-O's main flaw, that of being way-over-the-top friendly to anyone arriving at the front door. Be they friend or foe, relative or total stranger, she greeted each visitor with unbridled enthusiasm: spinning around like a whirling dervish; dancing on her hind feet, front paws tap-dancing on the new arrival's stomach or chest; and not infrequently piddling on their shoes out of sheer excitement.

The only solution was to keep a leash by the front door so if someone knocked or got the mostly non-functioning doorbell to ring, one of us could join Paddy-O at the door (she always got there first), hook her to the leash, call "just a minute" through the door, pull Paddy-O out to the fenced back yard, and then answer the door.

If the person at the door was an uninvited solicitor, I sometimes wished Paddy-O was there to do her thing.

Paddy-O was also a runner. If a gate to the back yard was left open she spotted it immediately and the chase was on. She was *fast*. I never could beat her to the gate before she got out. When she did, she headed straight for the street and took off. Fortunately, she usually turned to the west and sprinted down our very long block toward the dead-end before turning around and racing back my way, tongue lolling as I tried to stop her. I failed at least 19 out of 20 times.

"How can I safely run Paddy-O?" Jeannie asked me. Her motto for as long as I had known her had been, *where there's a will there's a way.*

I shook my head. "Get training wheels?"

The kids came up with a solution. Kelly and Brandy knew the owner of Bakersfield's largest bicycle shop. They worked out a deal to surprise Jeannie with a gift for Mothers' Day of an adult tricycle. Paddy-O would need to take steroids to pull that thing over.

For several weeks, Jeannie and Paddy-O romped all around the neighborhood, stopping frequently to chat with anyone they came across. Then one night, some dastardly soul cut the cable lock and the three-wheeler was gone, never to be seen again.

I bought her a new one in Idaho.

Sixty-Three

Retirement Home

After we bought the five-acre lot Jeannie had found down the lake from Twin Lakes Village, we mused about what we might eventually build on it. Her ideas and mine bore no resemblance to one another. She envisioned a place where each of our children and their families, together with her mother, had a comfortable place to stay when they all came at the same time. I figured two guest rooms were plenty—but one sounded better.

Jeannie made her pitch. "We could have a dormitory for the grandkids, a bedroom for each of the children, a bedroom for my mom, and one for us." She drew her plan. For as good an artist as she had become, it failed to capture my interest. Hallways didn't exist, nor did storage areas. But she did include bathrooms. Six of them.

"If you win the lottery (my standard line), we can do it. Otherwise, we have to get real." I sketched my idea for a perfect retirement home.

"No way." She furrowed her brow. "We have more room in the condo than that."

Not quite true, but close.

We then moved on to the type of structure, whatever the size this palace might be. There, we found agreement. A log home.

Jeannie began collecting log home magazines and pictures of various styles. They were popular at the time. Log home companies seemed to spring up everywhere. In the summer of 2004, we visited ten of them in Oregon, Idaho, and Montana. Then we met with a log home builder in Coeur d'Alene.

Based on the prices we had seen for various models, Jeannie's plan might be in reach. Wrong! Wrong! Wrong! The builder popped our dream balloon. "The prices you've seen are for the logs only. Delivered to your lot, not assembled. The roof, doors, floors, windows, plumbing, electrical, appliances, and on and on are not included. The logs are just the shell, and maybe some inside walls. Then there's engineering. For the two-story you want, that's a lot."

He took us to a two-story house he was building on Lake Pend Oreille and showed us all the special things he had to do because of settlement that occurs as the logs dry out and shrink. "Don't let anybody tell you their logs won't settle. They will."

Then he gave us an estimate of the cost per square foot of something like what Jeannie had in mind. Log home living had no place in our future.

After giving up on our dream of a log home, we started searching for a contractor to build a more conventional house. This led us to a former neighbor and her mother, both of whom were in the real estate business. The mother had just moved into a new house that had been constructed by Tom Sjoblom, a local builder. She showed us around her house, all the while singing Tom's praises. "He was a joy to work with," she told us several times.

We arranged a meeting with Tom at a home he was building in Twin Lakes Village to see if he was willing to work with us. He was. At that time, none of us knew Jeannie would soon be facing her breast cancer ordeal.

* * *

Two years went by as Jeannie underwent three surgeries and prolonged chemotherapy. Tom hung in there with us, exchanging design ideas on almost a weekly basis. In the spring of 2008, Jim Bergeson, a long-time fly-fishing friend and retired architect, helped finalize the design and I went to the bank to beg for construction financing. Tom brought in heavy equipment to clear trees from the construction site, excavate the basement, and dig the utility trench. No turning back now.

Jeannie and I made daily trips to the lot to watch the progress. When she saw the excavated footing trenches for the detached garage, she shook her head. "I don't like that."

"What?" I asked.

"I don't want the garage squared up to the house like that. I think it would look much nicer turned at an angle."

Tom was happy to accommodate her. As was I. With what she'd been through, I couldn't deny her anything. Except that sixth bathroom.

* * *

Everyone in the family except Kelly thought we were nuts to be building this home. "If that's what you want, go for it," she said. She and Bill had just celebrated their tenth wedding anniversary by going on a white-water rafting trip somewhere in California and sent us a picture of them with her holding up ten fingers.

Kelly and Bill's 10th anniversary.

"She's so cute and so positive," Jeannie said. "Our family optimist."

Sixty-Four

11-11

The events beginning Monday, November 10, 2008, are burned into my memory as if they just happened.

It started with a phone call from our son-in-law, Marty, that Jeannie answered. "Jim, Jim!" she called out, panic in her voice, "Marty just called. Kelly's in the hospital. Her kidneys have failed. He wants us to fly home right away." She appeared to be on the verge of hysteria.

I ran inside from my winterizing project of covering the little pond outside the front door of our condo. "What did he say, exactly?" My mind was reeling over how we could get home the fastest.

"He said Bill called to tell him he took Kelly to Doctor Young for the flu. She was running a 103 fever. John couldn't get a blood pressure and rushed her to the hospital ER. She was in complete kidney failure." Tears welled up in Jeannie's eyes. "What will we do with Paddy-O?"

"We'll board her at the vet's," was all I could think to say. "Call the airport and see what flights are available. I'm going to call Clifford to see if he can get more information." I went outside where I could get cell phone reception to call my long-time partner, Steve Clifford, who was on the Board of Directors for the hospital where Kelly was taken.

I told Steve what I knew and asked if he could get the ER doctor to talk to me. I knew the patient privacy laws didn't let the hospital give out any information, even to a patient's father. A few minutes later,

Steve called back and said to expect the ER doctor to call me in a few minutes.

I paced the parking area of the condo association, checking my phone often to make sure I was still getting a signal. It seemed like forever before the phone rang. The doctor verified who I was before he told me anything. When he did, my heart dropped even further. "We're going to put her into a drug-induced coma. I have five specialists working to find out what's causing her fever. IV antibiotics haven't brought it down."

I didn't want to ask the question, but I had to. "What's her prognosis?"

"It's too early to tell." His tone was ominous. Kelly was in deep trouble.

The building project of our retirement home a mile down the lake was under way after eight years of saving and planning. It was the reason we were still in Idaho. That house was no longer important. Getting home to Kelly was all that mattered.

With our nerves frazzled and our brains running on overdrive, we made the decision to drive the 1200 miles to Bakersfield as there were no flights we could take until the next morning. We had driven straight through before, but not for several years.

We threw some clothes and the dog in the car, locked the condo door and took off.

Jeannie sat beside me, shaking from nerves. When we approached Spokane and had a good signal, she called our daughter, Brandy, who was at the hospital with Kelly's husband, Bill.

"Calm down, Brandy. Tell me what's happening."

I could only hear Jeannie's end of the conversation. It didn't sound good.

When the call ended, Jeannie let out a pitiful moan. "I knew we shouldn't be building that stupid house. If we'd been home, I would've gotten her to the doctor sooner."

"What did Brandy say?"

"They only let her in with Kelly a few minutes at a time. Nobody seems to know what to do."

Jeannie and I prayed constantly as the highway seemed to slowly creep by under us.

Brandy called with frequent updates, none of them encouraging. The doctors hadn't been able to get Kelly's kidneys to function, and her other organs were showing signs of distress. Cell phone reception came and went, leaving Jeannie frustrated as her questions went into the ether, unanswered due to a lost signal.

Good weather and road conditions turned bad in central Oregon. The highway began to ice over. The few headlights coming our way bounced off the slick surface, nearly blinding me. By two o'clock in the morning, we limped into Grants Pass, Oregon.

"I can't go any further," I said. "I need to get a couple hours rest and start again at daylight." We had stayed in Grants Pass before at a motel that accepted pets. Jeannie called to see if they had a room. They did. As soon as we were in the room, she called Brandy. No improvement.

Physically and mentally spent, we plopped on the bed, but sleep didn't come. Shortly after four o'clock, the phone rang. Jeannie answered it. I stood beside her.

"No! No! Jim, Kelly's gone. She's dead."

My knees buckled and I fell hard to the floor. I didn't want to get up. But I had to. I had to be strong for Jeannie.

Jeannie was still holding the phone to her ear, her face void of expression. She motioned me to her and held the phone so we could both hear. Father Craig was saying a prayer over Kelly. He then got on the phone to talk to us. These words still ring in the ears of my mind: "The most amazing thing," he said. "I've been with a lot of people when they died, but this was special. I could feel her soul depart her body."

I flopped back on the bed and squeezed my eyes shut. I wanted this to be a nightmare. Instead, a vision of Kelly appeared with her radiant smile directed not at me, but at a figure with arms outstretched. She moved toward those outstretched arms. I have no doubt those were the arms of Jesus.

I told Jeannie what I had seen as we hugged and cried, and cried, and cried.

"The boys… Oh, those poor little boys." Jeannie's body shook with each word. Spencer was nine and Mason was six.

As soon as I was able, I called Steve Clifford. I didn't care that it was not yet five o'clock.

"Hello."

"She didn't make it," was all I could get out.

"What!?"

"Kelly died."

"Oh, Jim, I can't believe it. Where are you?"

"Grants Pass. Can you call Jack and see if he can fly up and get us?"

"I will. And I'll call you right back."

I didn't think to give him the motel number.

A couple minutes later, my cell phone rang. It was Steve. "Jack said the icing conditions won't let him get to Grants Pass. Can you make it down to Redding?"

"I'll try."

Jeannie sat silently in the chair by the phone, holding her head in her hands, tears dripping through her fingers.

"We have to drive to Redding. Jack can't fly up here because of icing."

She looked up at me. Her beautiful green eyes were puffy and red. In a pitiful small voice she said, "Why couldn't it have been me? Why did He have to take Kelly?"

I didn't know what to say so I just knelt beside her and hugged her as we both wept tears of anguish.

* * *

Only bits and pieces of what happened in the next several hours remain with me. How I was able to drive the 180 miles from Grants Pass, Oregon, to Redding, California, remains a mystery.

I do remember arriving at the airport parking lot and being met by Jack and his wife, Sharon. Sharon took the car keys and the dog's leash and told us she'd drive our car to Bakersfield. Jack led us to the plane.

The next thing I remember is the car we were in pulling into the cul-de-sac at Brandy's house. I don't know who met us at the airport and drove us there. What I recall is that the street leading to Brandy's house was filled with people who gave us hugs and condolences as we made our way to the front door. The scene inside was surreal. A TV reporter and cameraman were there interviewing Bill, who sat on a couch between his two boys, Spencer and Mason.

Brandy and Matt were happy we made it but racked with grief over the loss of their big sister. Jeannie, Brandy, Matt, and I hugged for a long, long time, as our collective despair pressed down on us.

Father Craig was there, sitting next to our pastor, Milt Cole. Both got up and came to join in the group hug.

When the TV people left, we had another group hug with Spencer and Mason. Spencer then looked up at Jeannie and said, "Who's going to be our mom now?"

From there, my memory fades again.

I don't know when or where Sharon arrived with Paddy-O, or when or how we got home.

* * *

The next couple weeks are a blur of relatives arriving from around the country, food and flowers pouring in at our house and Brandy's, and the mailbox stuffed with cards and letters, many from folks we didn't know but whose lives Kelly had touched.

Sixty-Five

Grief

The order of events in the months following Kelly's death are not at all clear in my memory. The English language doesn't contain words sufficient to describe the emotional upheaval brought on by the death of a beloved child. Words like anguish, devastation, despair, or agony don't come close. God's comfort seemed far away, unreachable.

Jumbled bits and pieces of various happenings are with me, but as to most of them I'm not sure of their proper sequence. So I will lay them out as they come to mind.

Kelly's Memorial Service

I don't know who did the planning for Kelly's memorial service. What I remember is riding to RiverLakes Community Church in a limousine with Jeannie, Spencer, and Mason. The limo service came as a gift from Raji Sanghera, one of Kelly's closest friends. Jeannie whispered in my ear, "Doesn't Spencer look just like Kelly did at that age?" He did. He really did. He also looked forlorn, as did Mason.

Milt Cole held the position of senior pastor at RiverLakes, the church Jeannie and I attended when we were in Bakersfield. He had also been a dear friend and tennis opponent for more than twenty years. Milt and Father Craig jointly presided over the service attended by a crowd of several hundred that overflowed the large auditorium.

Matt, Marty, and three of Kelly's close friends spoke about what she had meant to them. Jeannie and I went through a box of Kleenex. We needed another box when a baritone soloist sang *Fly to Jesus.*

I don't recall leaving the auditorium, but once outside, a flood of people came to express their sorrow. Many of them we didn't know. Over and over, we heard, "You don't know me, but Kelly . . ." followed by how she had impacted their lives in various ways.

Tina Pineda, Kelly's friend and doubles partner in high school, had come over from Santa Barbara. And a special young lady, Robynn Goodell, sister-in-law of one of Kelly's closest friends, had come down from Sacramento. Kelly had made a prayer quilt for Robynn who was suffering from a rare form of cancer. She wanted us to know how much that meant to her.

Robynn made her flight to Jesus one month after Kelly.

Garden Plan

Not many days after Kelly's Memorial Service, the bells on the front door jingled in a pre-dawn hour. Jeannie's side of the bed was vacant, covers tossed back. We had just cried ourselves to sleep, or so it seemed.

I scrambled to put on my robe and slippers and hurried down the stairs. No sign of her in the living room, den or kitchen.

Peering through the living room window into the near-darkness of the front yard, I saw her standing at the edge of her street-side garden, the box of Kelly's ashes held close to her chest. She reached into the box and sprinkled some of the ashes around the plants. She did it again as I came to her side.

"What are you doing?"

She turned to me with a faraway look in her eyes. "We'll make this *Kelly's Garden.*" Tears streamed down her cheeks, dripping onto her nightgown and bare feet.

"Good idea. But let's get you back inside. It's cold out here."

I led her back to bed and we hugged away her shivers but not her tears.

"Oh, Jim. Why?"

"I don't know. Probably never will until we get there."

<u>Norm Wright</u>

A few days after Kelly died, Jeannie and I attended a get-together of our church home group at Bob and Barb Harding's house. Bob had been my friend as well as one of my law partners for decades. He invited one of his neighbors, Norm Wright, to join us. Norm became a true blessing. He had moved to Bakersfield after retiring from the graduate school faculty at Biola University. His specialty was grief and trauma counselling.

Our loss of Kelly dominated the home group conversation. Norm joined in by presenting us with a *memory box* for Kelly's boys. He also gave us a large bundle of *memory cards* to be handed out at Kelly's Memorial Service with the request that attendees jot down a special memory of Kelly. The returned cards to go into the memory box.

We later learned that Norm was nationally known and well-respected in his field. He had provided counselling to many of those affected by disasters such as 9/11 and Katrina. Locally, as part of what he called his retirement ministry, he helped folks like us who grieved the loss of a loved one.

He invited us to meet with him weekly, which we did for quite some time. During those sessions, we became friends. We learned that he had experienced the loss of a 22-year-old son many years earlier and the loss of his wife recently. Somewhere during this time—when he said he thought we were ready—he gave us copies of a little book, *Experiencing Grief,* one of the more than 70 books he had written. I have read it at least five times and have given out dozens of copies to others who are saddled with grief.

Norm also met one-on-one with Brandy and with Matt to help them deal with the loss of their older sister. He told all of us about GriefShare, saying something like, "It's a 13-week program, sponsored by many churches, for people who have lost a loved-one. Each session has a 40-to-45-minute video followed by a group discussion of topics contained in a workbook." Jeannie, Brandy, and I signed up.

When we arrived at the first session, Norm Wright was there, attending as a grieving person, not as a leader or facilitator.

After introductory remarks, the video began. One grief expert after another, from all around the country, spoke from the screen about the GriefShare program and various aspects of the grieving process. Then a familiar face popped up—that of Norm Wright. I often wondered how Norm felt about receiving advice from himself. But I never asked.

Sandwiches

A year or so after Kelly and her friend Shannon sold Dagny's, a well-known coffee house in downtown Bakersfield, the opportunity presented itself for Kelly to design, build, and operate a similar café in the office building where her husband Bill worked. Bill's boss owned the multi-story office building and offered to pay for everything required to get it up and running. Kelly jumped at the chance. Before long the place Kelly named *Ristretto's* had customers lined up out the door.

In addition to running *Ristretto's* on site, Kelly provided a catering service for lunch-time meetings of all sorts. The lunches included a sandwich, salad, cookie, and soft drink. Shortly before she died, she had booked her largest event (more than 100 lunches). At that time, Matt worked for Kelly doing food preparation in the morning before his afternoon and evening job. He enlisted Jeannie and me as his assistants in making the sandwiches for this big gathering.

One of Kelly's employees took us back to the small kitchen where Matt was doing his prep work. She told us, "Kelly always insisted on full coverage for her sandwiches, condiments on up. No lump of meat in the middle with nothing at the edges." Then she gave us the "order list" for the choices of fillings and breads, including croissants.

"Full coverage," we reminded each other, as we did our best to keep our tears from salting the sandwiches. Someone else had the task of matching our sandwiches with the right salad, cookie, and soft drink before closing the box. We made the delivery on time—just barely.

<u>Return to Idaho</u>

Kelly and Bill had moved from downtown to the southwest part of Bakersfield, just a few houses away from Brandy and Marty. But Spencer and Mason still went to the Downtown School, near our home. Bill took them to school in the morning. We volunteered to do pick-up duty and help them with homework. Bill often joined us for dinner before taking the boys home.

One morning after Christmas vacation started for the boys, Jeannie woke me with, "What are we going to do? We didn't winterize the condo." She tossed back the covers and slid out of bed.

I rolled over and propped up on an elbow. "I guess we need to drive back up there, huh?"

She sat back down and burst into tears. "Why did this have to happen?"

I had no answer.

We packed the car and started the drive north. The roads were open and dry until about six o'clock the evening of our second day of travel. Then, snow started to fall. We were at Ritzville, 60 miles west of Spokane. Under ordinary conditions we could get to the condo in about an hour and a half, so we pressed on. The snow came down heavier and traffic slowed to a near halt by the time we reached Spokane. Our car had 4-wheel drive so I decided to get off the Interstate and take a back road. Not one of my best ideas. We pulled into our carport five hours later, shortly after midnight. The snow continued to dump from the sky as we slogged our way to the front door.

I turned up the electric heat to take the bite out of the heavy chill that greeted us inside the condo. Jeannie tried to get water to make coffee. Nothing came out of the tap. The snow fall didn't let up. By daylight, 20 inches of new snow covered everything.

When the condo began to warm and the water pipes thawed enough for us to get a trickle, Jeannie said, "I hear a hiss coming from under the stairs."

Not good.

A copper pipe leading to the water-heater had split, spewing a fine mist against the wall of the water-heater closet. Jeannie called the plumber we had used for years. "He says he can't get out of his driveway." The next call went to our builder, Tom Sjoblom. Tom came right away with his plow, cleaned out the whole condo association driveway and parking places, then waded through the snow to find the entrance to the crawl-space. He cleared away the snow, slid in and turned off the water. Then he had his plumber make temporary repairs. No charge.

I draw a complete blank when it comes to the trip back to Bakersfield or to the Christmas and New Year's holidays.

<u>Back to Work (or not)</u>

At some point in early 2009, I put on a suit and tie and drove to the office as a test. I failed.

All I did for many minutes was look out the window of my tenth-floor office and watch traffic on the streets below. How could people be going about their everyday lives as if nothing had changed? As if Kelly hadn't died?

I drove home, changed clothes, and waited until the time came to pick up the boys from school.

Sixty-Six

Taking the Boys to Idaho

I don't know how long Spencer and Mason missed school after their mother died, but when they went back, Jeannie and I usually went together to picked them up. They liked to spend some time playing before we left, either shooting baskets, kicking a ball on the grass field, or climbing on the monkey bars. During this play time, Jeannie and I visited with other parents or grandparents.

One Monday for some reason I didn't go. When Jeannie and the boys came in the door, they all held Starbuck's cups. "Amma took us to Starbuck's. These are really good." Mason slurped the last of his pink foam and then licked the end of his straw.

Jeannie had her usual *Grande Mocha Cappuccino Light with Whipped Cream* in hand. "They have non-caffeinated drinks for kids. We're going to go every Monday." So *Starbuck's Monday* was born. The boys never let us forget.

Next came *Moo Creamery Friday*. Moo Creamery not only served ice cream in a wide variety of flavors, but their menu also listed hamburgers, hot dogs, fries, chili, and more. An adventurous order included a bacon or Guinness flavored milkshake.

It only took one Friday visit for the Moo to become a tradition. The owners and their staff treated us like royalty. Brandy and her kids often joined us there. If for some reason or other, we didn't show up on a Friday afternoon, we heard about it the next time.

* * *

When school ended for Spencer and Mason in the spring of 2009, we asked Bill if we could take them to Idaho for the summer. He agreed. Our Honda Pilot barely held all the things he packed for them.

They were good travelers in part because Bill had outfitted each of them with a little TV monitor and a bunch of movies to watch on the road. Only in the last couple of hours of the two-day trip did they ask, "How much longer before we get there?"

Fishing, swimming, watching for deer at the feeder, spending time with neighbor Jayne's horses, and prowling around in the woods took up most of each day. They seemed happy.

Mason and Spencer with Fish They Caught and Cleaned

Jeannie and I did our best to hide the tears that popped up from time to time without an invitation. At night, Jeannie tucked the little guys in, and each of the three said a prayer. Then they joined together in saying the Lord's Prayer.

"I think I'll teach them the 23rd Psalm," Jeannie said one night. She had taught it to a Sunday school class when our kids were little. It took them a while, but Spencer and Mason both memorized it and understood the meaning of each verse.

One evening, we roasted hot dogs and made s'mores at the fire pit. Mason liked it when his marshmallow caught on fire so he could blow it out. "How about we go to Priest Lake tomorrow?" I asked.

"Good idea," Jeannie said. "The boys have never been there."

We pulled the boat out of the lake the next morning, loaded up the picnic lunch Jeannie made, and took the hour and a half drive to the boat launch at the south end of Priest Lake.

"This is a big lake. How big is it?" Spencer always had questions like that.

"It's about 18 miles to the other end. Then we'll go up a two-mile long river to the upper lake." I backed the trailer into the clear, cold water, slid off the boat and tied it up.

"How big is the upper lake?" Spencer, again.

"About the size of our lake."

With all the supplies aboard, we pushed off for the cruise up the island-dotted lake. Very few other boats were on the water.

Jeannie spotted an osprey nest atop a tree on one of the larger islands. A fledgling perched on the edge of the nest and fluttered its wings. Jeannie put her binoculars to her eyes. "I think it's getting ready to fly. Let's watch."

I stopped the boat. "Come on bird, you can do it," Spencer called out.

Mason clapped his hands. "Fly."

That was all the encouragement the osprey seemed to need. After a few more practice wing-flaps, the young bird let go of the nest and went airborne to a branch about 20 feet below the nest. At least ten minutes passed before the wing fluttering resumed. Both boys—and Jeannie—called for the bird to take off. It did. This time gaining altitude and flying into the trees, disappearing from sight.

Spencer gave Mason a high-five. "That was so cool."

I fired up the engine and aimed the prow north. A large expanse of open water lay ahead, chopped by a stout westerly breeze. Floating debris could cause a problem, so I kept a close watch. Before long, I saw it. "Can you see that floating log up there?" I pointed to a dark line on the lake dead ahead about a mile. Before long, they all saw what I was pointing at.

Log in the distance

Then the log wiggled its ears. A female moose! I pulled up close enough for Jeannie to take some pictures.

Moose up close

The boys stayed with us in our new, almost-completed home in Idaho for seven weeks before Bill called to say he couldn't stand being without them any longer. And they were ready to see their dad, so we drove them back to Bakersfield.

Sixty-Seven

Kelly's Garden

Jeannie started her search for someone to make a stone marker to place in Kelly's Garden in the spring of 2009. She came into the den after spending a long time on the phone in the kitchen. "I just talked to a man who does marble work. He'll be in his shop all day if we want to go see him."

We found his place of business in an industrial park. A nicer fellow you couldn't ask for. Jeannie found a block of rose-colored stone that she liked, rough around the edges with a polished face. "We need another block to mount it on," she told him. He showed us an area behind his shop where he stored remnants from his prior projects.

"If I cut a notch like this." He showed us with his hands. "The other piece will stand up nicely." We worked out a price after Jeannie sketched what she wanted carved into the stone.

* * *

Kelly's Garden became the gathering place for family and friends on her birthday, Mothers' Day, and the day she left us. Jeannie always came up with something special for the occasion. One time she rented a helium tank and filled big balloons with it. She handed out marking pens and told everyone to write something to Kelly on their balloon.

Mason, then age nine, filled every part of his balloon with a letter to his mom.

When all had been written, Jeannie gave the signal to release the balloons. Up they went, a myriad of colors, high into the sky—Except for Mason's. His got stuck in the upper branches of our liquid amber tree, 60 or 70 feet from the ground.

"Blow it free, Mom," Mason called up to the sky. The words were barely out of his mouth when a puff of wind shook the branches of the tree and the balloon rolled free, sailing up after the others. We watched until they all disappeared into the blue.

"Can I do another one, Amma?" Mason asked.

Jeannie filled another balloon for him, and he wrote a second long note before letting it go. This time, our camphor tree grabbed it.

Mason clapped his hands. "Do it again, Mom."

Breeze wiggled the clutching branches. Up went the balloon.

We all watched in amazement.

* * *

On the fourth anniversary of November 11, Jeannie wanted everyone to release a butterfly. She searched for and found a place that sold beautiful butterflies individually housed in little pyramid-shaped boxes. On her signal, everyone opened their box and set the butterflies free. With each get-together, after some hugs and remembrances, we all headed to the Mexicali for food and drink at a long table in the back room. Many sipped on Cadillac Margaritas, Kelly's favorite. Others ordered food, specially prepared as Kelly would have requested. Stories told of Kelly's antics brought laughter despite our collective sadness. They were good times, times of healing.

Sixty-Eight

Knee Surgery & More

In early 2011, Jeannie clomped into the den leaning heavily on her cane. "My knees really hurt when I'm on my feet for very long. I think I need to go back to Doctor Hamilton." Painful knees had plagued Jeannie since her mid-fifties. The pain lessened after her bypass surgery in 2001 to the point that she rarely used her cane.

She had seen Dr. Hamilton several years earlier and been told her knees were "bone on bone," but to wait until the pain got worse before having surgery. Ten years after bypass surgery the cane had again become her constant companion. "I think I'm ready," she said and made an appointment. A few days later, she announced, "There's a group of doctors at Good Samaritan Hospital in Los Angeles that do nothing but knee replacement surgery. They're putting on a seminar in Bakersfield this weekend. I'd like to go."

We went.

Two of the group's doctors spoke in person and a third addressed us by way of video. They were all impressive, but Jeannie took a liking to the first one to speak and approached him with questions after the seminar. He talked with her for at least half an hour, not seeming to be in any hurry to get back over the hill to LA. She cancelled her appointment with Dr. Hamilton and made one with her new friend.

At Good Sam, the doctor took X-rays, made precise measurements, and showed us the surgery suite and the robotic equipment he used to reconstruct knee joints.

"When can we do it?" Jeannie asked. She was ready.

His assistant gave her a surgery date and told her to plan on four or five days of post-op physical therapy at the hospital before going home.

"Can't I do the PT in Bakersfield?" Jeannie asked.

"No, dear. Trust me. You don't want to be getting in a car for a two-hour ride over the Grapevine. You'll want the pain meds they'll give you here."

* * *

The day for surgery came, and off we went for another hospital stay in Los Angeles. The surgery went well as did the PT. "She was telling the truth about the pain meds. They really work," Jeannie said when we came back from a walk in the hall. The hall made a big loop around her floor.

After one night sleeping in a chair in Jeannie's room, I asked a nurse if they had a recliner. She told me that the small hotel next-door was part of the hospital complex, and I could sleep there and come and go as I pleased. The price was right, and a few hours on a mattress each night felt good.

* * *

The first three months after her knee surgery, Jeannie questioned whether or not she made a mistake by not leaving her knee well enough alone. "Now, I have to use *two* canes." Then, like magic, rapid improvement kicked in. Before long, she was back on the golf course at Twin Lakes Village and talking about getting her left knee done.

Sixty-Nine

More Bad News

Jeannie's ovarian and breast cancer markers remained good, but her borderline anemia numbers gradually got worse. Dr. Cartmell expressed concern. "I want you to take some iron supplements. If that doesn't help, we'll do some other tests."

The iron didn't help. Her numbers continued to drift lower. Dr. Cartmell ordered a series of other tests in an attempt to see if Jeannie was losing blood somewhere. The last was a repeat colonoscopy. She had one the year before that disclosed nothing of concern.

After the colonoscopy, with Jeannie on the gurney recovering from what I call the "happy juice," I sat next to her trying to see if I could get her to make sense. It took a while.

Then the doctor came in with a handful of documents and all the bedside manner of Attila the Hun. "You have cancer . . . here." He pointed to one of the pictures. "Talk to Doctor Cartmell about what to do next." With those words, he turned, pulled back the curtain, and walked away.

"Oh, Jim. I'm so sorry to put you through more of this." It wasn't the happy juice talking.

Her next surgery was not to be her left knee.

* * *

We talked to Dr. Cartmell about what Jeannie faced with the diagnosis of colon cancer. "I don't want to go out of town again. Is there a surgeon here you can recommend?" She asked.

"There are several good ones." He gave us a list of general surgeons that included Dr. Vince Phillips, the husband of the daughter of long-time neighbors of ours. She babysat our children when they were little.

Dr. Phillips agreed to see us right away. Jeannie brought with her the colonoscopy pictures. He talked to Jeannie as if I weren't there. That was good. "The tumor doesn't appear to have penetrated the outer wall of the colon, but we can't be sure. If it hasn't; we'll just resect the colon."

She winced. "Will I need to wear a colostomy bag?"

"Hopefully not. If the tumor hasn't spread outside the colon, I'll take out the bad part—about eight to ten inches—and do an anastomosis. But you will have a big scar."

"Bigger than these?" Jeannie pulled up her shirt exposing her multiple surgical scars.

"Whoa." He laughed. "Someone's been here before."

"I should have had them put in a zipper the first time," she said.

Dr. Phillips seemed to give that concept some thought. "I won't add anything. In fact, I'll remove some of the old scar tissue."

"How long will I be in the hospital?"

A smile crossed his face. "Until you pass gas. Believe it or not, that's the test we use to see if the bowels are functioning."

November 12, 2012—the day after we released the butterflies—Jeannie checked into Memorial hospital. I stayed with her until she was wheeled off for yet another cancer surgery. Then I joined Brandy and Matt in the waiting room. No one else was there. After a few minutes, my cell phone rang. My queasy stomach clutched. Could something have gone wrong?

I answered. It was Judy, Jeannie's sister. "Is Jeannie in surgery?"

"Yes. It just started."

"I have some bad news about mom; she fell and broke her pelvis yesterday, and she's in the hospital. She didn't want Jeannie to cancel her surgery and come running out here."

"That's terrible. How did it happen?" I knew a fracture of the pelvis didn't bode well for someone Bertha's age. She was then less than two months shy of turning 93.

Judy explained that she got a call from Bertha's neighbor who said he found her sitting in her car not looking well. Bertha had told him she was in so much pain that she couldn't get out to go into her house. He called 911, and she was taken to the hospital.

Judy drove down to Houston from her home in Dallas and got the rest of the story directly from her mother.

Bertha told Judy she had lost her balance and fallen backward after stepping up the curb in front of the beauty shop where she was going to get her hair done. She somehow managed to get into her car and drive herself home. When she got there, it hurt too much to move, so she sat there about 5 hours before her neighbor found her.

When and how to tell Jeannie?

I didn't know. She would want to get out of bed, gas or no gas, and catch the first plane to Houston to be with her mom. Maybe Judy should tell her. Or maybe Bertha herself. I don't remember who did.

What I do remember is that Jeannie, Brandy, and I flew back and forth between Bakersfield and Houston through the holidays and into 2013. During these two months, Jeannie started chemotherapy, and Bertha was transferred six or seven times from the hospital ICU to a long-term care facility. Each time she went to long-term care she had a set-back and was returned to the ICU.

On our last trip to Houston, we celebrated Bertha's 93rd birthday, December 30, 2012. A few days later she took 17 steps with her physical therapist, her longest walk since her fall. Things were looking up.

The chemotherapy schedule at CBCC controlled Jeannie's time, so we had to fly back home in early January for another session.

"She looked good, didn't she?" Jeannie said when we left Bertha's hospital room and headed for the airport.

"She sure did. Maybe she'll take 19 steps tomorrow."

She didn't. Those 17 steps were her last.

A few days later, Judy called to give Jeannie the news of Bertha's passing.

Seventy

More Chemo – Code Blue

After Bertha died, Jeannie underwent more of her chemotherapy, this time with severe complications. Nausea and vomiting became uncontrollable. She couldn't eat or drink anything without throwing up and became weaker as time went on.

Dr. Cartmell admitted her to Bakersfield Memorial Hospital. Much to our chagrin, we then learned about the role of "House Doctor." Jeannie's care left the hands of Dr. Cartmell and went into those of doctors employed by the hospital, people we had never met. They tried different medications to control her vomiting. None worked. The only nutrition Jeannie got came through her IV in the form of what I called "sugar water."

After a week of no food, with hydration coming only by way of IV drip, Jeannie's condition had deteriorated. She began running a low-grade fever. Because of her fear of bladder infection, she refused to be catheterized. In order to use the toilet, she had to be unplugged from all her monitors and be helped by a nurse to get herself, her IV pole, and the nurse into the tiny restroom. I was told to wait in the hall.

While waiting in the hall on one of those occasions, the intercom blared, "CODE BLUE, CODE BLUE, room . . ." Jeannie's room.

A storm of people appeared from everywhere, one pushing a crash cart, some with stethoscopes around their necks, others carrying things. All of them raced into Jeannie's room until it seemed no more could fit.

Is this it? Am I losing her? My pulse pounded in my ears.

I could hear voices coming from the room—instructions to do this or that. Other noises as well that sounded like the rattle of the bed or maybe the crash cart. Not knowing what was happening put a vise-grip on my heart. I wanted to go in but knew better.

Then a trickle of people left the room. None looked my way. Was it over? What happened? I couldn't bring myself to ask.

The next thing I knew, Dr. Cartmell was there, confronting one of the house doctors. Jeannie had been revived and was back in her bed.

From that point on, Dr. Cartmell took charge. He saw to it that Jeannie received nutrients through her IV—something more than sugar water. It came in a large bag of amber-colored fluid. Within a few days, she was able to keep down Jell-O, crackers, and chicken broth. Soon, she tolerated a regular diet and was discharged to resume her chemo. "That was rough," she said—as close to a complaint as ever came from her.

* * *

Bertha's memorial service took place in the spring of 2013 in Oklahoma City where the Ratliff family's burial plot was located. Even though 55 years had passed since Jeannie had lived in Oklahoma City, some of her high school friends showed up to lend their support. It touched me to see how much they cared for her.

Bertha's great-granddaughter, Ryan, then 14, gave a moving recount of what "Big Amma" had meant to her young life. Ryan had written notes about what she planned to say but never once looked at them as she addressed the fairly large crowd in a confident voice. Bertha had spent three months or so in Bakersfield every year since Ryan was born. They were very close even though otherwise separated by more than 1500 miles. I don't know if Ryan knew then the role Big Amma played in her not being aborted—but she does now.

Seventy-One

What's Wrong with Jim?

October of 2013 found us on the road to Rochester, Minnesota, and the Mayo Clinic. We hoped a week's worth of testing, and a fleet of doctors, might tell us the cause of my frequent loss of balance as well as the speech difficulty that often accompanied my balance problem. The visit to Mayo had been arranged by a neurologist at the Sansum Clinic in Santa Barbara.

The balance difficulties first became apparent on the tennis courts of the Bakersfield Racquet Club during my regular Thursday "Old Guys" doubles matches. I asked Dr. Young about it and he first thought it might have something to do with my heart. He hooked me up to what he called a Holter monitor, a portable device with lots of wires taped to my chest and stomach. I was to wear it for a day or two while it recorded my heart activity.

"I'm playing tennis this afternoon. Is that okay?" I asked.

"That'll be good," he said. He was an old guy tennis player himself, a level or three above the group I played with. "That should give me some good information."

It gave him more than he probably thought.

My earlier balance bouts caused me to stagger and stumble but resulted in no bad falls. This time was different. I put a significant dent in the hard-court surface of Court Three with my face.

Dr. Young patched me up and reconnected the wires that had been pulled loose. "Go home and take it easy for a while. Come back tomorrow afternoon and we'll see what the monitor has to say."

The next day Dr. Young said, "The monitor says your heart works fine. I recommend you see Greg Pineda for a neurological work-up." He patted me on the shoulder. "Meanwhile, take it easy."

Dr. Pineda, the neurologist who checked out Brandy after she totaled Kelly's car, ordered a battery of tests. Jeannie went with me to find out the results. The three of us chatted for a few minutes before Greg opened my chart. Then his cell phone rang. "I have to take this," he said.

He didn't leave the room or even step away from us as he listened to the call for some time before saying anything. His facial expression left no doubt that he was receiving bad news. "I love you," he said to the caller. "We'll be there tonight."

His head dropped and he sat silently for a moment. "That was my daughter, Tina . . . she has brain cancer . . . treatment isn't working . . . she's getting worse."

Jeannie went to him and gave him a long hug. "I'm so sorry, Greg. You and Ann need to get to Santa Barbara. We can come back another time."

That other time never happened. Tina died a few weeks later, and Greg arranged for another neurologist in Bakersfield to take over my evaluation.

Jeannie and I had last seen Tina at Kelly's memorial service less than a year earlier. She had come from her home in Santa Barbara and looked to be in the best of health as she told us about her three young children and how much Kelly meant to her. Now, she was gone.

"What's going on? First Kelly, then Robynn, and now Tina. It's not right." Jeannie knuckled a tear from her eye.

* * *

The new neurologist was a bright young man, new to me, new to Bakersfield, and new to the practice of medicine after completing his residency. He reviewed the test results in Dr. Pineda's chart, including an MRI of the brain (mine, that is). "I see nothing there," he said.

Jeannie sputtered a laugh. "That's just what I thought."

The young doctor looked puzzled. Then he got it. "No. I mean everything looks normal."

I explained to him that about twice a day my balance became noticeably worse and after 30 to 45 minutes the problem went away. Usually when this happened, I also had difficulty speaking clearly.

He had me squeeze his fingers, walk up and down the hall, smile, move my tongue, and a few other things before admitting he had no idea what was causing my balance and speech problems.

* * *

The next stop was in Santa Barbara to see another neurologist, Dr. Chang, on the recommendation of Pete Lewis. Jeannie was again with me. I had sent Dr. Chang a summary of the history and progression of my symptoms along with the brain MRI and other medical records.

After asking me a few questions about what I had sent him, he had me take off my shirt. Then he slapped the backs of my arms. "Um-hum, um-hum." Then he slapped my back. "You have fasciculation," he said.

"What's that?" I asked, thinking it must be some kind of disease.

"Small, involuntary muscle contractions. Can you feel them?"

"No."

"Um-hum, um-hum."

He then pulled out some kind of electrical contraption that had a wire leading to a long needle. Needles weren't my friend, especially long ones intended to be stuck into me. It didn't hurt as much going in as it did when he wiggled it around while watching the dial on his thingamajig. He poked it into my arms, my legs, my back, and then inserted it under my chin into the base of my tongue.

"Um-hum, um-hum. I think you have ALS."

I had been looking for a diagnosis, but not that one.

Jeannie looked like she had been zapped with a Taser.

Then Dr. Chang added, "If it is ALS you should already be dead. I'd like to run some more tests, but I can't do them right now. Go get something to eat and come back at noon."

The thought of having Lou Gehrig's disease is not the best appetite stimulator. Nor is the thought of already being dead.

Jeannie and I found a café nearby and ordered food that went untouched. At noon, we went back to see what Dr. Chang had in mind. He did his extra tests without any more 'um-hums.' When he finished, he wagged his head a bit. "If I plugged all the findings into a computer, it would say you have ALS . . . but I don't believe you do. You need to get worked up at a major medical facility."

So, here we were on our way from Idaho to Rochester, having passed through Montana, Wyoming, and South Dakota. A new adventure—this time I was the patient, not Jeannie.

Seventy-Two

Mayo Clinic

A Welcome to Minnesota sign came into view ten miles east of Sioux Falls, South Dakota. "Only about three and a half hours to go," I announced to Jeannie.

"Huh?"

"Sorry. Go back to sleep." She did.

Interstate 90 crossed into the southwest corner of Minnesota. If you threw an apple core out the passenger window, it wouldn't land in Iowa, but would land close enough that an Iowa critter might have it for lunch. Stumps of corn stalks poked out of some of the fields. Others, freshly plowed, displayed rich soil ready to soak up moisture from winter snow.

Streetlights popped on as we entered the outskirts of Rochester, a city of over 100,000—most of whom had something to do with the Mayo Clinic, known to the locals as simply *the Clinic*. The GPS took us to the squat hotel we were to call home for the week. "Wake up, Jeannie. We're here."

"Already?"

I pulled into the underground garage and parked next to the elevator. Our Honda Pilot sagged in the rear. I took out six suitcases—one of them mine—and the Pilot recovered.

"Just bring in that one and my overnight case for now. You can get the others later." She picked up my little bag and pushed the elevator button. The door opened right away. "Hurry up." The door pushed against her foot several times before I joined her for the ride up.

"Did you lock the car?"

"Yup."

"I didn't hear it beep."

I pushed the lock button on the fob a couple times and a faint *beep* came through the elevator door.

"Thanks."

After checking in and getting directions to the closest restaurant, we boarded a different elevator that rattled its way to the top floor—the fourth—and deposited us a few steps from our room. *Clean and spacious* the AAA book said. Right on. With a shuttle to the Clinic, the book promised. Also right on. Every hotel, motel, B&B, and flophouse in Rochester had shuttle service to the Clinic. The Clinic had its own transit system. The trick was to know which bus took us back to our hotel.

"You hungry yet?" Jeannie asked when she hung her last item in the closet.

"Yeah. You?"

She put on her coat. "Let's go."

The rattling elevator took us to the lobby. "Going for dinner?" the cheery young lady at the desk asked.

We both nodded. Jeannie pulled open the outside door, then pushed it closed. She flipped up her collar and tugged her knit cap over her ears. "Let's hurry."

A block and a half of huffing and puffing down the street took us to the warmth of the recommended restaurant. One open booth remained. We took it. Our server brought menus and water. "Our specials for the day are -"

"Walleye!" Jeannie's eyes went wide looking at her menu.

That's all it took. "We'll both have walleye," I said. "No need to tell us the specials."

* * *

Bright and early the next morning we boarded the bus to the Clinic. Several others from the hotel joined us. The bus was already half-full. After a few more stops, only a couple seats remained open.

"Vhere you from?" the gentleman next to me asked with a strong Germen accent.

"Rathdrum, Idaho," I replied. "And you must be from Ireland?"

"Nein." He laughed. "Ve are from Dusseldorf."

* * *

The first day at the Clinic was like Disneyland—lots of standing in line, only to find out I was in the wrong line—but at least I was in the right building. I earned a gold star for that. The Clinic occupies most of downtown Rochester.

I checked the map I had picked up at the entrance, searching for a route to the neurology section. Only a few wrong turns later, I found it. The waiting room resembled something from a major airport, complete with voices over a garbled intercom. My impaired hearing didn't help.

I checked in a few minutes before my scheduled appointment and settled into a comfortable chair next to Jeannie. Two or three dozen other chairs held waiting folks. "Looks like we might be here a while," I said.

My words hadn't even landed on Jeannie's eardrums before "James" crackled over the loudspeaker. I stood up, as did another man in the waiting section to our right. Another James, no doubt. We both approached the woman in the doorway with a chart in her hands. The call turned out to be for me. I motioned for Jeannie to come along, and the woman with the chart escorted us to the doctor's office.

Dr. Lagerlund remained seated behind his desk as the lady made introductions. He wore a tweed jacket with elbow patches. His receding hair, peppered with gray, needed a trim. Everything about him shouted a silent 'You are in the best of hands.'

After an hour or so going over my symptom history and his plan of attack, he said, "Check back at the reception desk in a couple hours to pick up your schedule."

I nodded at the other James on our way out, not knowing if he was still waiting to see a doctor or waiting for his schedule.

"Let's go to the bottom level," Jeannie said, folding her *Clinic Map* and stuffing it in her pocket. "They have shops down there." Shopping topped our short incompatibility list. She loved it. I preferred watching grass grow or ants collecting sugar.

As a seasoned pathfinder, I guided us back to the entry level and located the escalator going down to the shops. We stepped off into a veritable shopping mall. Jeannie raised her eyebrows and smiled. "Why don't you get a cup of coffee and sit over there?"

I did.

A talented gent sat at a grand piano playing soothing music. Plush chairs and couches surrounded the piano.

Two hours later, we lugged Jeannie's purchases to the neurology section and picked up my schedule for the rest of the week. Nothing until 6:30 the next morning for "blood draw."

After wending our way to the exit doors, we stepped into bright sunshine that took some of the chill out of the late October Minnesota air. A handful of people were boarding a bus bearing a big letter A. We needed the C bus. A few minutes later the D bus pulled in, the C bus hot on its tail. The busses apparently didn't arrive in alphabetical order.

Back at the hotel, I lugged up the rest of Jeannie's luggage. She went to the lobby in search of a newspaper.

"How far away is Austin?" she asked when I came in with the last two bags. She sat at the writing desk circling something in the newspaper.

"Not too far. Why?"

"There's an ad for Golden Doodle puppies. Eight weeks old."

* * *

Cancer had taken Paddy-O in September, shortly after Jeannie finished her chemo for colon cancer. We had driven to Idaho a week later, dogless for the first time in what seemed like forever. Jeannie began her hunt for a new puppy as soon as we pulled in.

One breeder in Coeur d'Alene said she expected to have a litter ready for adoption in about three months with a price tag slightly less than the national debt. Another in Deer Park, Washington, had what she claimed were Golden Doodle puppies at a reasonable price. We drove to Deer Park hoping to bring one home. It was not to be.

"Well . . ." Jeannie said as we drove away. "They were puppies."

That's about as close as they came to being Golden Doodle puppies.

* * *

Jeannie had now moved her hunt to Minnesota. "We don't have anything else to do this afternoon. I'm going to call this number." She tapped the newspaper where she had circled the ad.

I sat on the bed and Googled the distance to Austin while Jeannie made the call.

Jeannie hung up the hotel phone. "A girl answered. Said her mom usually comes home about three. We can look at the puppies then. I got the address." She handed me the slip of paper where she'd written it down. "Can we get there by three?"

"Oh, sure. It's only about a 45-minute drive. You want to get some lunch?"

"Let's eat in Austin. Check out the town."

* * *

On the short drive to Austin, Jeannie asked, "Do you think we're being silly, thinking about buying an eight-week-old puppy here—with a three-day drive to get back to Idaho?"

I pondered this query.

What can I say other than a flat-out lie? Hmmm?

"Silly is normal for us, isn't it? Let's see what they look like."

"What if I fall in love with one like I did with Paddy-O?"

I shrugged and pulled off at the first Austin exit. "We'll figure something out."

Austin proved to be a trivia town. The Spam Museum is located there? We learned this tidbit of information at the café Jeannie picked for lunch—after cruising every street that held promise for an eatery. "Let's go here. Look at all those cars in the lot," she said.

"Might be crowded."

"Oh, you . . ."

I found a place to park and took Jeannie's hand as we walked to the front door of a white stand-alone building with green awnings. Every seat was taken.

A waitress hustled past us carrying a load of filled plates on each arm. "We'll have a booth for you in just a minute." The food looked and smelled amazing.

Jeannie glanced at me with wide eyes and raised eyebrows. "I done good, didn't I?" A line from either a movie or TV show we had seen many moons earlier.

"You done good, real good."

The waitress came back and told us Fred and Ethyl—or whatever their names were—had finished and she would clean the booth right away. "Here's menus you can look at." The lilt of her voice came right out of the movie *Fargo*.

Jeannie opened her menu and sputtered. "Look. Spam."

Not the email kind, the meat-in-a-can kind. Austin was the home of Spam. Quite an accomplishment for a town of barely 20,000 people, half of whom were probably employed by Hormel—or the Spam Museum.

After a Spamless lunch, I loaded the puppy address into our GPS and drove by the house so Jeannie could check for any sign a serial killer might lurk there. "It looks okay," she opined. She had a good eye for things like that.

We had time to kill before three o'clock, so we set off in search of the Spam Museum. It was closed. What a pity. Jeannie could have told them all the ways Bertha had served Spam back in Oklahoma.

At about five minutes to three, I parked at the curb in front of the puppy house. Two pre-teen girls were playing with a puppy in the front yard. Jeannie lowered her window. "Is your mom home?"

"Not yet. Are you the lady who called about the puppies?"

"Uh-huh. We'll wait for your mom."

"There she is." The girl pointed down the street at a car turning the corner.

After introductions, it didn't take long for Jeannie to fall in love with one of the pups. "Can we pay for her now and pick her up Saturday morning?"

The lady kind of squinted one eye as if something about that idea bothered her.

"We'll pay extra for food between now and then," Jeannie added. I sensed desperation on her part.

"No need for that. They all eat outa the same dish. Can you pick her up before eight? I have to be at work by eight-thirty." *Jeannie time* wouldn't do.

Jeannie looked at me. I nodded. She wrote the check, gave her new puppy a hug, and we headed back to Rochester for another walleye dinner.

Seventy-Three

Kabby

Jeannie slept in on our second morning in Rochester. I caught the C bus in the dark to be sure I got to The Clinic before the doors opened at 6:30 a.m. A cluster of folks were already polluting the air with steamy breath when the bus pulled in. A few minutes before 6:30, a uniformed man unlocked the doors. By then, there were about fifty of us waiting to get in. I thought I knew a shortcut to the blood draw section. Somehow, I made a wrong turn down a dead-end hallway. By the time I found the right route, the line at the check-in desk looked like it was for Space Mountain.

Disneyland could learn something about efficiency from The Clinic. They checked me in, extracted twenty vials of blood, brought me back to consciousness, and sent me off to my next appointment before 7:00 a.m.

The next appointment was a doozy. Dr. Chang all over again—in spades. Except a nice young lady from North Dakota wielded the needle. We had a good visit about North Dakota before she stuck the needle into places I didn't even know I had places. She was done in about 45 minutes. So was I.

The rest of the week took me—I believe—to every department at The Clinic except maternity and pediatrics. Then Jeannie and I went back to Dr. Lagerlund to wrap things up.

"You have episodic ataxia with ataxic dysarthria—and some mild peripheral neuropathy," he said.

Jeannie seemed to understand. "What causes that?" she asked.

"Episodes of ataxia are, we think, triggered by a variety of factors, alcohol, caffeine, fatigue, and stress among them. But the underlying cause is unknown."

I assumed the 'we' referred to medical science generally, not just The Clinic.

Jeannie pressed on. "You're sure it's not ALS?"

Dr. Lagerlund nodded. "It's not ALS."

"Is there any medication he can take that will help?"

"No."

"Will it get worse?"

"Probably not much." He turned to me. "You've lived with it a few years now, and you'll have to keep living with it. I'm sorry there's not better news."

We thanked him and made our way back to the hotel. On the bus, I asked Jeannie what we came all this way for. "He just put what I told him into medical terms."

Her grin went all the way to her eyes. "Look on the bright side. It's not ALS. We found a puppy. And we get to eat walleye. You up for more?"

The bus driver agreed to drop us off at the restaurant.

* * *

My alarm jangled early Saturday morning. Time to get Jeannie moving so we could get to her new love before eight o'clock. I reached to her side of the bed. No Jeannie.

"Good morning, sleepy head." She stood in the bathroom doorway, fully dressed with her closed overnight case in hand.

I dressed as fast as I could, hauled packed suitcases down the rattletrap elevator and checked out of the hotel.

Before 7:30 we arrived at *Puppy Central* and collected Kabby. Brandy came up with the name since Kelly's initials were KAB. For three days,

Kabby rode on Jeannie's lap. Somewhere along the way, we stopped to buy a little cage to take into the motel rooms. Puppy food and water, we had already been given. I tried to get Jeannie's bladder and Kabby's in sync but failed. Potty stops came every hour or so.

Early snow greeted us in North Idaho, and quickly piled up. Kabby loved it. And we loved her, our eighth and last dog.

Seventy-Four

Ringing in 2014

Snow continued to pile up through November and into December. Kabby liked to climb to the top of the highest heap, plop down, and chew on a stick.

We devoted ourselves to getting ready for family to arrive. Jeannie, as usual, over-prepared for company. She cooked, cleaned, and planned activities to a fare-thee-well. Everything had to be just so.

The day after Christmas, Brandy and family plus our son Matt flew to Spokane to spend the rest of the grandkids' vacation with us. They rented a car at the airport and drove to our house. Jeannie had asked them to come for a white Christmas with us, but the little ones wanted to celebrate at home—presumably because of the stack of presents building up beneath their tree, or maybe it was to avoid the need to redirect Santa to Idaho for him to drop off his load.

While the family was with us, we went on a horse-drawn sleigh ride through forested hills followed by a *Bar-B-Que in the Barn* that Jeannie had booked. The only down-side to that adventure was getting our car stuck in the snow on the last hill leading to the barn. Some other folks helped push us free.

The next day, the kids played in the snow or cleared it from the frozen lake below our house so they could slide on the ice. Time flew by, and soon New Year's Eve showed up. Jeannie had chilled Champaign for the adults and sparkling grape juice for me and the youngsters. The countdown to 2014 began. 10!-9!-8!-7!-6!-5!-4!-3!-2!-1! Happy New Year! Everyone toasted, hugged, and smooched to welcome in 2014.

* * *

On January 2nd, the kids and grandkids flew home. The house felt empty and quiet as we settled into our old routine. Kabby kept us entertained but spent most of the day outside. Toward evening, Jeannie lay down on the couch. "I'm really tired. I can't seem to catch my breath."

Then her breathing became more labored. She took her temperature—101 plus. I bundled her up, helped her to the car, and drove as fast as the road conditions allowed to the Urgent Care Center in Hayden, about ten miles away. The waiting room was empty when we came through the door and an attendant took Jeannie to the back while I settled uneasily into a chair.

When Jeannie returned, someone wearing a white jacket accompanied her. "From the X-ray, it looks like pneumonia," White Jacket said. "But I think you need to go to the Emergency Room at Kootenai Medical Center for a complete work-up. I'll let them know you're coming and forward the x-ray."

Off we went.

It wasn't pneumonia. It was congestive heart failure.

* * *

During the next three days Jeannie was subjected to multiple tests, including a coronary angiogram where a catheter was threaded through a blood vessel into her heart. The doctors determined that her heart didn't need surgery.

I sat on proverbial *pins and needles* at her bedside in the hospital and for several days thereafter as Jeannie's strength returned bit-by-bit. "I guess I'll have to go to that cardiologist in Bakersfield," she said. "The one Doctor Cartmell sent me to."

* * *

A few weeks later, we packed up for the drive south to Bakersfield in order to attend Jeannie's regular follow-up blood work and visit with Dr. Cartmell. Everything looked good with her cancer markers. She also saw the heart doctor who ran tests and pronounced her heart-healthy. "I must be pretty tough," she said.

A few days later, the house phone rang. Jeannie answered and talked for several minutes. She came into the den and stood with hands on her hips. "Judy wants us to come to Houston to take care of mother's things and get her house ready to sell." With pinched lips she gave her head a shake.

Judy had been looking after Bertha's affairs for more than a year.

Jeannie gathered up Kabby's dishes, food, toys, and crate. Kabby pranced over, tail wagging. "I guess it's time for us to do our part, Kabby girl. Are you ready for another long drive? We're going to Texas."

Seventy-Five

To Houston

The day after Judy's call, I packed my suitcase and settled into a comfy chair prepared to wait however long it took for Jeannie to get ready to roll.

"I'm just going to take old clothes," she said. "It won't take long to pack."

To my surprise, it didn't.

I loaded the car and backed out of the driveway of our Bakersfield home. "We can probably make Tucson by about ten." I turned east on Highway 58 and stepped on the gas. "Is that too late?"

"No, that's fine. What about tomorrow night?"

"If we get an early start, we can make it to Fredericksburg. Then we can get to your mom's the next day before dark."

* * *

Judy was there when we arrived in Houston, going through things to put out for a yard sale. "Pick out what you want to take to Idaho or Bakersfield. We'll put price stickers on the rest."

Jeannie wandered through the house making comments about almost every piece of furniture and knick-knack. "Oh, I remember this" or "I want to keep this."

I contemplated how much might fit inside the biggest U-Haul trailer our Honda Pilot could tow, leaving room for the toolbox I had my eye on. "I don't think we can take everything you want, Jeannie."

"Why not?"

I told her I called U-Haul and got the largest enclosed trailer they said could be pulled by our car.

"Can we get a bigger one from somebody else?"

"Probably, but the Pilot couldn't handle it."

"How do you know?" She gave me *that look.*

"I don't. That's just what they told me at U-Haul."

* * *

Rain held off and the yard sale went well except for the people who arrived an hour early and those who went inside and wanted to buy some of *Jeannie's stuff.* One man even made an offer on the house "as is".

Near the end of the sale, a fellow bought a chest of drawers for $50 and asked if he could pick it up the next day. Judy told him that was okay. We moved the chest back inside.

Judy had arranged for a charity to pick up the items that didn't sell.

That evening, we sat on the floor eating take-out food.

Judy got up. "I'm going to clean that dresser the man said he'd pick up tomorrow." She disappeared down the hall. Jeannie and I continued our fast-food-feast.

Not more than five minutes passed before we heard Judy let out a whoop and gales of laughter. She bounded through the doorway holding an envelope in her hand. "Look what I found in this envelope taped to the under-side of a drawer." She pulled out the cash and counted it. "Mom paid this house off years ago, but this is the exact amount of her house payment. She must have forgotten it was there."

Judy divided the money into two piles, putting all three of the $100 bills in Jeannie's stack. We celebrated our good fortune that the guy left the dresser overnight, wondering if he would have ever found the money.

The following morning, I picked up the trailer from U-Haul. Jeannie and I crammed all we could into the trailer until the poor thing's sides started to bulge. The overflow of what Jeannie had picked out had to invade Kabby's space in the back of the Pilot. When Jeannie made her last walk-through Bertha's house and was satisfied we had loaded everything she wanted, our wheels started rolling—destination Idaho, 2100 miles away. I chuckled to myself over Jeannie asking before we left Bakersfield: "Is Houston on the way to Idaho?"

"What's so funny?"

"Nothing."

"You think I took too much?"

"Could be."

* * *

We stopped for the night in central Kansas. "I want to treat us to a nice dinner with one of mom's hundred-dollar bills." Jeannie asked the desk clerk at the motel for directions to the best restaurant in town. We ate our fill of delicious food. When time came to pay the bill, Jeannie proudly handed the server one of her 'C' notes. "Keep the change," she said.

We took our last sips of coffee and started to leave when the server returned with Jeannie's prize bill and a sheepish look on her face. "My manager says we can't accept this. It's too old and doesn't have the strip —whatever that means."

Plastic worked. Jeannie laughed all the way back to the motel, and a little more in the morning when we hit the road, oblivious to what the next few months held in store.

Seventy-Six

Our Fiftieth

Jeannie had been cleaning out the refrigerator in preparation for our trip back to Bakersfield when she came out of the kitchen and sat on the couch with her hand on her stomach and a pained expression on her face.

"What's wrong?" I set down my suitcase and sat beside her.

"Nothing. Just indigestion. I've been having a lot of that lately. It'll pass."

"How about seeing Doctor Lancaster when we get home?" He was an internal medicine specialist she had seen the year before.

"Maybe. It's probably my gallbladder."

I worried about something more serious.

Jeannie called and made an appointment. Before long, she was back in action, doing laundry, wiping down counters, and generally straightening things up. The same things she did before any trip.

My goal was to leave the next day, getting us home in time to unwind before our golden wedding anniversary. But Jeannie hadn't started packing yet. I shifted my goal accordingly, having been well-trained in the art of patience.

We did make it home before the big day, but bad news dampened our enthusiasm. Hours after we unpacked, we received word that "Grandma Sheila" had died in her sleep.

Sheila, one of the few to attend our wedding, had married my father—a man 23 years her senior—two years after my mother died. They divorced a few years later. Jeannie first met Sheila as my stepmother, but even after the divorce, Sheila remained part of the family and was one of our closest friends. Our kids called her Grandma Sheila.

* * *

There were no balloons or confetti on our 50th. We shared the evening alone, enjoying our traditional anniversary dinner—charcoal-grilled steaks, loaded baked potatoes, and salad. With full bellies, we reminisced about the paths we had travelled before and after our wedding.

"You never proposed." She frowned. "I worry that you didn't really want to marry me."

"Well, you're right about that. You trapped me by showing up a day late for our wedding."

We laughed and kissed. The tingle still went down to my toes.

Seventy-Seven

Test Results

We went to see Dr. Lancaster a few days after our anniversary. On arrival, Jeannie was taken back for an abdominal x-ray. When we were ushered into the doctor's office, he was looking at the x-ray on his computer screen. "Your gallbladder looks healthy and happy. I don't think that's your problem." He turned the screen toward us. "There's some shadow behind it." He pointed with his pen. "Have Doctor Cartmell check that out."

"I will," Jeannie said. "I have my regular follow-up with him next week."

***

Dr. Cartmell opened Jeannie's file—the fourth or fifth volume—and said her ovarian and breast cancer markers still looked good. However, he didn't like what he saw on the x-ray Dr. Lancaster had sent him. "There appears to be two tumors in your liver. I'm going to set you up for computer-assisted needle biopsies at San Joaquin Hospital and a CT-PET scan to be done here."

My gut knotted.

Training in patience didn't include waiting to find out about suspected tumors. Jeannie seemed more concerned about needle biopsies spreading cancer if the tumors were malignant.

At the appointed time, we drove to San Joaquin Hospital and Jeannie was prepped for the procedure. Dr. Cornforth, the one who had drained fluid from her abdomen 11 years earlier, came to talk to her.

"It's my brave lady, back for more. Nice to see you." He patted the back of her non-IV hand.

"Nice to see you, too." She smiled as he pulled down her blanket and examined her abdomen.

"Quite a lot of surgical scars here. You've really been through it." He pulled the blanket back up. "I won't add more than two little dots. We'll give you some medication to make you drowsy, then insert needles into your liver to collect tissue samples from the tumors. I'll send the results to Doctor Cartmell."

***

In early July, on a day that promised to be another scorcher in Bakersfield, Jeannie and I walked hand-in-hand into CBCC. We had come through those doors umpteen times in the past 11 years. After a brief stint in the waiting area, where our daughter Brandy joined us, we strolled down the hall toward Dr. Cartmell's examining room. Jeannie stopped off at the restroom.

Brandy and I settled into our usual chairs. When Jeannie came in, she took her assigned seat on the examination table. "The results must be good," she said in her up-beat manner. "I saw him in the hall, and he was smiling,"

Dr. Cartmell's nurse brought in a thick file. She took Jeannie's temperature, pulse and blood pressure and engaged us in friendly chatter. "Doctor Cartmell will be right in." Then she left and closed the door.

We were about to learn the results of the biopsies and CT-PET scan Jeannie had undergone the previous week. Dr. Cartmell had seen her through ovarian cancer, breast cancer, and colon cancer. In the process she had undergone six major surgeries and two dozen months of chemotherapy. By this time, he was almost part of the family.

When Dr. Cartmell walked in, he went through his customary routine. He greeted Brandy and me in turn before looking silently into

Jeannie's eyes, waiting for her to say something. This time he didn't have to wait long.

"Were the results good?" She asked with a grin.

"They were what they were," was his quiet response.

Jeannie must have only heard the first two words, *they were.*

"Oh, great." Her face beamed.

Then she looked at me and her bright smile wilted.

"What?" Her brow furrowed.

"He said they were *what they were.*"

Dr. Cartmell gently walked us through what Jeannie was facing. There were two large cancerous tumors in her liver—another primary cancer, not the spread of any of her others. Blood tests suggested this cancer was also in the pancreas. Surgery was not an option and chemotherapy might provide some pain relief, but nothing more.

His words, even though spoken with kindness, hit with withering ferocity. My worst fear had come true. Color seemed to disappear from the universe.

"Isn't there something you can do?" Brandy pleaded.

Dr. Cartmell shook his head. "I wish there were."

"How long do I have?" Jeannie's voice cracked as she spoke, but her eyes remained dry.

"Only God knows," he said.

"Can I travel to Idaho?" Her mouth appeared to try to smile.

"Whenever you want." He put his hand on her knee and gave her a kindly look. Then he stood up and motioned for all of us to do the same. It was his invitation for a group hug.

* * *

"I want to go fishing one more time," Jeannie said as we made our way to the car.

On the drive home, tears began to flow down Jeannie's cheeks and her shoulders bobbed up and down with silent sobs. She wiped the tears away and put her hand on my arm. "I'm sorry to put you through this," she said as only Jeannie could. *She* had cancer *again,* this time surely terminal, and she was concerned about *me.*

Seventy-Eight

Hospice

By late September, Jeannie no longer ate the poached egg on half an English muffin I fixed for her every morning. At best, she took a bite or two. Brandy and I urged her to eat more, but she silently refused.

With tears in her eyes, Brandy led me out of the den and into the living room. "Is it time to call hospice?"

Her question stabbed deep into my chest. I knew Jeannie was dying —had known it since July when Dr. Cartmell told us there was nothing more he could do. I just wasn't ready for this final step.

I took a deep breath and blew it out slowly, puffing my cheeks. Brandy had long since recognized this as a sign I was under stress. She gave me a strong hug, tears now running freely down her cheeks. "Oh, dad. I'm so sorry."

"Let's ask Doctor Cartmell," I whispered in her ear.

I put in the call, wiping my nose and eyes. After I explained Jeannie's situation, he agreed it was time.

The lady from hospice came to the house and went over the services they provided. I signed the forms without reading them, my mind reeling with despair.

That evening, hospice set up a hospital bed in the den next to a bed for me that son Matt and son-in-law Marty brought down from an upstairs bedroom. The man who set up the hospital bed showed us how to raise and lower the whole bed or different parts of it. A short while later, an RN stopped by to go over the pain medications available to keep Jeannie comfortable. When he got to morphine, Jeannie spoke up for the first time.

"No morphine. I had it once. It made me feel funny."

That broke the tension. We agreed to go with Fentanyl patches supplemented with Norco for break-through pain. Jeannie was fine with that. I wasn't. I did all I could to keep from becoming a blubbering mess.

On the Friday after we started hospice, Father Craig dropped in to see Jeannie. He pulled up a chair next to her and held her hand. She looked up at him, wide-eyed. "Oh, Father Craig, hi."

"I came to give you communion, and don't give me any of that 'I'm not a Catholic stuff.'"

I raised the head of the bed, and Father Craig gave her communion. He then settled in for a chat.

Before he left, Father Craig again took Jeannie's hand. "I'm on my way to Three Rivers for a Priests' Conference. There will be over a hundred priests praying for you."

Jeannie beamed. "Thank you, Father Craig… I mean Monsignor."

"Father Craig is just fine." He patted the hand he was holding. "I'll see you when I get back."

After walking with Father Craig to the door and thanking him, I returned to the den and asked Jeannie if she wanted me to lower the head of her bed.

"No. I'd like to stay up for a while." She had a far-away look in her eyes. "Isn't he nice?"

"Yes, he is. I think he has a thing for you."

* * *

Nightfall brought on silence broken only by the mellow bongs from the grandfather clock in the living room and Jeannie's soft breathing. Thin rays from the courtyard light slid through slits in the bamboo curtains covering the den door. Memories pelted my mind. I couldn't sleep.

I thought of the many golf courses we had played, counting them until I reached fifty in eleven states and five in Canada.

Then a fishing adventure came to mind. A trip to beautiful Priest Lake where we sought to learn the art of downrigger fishing for Lake Trout. We had arranged for a guide who wore the mantle of local expert. He showed up a little late, explaining he had been up all night in his EMT capacity making a run to take a heart attack victim to Spokane. Near the end of a fishless day, he asked Jeannie, "Missus Brown, could you face the front of the boat? I've had so much coffee, I need to relieve myself out the back." As soon as Jeannie turned around, her reel screamed.

"Grab Your pole. That's a big one," the guide shouted. A big fish seemed to outweigh his need for privacy.

Jeannie set the hook, and the fight was on. Then my reel buzzed loud and long. We had a double.

The guide cut the engine, looked at both our poles, and felt the tension in our lines. "You have a good fish, Missus Brown. Mister Brown has a great one." .

Jeannie with Big
Mac

Many minutes later, Jeannie landed a 36-inch lake trout. After a few more minutes, I pulled in a 15-foot pine bough that put up a strong tussle. Jeannie's fish is mounted near the fireplace in Idaho. Since I believed in *catch and release,* I sent my wooden monster back to the 192-foot depth from whence it came.

* * *

Three days after his last visit, Father Craig knocked on the door. "Hi, neighbor," he said. "I came to see Jeannie."

"Come on in." My face must have spoken volumes.

"Not going well?" he asked.

Father Craig had lost his mother to pancreatic cancer less than six months earlier. She lived with him, and he was one of her primary care givers. He knew the signs.

I ushered him into the den without responding. "Jeannie, Father Craig is here to see you."

She was pretty groggy but turned her head toward him and smiled.

"A hundred and thirty-two priests prayed for you this weekend," he said.

The smile stayed on her face. "That's nice." Her voice was barely audible.

Father Craig again gave her communion. Then he sat up straight as if hit with a sudden thought. "I think you two need to renew your wedding vows."

Without waiting for a response, he took Jeannie's hand. "Repeat after me – I, Jeannie, take thee, Jim."

"I, Jeannie, take thee, Jim," she repeated in her weak voice.

Father Craig continued phrase by phrase with Jeannie struggling to respond until he got to "Until death do us part."

Jeannie didn't respond.

"Until death do us part," Father Craig said a bit louder. He waited.

Jeannie just looked at him.

With that, Father Craig turned to me. "I, Jim, take thee, Jeannie…"

When he got to the end, he didn't say, "Until death do us part." Instead, he said, "All the days of my life."

"All the days of my life," I said.

Jeannie looked at me with those beautiful green eyes. The corners of her mouth lifted, and she gave me a small nod.

Before he left that day, Father Craig told Jeannie he had to go to Dallas to do a wedding. "I'll come see you when I get back."

Jeannie soon drifted off to sleep. As I gazed at her, my mind wandered back to the first time we exchanged vows. So much had happened in the half-century that followed.

* * *

Less than two weeks before our 50th wedding anniversary, six magnificent hours came our way. June in the North Country produces long days that end with an afterglow lingering in the northwest until nearly ten o'clock. We were still feeling the residual effects from the four thousand miles we had driven a few days earlier from California to Texas and then on to Idaho.

The rest of this story must be told metaphorically.

When we were young, as together we once were, there came times when passions ran wild. I liken it to the two of us racing up a hill to get to the top of a giant slide on which we would plummet down at breathtaking and exhilarating speed, deposited at the bottom drained for the moment but before long ready to race up the hill again.

Later, when not quite so young, we learned to climb the hill by a path leading through fields of clover and fragrant flowers and along a babbling stream; a path that reached the summit where the grass was green and lush and the songbirds sang. A place to enjoy the view and feel the soft breeze on our skin before mounting the last few steps to the top of the slide. We followed this path many times, taking in the delightful sights, sounds and aromas encountered along the way. But this time was different and so very, very special.

Although it was time for sleep and the last of the afterglow was fading from the sky, Jeannie and I slowly moved toward the entrance to the path up the hill. Guided by an unseen hand, she was leading me as I was leading her. Even in the deepening darkness we had no trouble making our way along the path that was soft and smooth as it wound gently upward. We knew it so well that even in the dark we were able to avoid the few roots and rocks that could cause one to stumble and fall. We stopped along the way and held each other close, talking quietly about what we knew lay ahead. We were in no hurry.

Time drifted past but we paid it no mind. The roses and wildflowers smelled sweeter than ever. A cool zephyr, fluttering the leaves and waving the grass, stroked our skin as we turned our faces into it. And as we contemplated how much further along the path our stroll might take us, we laughed the kind of laugh only two people so deeply in love could laugh.

Each bend and turn in the path was both familiar and new: familiar because we had walked, jogged or raced up this path hundreds of times before; and new because we were now taking it all in with heightened senses and without any urgency to get to the top.

As we drew near the end of the path, it opened to a moonlit expanse of verdant grass. There we found a blanket spread next to a low table holding wine and a selection of our favorite treats. We were at the summit with a panoramic view that seemed to stretch to eternity. We took rest on the blanket, drinking in both the wine and the sights from this magnificent vista. On the far side of the feast-laden table rose the stairway to the slide. If we made it up that stairway, fine. If not, also fine. We were together on this journey, this splendid, magical journey that didn't end until the faint light of dawn appeared and we drifted off to sleep in each other's arms—at the bottom of the slide.

The last time Jeannie was able to sit up next to me on the couch, and lay her head on my shoulder, we talked of that night some three months earlier and confirmed to each other just how special it was. "I'll love you forever and always," she said. "I'll love you forever and always," I said in return. She then closed her eyes and lay down with a lovely smile on her still beautiful face.

* * *

Jeannie's hospice voice snapped me out of my reverie.

"Norco," she said. I knew that meant she was having break-through pain. The Fentanyl patches weren't enough.

The Norco seemed to do its job. After a few minutes Jeannie closed her eyes and went back to sleep.

She didn't wait for Father Craig. She took her last breath the day he flew to Dallas.

* * *

October 7, 1960, to October 17, 2014

Fifty-four years and ten days

Not long enough

About the Author

Since the death of my beloved Jeannie, I have resided in North Idaho where I have been blessed with a warm and welcoming church home, wonderful neighbors, great fishing friends, and family that visit often.

My life took another major blow when son Matthew died less than two weeks before his 46th birthday. But I give thanks to God for a loving and caring daughter, Brandy, and six wonderful grandchildren. My only granddaughter, Ryan, graduated from Belmont University in 2021. She works as a surgical RN in Buffalo, New York, where her husband Michael attends dental school. Kelly's boys, Spencer and Mason, are both serving their country in the Air Force, Spencer in North Dakota and Mason in North Carolina. Brandy's three sons, Joseph, Jonathan, and Cooper are all fine young men and bring much joy to my life. In the spring of 2024, Joe will be graduating from California Baptist University, Johnny will be graduating from Garces Memorial High School, and Cooper will be graduating from O. J. Actis Junior High. All are good students and excellent water polo players.

I owe special thanks to my writing group, *The Red Inkers*, Bruce, Carol, Carrie, Joyce, Karen, Kathryn, and Randy, for their help and patience throughout this project.

After more than four decades at the bar, I retired from my career as a civil trial attorney. Under the name Enoch James, I have written two novels, *The Third Wrong* and *The Anniversary*. More are in the pipeline.

Comments, good or bad, are most welcome at jenochbrown@gmail.com.